The
GUIDE
to SUCCESSFUL LIVING

- by -

Obie R. Silverwood, Jr.

OCCIDENTAL
BOOKS

Published by
- OCCIDENTAL BOOKS -
P.O. Box 1361
La Jolla, California 92038

Library of Congress Catalog Card Number: 91-060941

ISBN 0-9629226-0-9

Printed in the United States of America
First Edition

- Table of Contents -

PART FIVE: Other Considerations.....................Page 241

[Note - The words *Man, his, he, him,* and *himself* herein refer to the species in general, with **no sexist connotation intended**.]

✳

Introduction

Successful Living is the adequate, consistent, and simultaneous fulfillment of one's health, family, money, and play needs.

This book provides practical suggestions and specific problem solving approaches that can help the reader to achieve a successful life.

Philosophical, health, family, money, and other considerations are addressed, with guidance for particular problems readily accessible through a detailed index.

The special value of the information offered herein, although often based upon common sense, lies in its unique organization and presentation. The accuracy of the technical subject matter, where appropriate, has been supported by research and expert review. Some of the opinions expressed are *avant-garde*, or speculative in nature.

PART ONE: Primary Considerations

- Contents -

PART ONE: Primary Considerations

PART ONE: Primary Considerations

SECTION A. Basic Concepts

Individuals use basic concepts such as *Existence*, *Time*, *Death*, and *Morality* as **reference points** to guide themselves through life. Comparatively, a mariner might use a compass, the stars, the wind, and the ocean swell direction, as "reference points", to guide his ship towards a desired destination.

Each day at sea, a mariner must maintain his ship and crew, and face nautical hazards. If a mariner uses **inaccurate** reference points, the ship's voyage might **take longer** to complete, consequently subjecting the mariner to **unnecessary** expenditures and risks. Similarly, if individuals use inaccurate basic concepts, they too might experience unnecessary time or material expenditures in the process of **fulfilling their life needs**.

Most individuals learn such basic concepts from their parents, peers, schools, church, television, and society. Often, such sources **fail** to provide accurate or effective guidance; in such instances, an individual might **flounder** upon life's seas, until he develops his own **functional** reference points.

The following **definitions** offer a **practical** perspective, through which the reader might **better** fulfill his or her life needs.

SUBJECT 1. What is the Universe?

The universe consists of one's body and all that surrounds it. Anything that Man can rationally sense is categorized as **matter** (and its related force fields), **energy**, or **void**, the latter being the medium in which all matter and energy are suspended.

The exact amount of all matter and energy, and its distribution throughout the void, is presently **unknown**; however, the amount appears to be

infinite in quantity and its universal distribution appears to be relatively **uniform**. The void appears to have no spatial limits, and is **inert** in physical character.

Matter's structure can be divided down into **infinitesimal** subatomic component levels, with one such structural level being **pure** energy. Likewise, energy can be **combined** into denser physical structures, with one such state being matter. Neither matter nor energy can be created from nothingness, or reduced to nothingness; they can only be **transmutated** from one state to the other (from matter to energy, and from energy to matter). Consistent with this reality, the total universal quantity of all matter and energy is **constant**; that is, all of the matter and energy that presently exists has **always** existed and **will** always exist. In basic terms, **the universe has no beginning and no end; it simply exists, in a continuous state of change.**

Gravity is one of matter's physical characteristics. Gravity is a force field that surrounds and holds matter **together**. The gravitational field of any body of matter will attempt to **attract** neighboring matter or energy.

The **mass** (or density) of matter **increases**, as its gravitational field pulls other matter and energy into it. The strength of matter's gravitational pull is **increased** as the matter increases in mass. Consequently, as a body of matter draws in surrounding matter (and energy), and as its gravitational field strengthens, a **self-feeding cycle** can develop if there is adequate neighboring matter and energy to feed it. This phenomenon is commonly referred to as a ***black hole.***

The descriptive name black hole is derived from its effect on ***light*** (photons); that is, the mass of a black hole creates such a strong gravitational field that light becomes **incapable** of escaping such bodies. Consequently, such phenomena literally **appear** as black holes, against a uniformly lit heaven.

Black holes gravitationally pull in all surrounding matter and energy (of lesser mass), and continue to increase in gravitational strength. As their matter and energy are **compressed** under their increasing gravitational field, any existing atomic structure is **crushed**. Eventually, the black hole becomes a celestial ball of subatomic **nuclear fluid**.

The present assumption is that such super-compressed nuclear fluid eventually reaches an **unstable** state (*a critical mass*), that is incapable of being contained by its own gravitational field. As a result, the mass of the black hole **explodes**, therein **redistributing** raw subatomic materials throughout the universe. Such materials then start **recombining** into complex matter and energy structures, which will eventually undergo the same **attraction/compression/explosion cycle**.

This process may be functioning on a regional and universal scale, **concurrently**. Isolated sections of the universe may be undergoing repetitive black hole compression/explosion cycles, while the **entire** universe is **also** undergoing repetitive compression/explosion cycles.

The certainty of this phenomenon cannot be demonstrated in the laboratory; however, its occurrence is **strongly suggested** by Man's present understanding of the physical laws governing the universe.

SUBJECT 2. Why Does the Universe Exist?

This question might be asked in **two** respects: "Why does the universe exist, **as perceived by Man**?" and "Why does the universe exist **at all**?"

a. The reason that the universe exists, as perceived by Man (for example, as it is at **this** moment), can be explained through the field of mathematics referred to as **probability theory**. Probability theory can be used to assist one in predicting or understanding the occurrence of **random events**. For example, the occurrence of different outcomes in the throwing of game dice is typically explained through probability theory:

> Each surface of a cubical game die is numbered one through six. If an individual throws the two dice onto a table and looks at the resulting numbers on the top surface of each die, there are thirty-six (6x6) possible combinations that might occur; that is, any one of each die's six surfaces might come up in combination with the other die's six surfaces.

> With three dice, the number of possible combinations would be 6x6x6, or 216. With four dice, it would be 6x6x6x6, or 1,296; and so on, **increasing by six-fold** with each additional die thrown.

An individual might better comprehend the reasons for the universe's complex configurations by drawing an **analogy** to the throwing of game dice; that is, one might envision each existing **atom of matter** and **radiation of energy** as an individual multisided game die. One might further imagine that upon each progressive tick of time, these countless multisided game dice are continuously **re-thrown** onto a universal playing table. Obviously, **the possible combinations are infinite**. Therefore, with regard to the question *Why does the universe exist, as presently perceived by Man?*, by analogy, it is simply a **roll of the dice**, a **random configuration** of matter and energy.

This concept of **random configurations**, regardless of its mathematical reality, is difficult for many individuals to comprehend. People look around themselves and observe that there is air to breath, food to eat, and that everything appears to be quite **harmonious** and **well-planned**. Such observations prompt one to ask **"is there some universal master plan, with divine guidance?"** - the answer is "no." The universe is simply a product of random configuration, and there is a very **logical** and **comfortable** explanation as to why it appears to be so *pleasant* and *harmonious*:

> All forms of life need **certain** environmental conditions to survive. As their environments change, living objects try to **adapt**, through **selective breeding** and **mutation**. Man has undergone millions of years of **genetic evolution**, in order to **adapt to his environment**.

> Man's environment **seems** pleasant because he has physically adapted to it, through selective breeding and mutation. There are many other species that did **not** make the **right** selective breeding choices, nor beneficial mutations; **they no longer exist!**

> Members of many present species (the whale, the elephant, the grizzly bear, et cetera) **do not** perceive the environment to be harmonious and wonderful, relative to **their** needs, because Man is **pushing *them* off of the planet**.

b. With regard to the second part of the question, "Why does the universe exist at all?", the question is **invalidated** by known physical laws; that is, the word "why" presupposes that the universe did not exist at some previous time and then **later** came into existence. As previously stated (see *What is the Universe?*), matter and energy cannot be created or destroyed, they can only be transmutated; therefore, **the universe has always existed, and will always exist.**

SUBJECT 3. What is Infinity?

Infinity is a **concept** that, when considered, tends to give one a *headache.* In reality, infinity is a comfortable and logical aspect of the universe, relative to its **quantitative** characteristics.

In simple terms, infinity means **without limit.** Most people find it difficult to grasp this concept, because their **daily** lives are guided by and filled with limits. As one thinks of objects and situations, common to his daily life, such items are typically perceived in terms of **beginnings, endings, boundaries,** and **finite quantities.** As an example, when one thinks of an *ink pen,* he might think that the pen **began** to exist when it was manufactured and that its existence **ends** when it is thrown in the trash or incinerated. In reality, the elemental components of the ink pen (the atoms composing the plastic and metal and ink) existed **before** they were combined into the form of an ink pen, and will **continue** to exist after the ink pen form has been destroyed.

The **configuration** of material that one calls an ink pen does have a beginning and end, but the pen's basic components (its molecules, atoms, and subatomic particles) previously existed for **all time,** prior to being assembled into an ink pen form, and will **continue** to exist for all time, after they are disassembled from an ink pen configuration.

Most earthly objects (such as houses, neighborhoods, nations, et cetera) have physical boundaries (such as walls, streets, or oceans), beyond which they cease to exist, consequently giving Man a **boundary-oriented** mentality. This **Earth-referenced** spatial relationship mentality invites the **misperception** that the universe also has a boundary beyond which it ceases to exist. In reality, there is **always** an additional portion of the universe beyond any apparent boundary - if not matter or energy, then continued limitless space (which is **also** part of the universe).

Similarly, Man's Earth-referenced mentality invites a misperception of quantitative infinity as it relates to universal **mass;** that is, because there are limited (finite) numbers of objects (such as cars, people, trees, et cetera) on Earth, Man mistakenly assumes that there is also a finite mass to the universe. In reality, there may be an infinite amount of mass (matter and energy) in the universe.

SUBJECT 4. What is Time?

Time is a man-made **measurement** concept. The word *time* is used to **label** Man's process for relating the physical and spatial **interaction** of various components of the universe. This process involves:

a. The arbitrary selection of a relatively **consistent** and **convenient** event, such as the rotation of the earth about its axis, or the rotation of the earth about the sun, et cetera.

b. The formal establishment of such an event as a **"time standard"**, and the designation of increment (years, months, days, et cetera) terminology.

c. The **comparison** of other universal events against such time standards.

To exemplify the usage of the time concept, consider how a person's date of birth and age are determined:

> First, a civilization selects a time standard; for instance, the period of the earth's orbit about the sun (arbitrarily designated as a **year**). Next, they select an event for their **calendar starting point**, such as the birth of Christ.

> If an individual was **born in 1962**, it simply means that the earth had made 1,962 revolutions about the sun prior to the birth of the subject individual and subsequent to the arbitrary commencement of his civilization's calendar.

> Likewise, if an individual is **fifty years old**, it simply means that the individual's life span is thus far coincident with fifty consecutive revolutions of the earth about the sun.

In reiteration, **Time is a measurement concept that uses arbitrary standards, devised by and for the convenience of Man, and in the absence of Man, there is no time!**

A similar methodology applies to many other measurement concepts, such as *distance*, *volume*, *voltage*, *speed*, et cetera. Again, Man arbitrarily selects some convenient event or object as a standard, and then describes other related events or objects in comparison to the designated standard.

SUBJECT 5. What is Life?

The concept of Life, although complex in consideration, is a highly probable and natural phenomenon.

The universe is in constant **rearrangement**. Each instant, something moves or combines, or cools, or heats up, or there is a change in gravity, radiation, or magnetism, et cetera. Each new arrangement is **different** from the previous. Granted, there are repetitive cycles that produce **similar** phenomena, like sunsets or snowflakes, but no two are the same (see *Why Does the Universe Exist?*).

Man observes these randomly different matter/energy arrangements, and descriptively **labels** those that are of particular interest. **Life** is the word that Man uses to label one such interesting configuration of matter/energy.

Given infinite time, the probability of such spontaneous and repetitive *life* occurrences throughout the universe is **extremely high**. To exemplify this point, imagine a blind person at a rifle range. Given unlimited bullets and unlimited time, it is extremely probable that the blind person will **eventually** hit a *bulls-eye*.

The same mathematical principle applies on universal scales; to create spontaneous life, certain materials, in certain quantities, under certain environmental conditions (temperature, electromagnetic field, gravity, light, radiation exposure, et cetera) are necessary. One need not be a mathematician to understand that, given an **infinite** amount of matter/energy and **infinite** time to randomly rearrange itself, the **life combination** is **very probable**.

The reader should understand that the above comments are not suggesting that a dog, bird, fish, et cetera might spontaneously appear as the result of a random combination of matter and energy. The term *life combination*, as above used, is referring to initial **quasi-life** chemical processes, such as **enzymatic reaction chains** or **basic polyamino acid processes**, et cetera. Such basic quasi-life combinations are the **chemical forebears** to higher life forms, such as Earth's **DNA-protein-carbon-based** life process. Such basic quasi-life combinations, once initiated, require billions of years to evolve into familiar higher life forms (mammals, fish, et cetera).

SUBJECT 6. What is Death?

Life forms range from single cell to extreme multicell complexity and are generally categorized as plant or animal. One of life's unique characteristics is its **innate desire** to continue to exist. To this end, life interacts with its surrounding environment, nourishing, mutating, and propagating itself.

The **life process** starts when certain materials combine under certain environmental conditions. Once started, a life organism begins to ingest sustenance from the surrounding universe. It incorporates certain new material and excretes unwanted materials. It grows, reproduces, and then (on genetic cue) begins to **slow** in its metabolic functions, until these functions completely **cease**.

Death is that final state in which a body no longer functions as a living organism. Any intelligence or persona is **lost** through death. After death, the body simply decays into the soil, or is cremated. Regardless of how a body is disposed of, the residual non-life materials eventually **diffuse** throughout the universe, in the continuance of their perpetual existence. **In this respect, one might say that each individual has existed and will continue to exist forever, in a subatomic particle, random configuration fashion.**

In simplest terms, Man (and any life form) is a **temporary holding pattern** and **conduit** for certain **transient** materials. Upon death, Life has no residual character other than its **latent** interactive effects on other universal objects and the random redistribution of its decaying residual materials.

Life, like any other object in the universe, is simply a **temporal** combination of matter and energy.

SUBJECT 7. What is the Purpose for Existing?

This question might be approached from a biological and philosophical perspective:

a. From a **biological** point of view, the ***purpose*** for existing (one's reason **to be**) is **genetically inherent**; that is, every individual's *purpose* is to **continue to exist** (to stay alive). This purpose is **common** to **all** life forms.

Man's basic functions (to eat, excrete, rest, and reproduce) are not learned, they are genetically pre-programmed into his psyche. People do not contemplate, "do I want to be hungry, or not?" nor ask "do I want to stay warm, or not?"; they **involuntarily** sense such needs.

The fulfillment of an individual's basic needs is his **functional** purpose for existence. One's daily actions are **motivated** and **governed** by this purpose.

One can enhance (or obscure) his biological purpose for existing through the fulfillment of **higher** level needs, such as friendships, creative endeavor, game playing, et cetera.

b. From a **philosophical** point of view, each individual's purpose for existence (and that of the species as a whole) is absolutely **arbitrary**; that is, the philosophical value, meaning, or purpose of life is **subjective**, and **personal** to each individual.

The question sometimes arises, "how **significant** can **Man** be, compared to the **vastness** of the universe?", implying Man's **diminutive** purpose. In reality, Man's significance (as an individual or as a species) is always **equal** to that of any other universal object, regardless of comparative physical qualities.

In **spatial** dimensions, the universe extends infinitely beyond Man; however, the atoms that comprise each individual's body can be **infinitesimally** divided into subatomic materials. Logically then, the infinite nature of the **macro-universe** is **reciprocally** complemented by the infinitesimal nature of the **micro-universe**; consequently, every individual (and object) **is relatively (and always) in the middle** when compared on a physical or philosophical significance basis.

In effect, each individual is **always** at the **center** of the universe (relative to his **personal** perspective). To exemplify this point, the reader might envision a **continuous** and **infinitely** long piece of string, that extends straight out to his left and right. The reader might further envision that a **sliding bead** has been placed on the string, directly in front of him. Now, regardless of how far the reader slides the bead to his left or right, the bead will **always** be in the **middle** of the string, **relative to the overall and infinite length of the string**.

Likewise, each universal object, regardless of its size or location, is always **at the center** of the physical universe. Consequently, although objects may have comparative differences, they are **always equal** in universal **significance**.

SUBJECT 8. What is Morality? - **[knowing *right* from *wrong*]**

Morality refers to the **nature** of a **problem solving approach**, with regard to its **overall effectiveness** (see *Problem Solving Skills*).

In order to fulfill one's daily needs, one must interact with other people, other animals, plants, and his surrounding environment. Such interactions are typically guided by one's **problem solving approaches**.

Some problem solving approaches are more, or less, effective than others. Individuals and societies refine the effectiveness of their problem solving approaches through trial and error. Eventually, as the relative benefits of effective problem solving approaches are realized, they become commonly accepted and practiced. Such knowledge, when formalized in its organization and presentation, is referred to as a **morality system**.

Moral problem solving approaches should embody the following characteristics:

- They are **efficient**; that is, they do not waste **time, energy**, or **materials**.

- They accommodate the **consistent** fulfillment of the user's **immediate** and **future** needs.

- They **minimize** the detrimental effects that might result from the **conflicting** need fulfillment activities of various individuals, groups, or life forms.

- They **minimize** damage to, or waste of, the environment.

Individuals, by adhering to **established** and **functional** morality systems, lessen their need to devise and contemplate the moral consequences of routine problem solving approaches.

On occasion, some individuals employ problem solving approaches that **defy** the precepts of traditional morality; representative of such actions are **thievery, rape, murder**, et cetera. Due to **irrationality** or ignorance, such perpetrators often fail to comprehend the **certain** inefficiency of their actions. For example, a **shoplifter**, if not immediately apprehended, might **mistakenly** assume that he has escaped any negative moral consequences. In reality, the moral consequences of his actions might be **subtle**, yet **substantial**. For example, the shoplifter's actions may force the victim retail store to **increase** its **prices**, in compensation for the cost of the stolen merchandise. Such merchandise price increases tend to **induce** general cost of living increases, therein eventually subjecting the shoplifter to higher retail prices for **all** of his consumer needs. Additionally, a high incident of shoplifting typically prompts **stringent** security measures and related costs, thereby **inconveniencing** the shoplifter's normal shopping activities, and further increasing merchandise prices.

It is highly probable that the perpetrator of an immoral act will suffer **negative** material consequences, in addition to the **mental discomfort** of any associated guilt that he is capable of sensing.

From a **philosophical** point of view, an individual might ask himself, "if morality systems are man-made and arbitrary, **why** then should one act in a **moral manner?**" In reiteration, morality systems by definition are formal groupings of effective problem solving routines. It is in an individual's personal **best interest** to use and benefit from available knowledge, rather than take the time to create a unique problem solving approach for **each** new life situation. Furthermore, every problem solving action affects one's surroundings - other people, other animals, the environment, et cetera. When one acts in a moral manner, he **minimize**s damage to other life forms and **minimize**s the waste or spoilage of natural resources, thereby maintaining a **healthier** world.

By maintaining a healthier world, individuals **increase** the probability that natural resources will be available to accommodate their future survival. Furthermore, the moral consequences of one's actions are ultimately **inescapable**; they are like the casting of a pebble into a pond. When the pebble strikes the water, its impact rings radiate out, touching other objects in the pond and eventually reverberating to their source of origin (the individual that cast the pebble). In life, **"what goes around, comes around!"**

SUBJECT 9. Which Morality System is Best?

The **best** morality system is the one that **most effectively** fulfills an individual's needs.

Most individuals are **children** when **indoctrinated** into their parents' or their society's morality system. Consequently, they seldom possess the intellectual maturity to **question** its logic or effectiveness. Such morality systems may be **obsolete**, or **flawed** in design; that is, their suggested problem solving routines may be relatively **ineffective** when compared to other morality systems. Although ineffective morality systems tend to be **self-correcting** (because they are either corrected when they fail to fulfill needs, or they are abandoned), the quality of **many** lives may be **diminished** during the years or centuries that are required for such faulty systems to self-correct. For this reason, each individual should **think seriously**, before **blindly** accepting and practicing any established morality system.

As an individual approaches **adulthood**, he should make a **conscious** effort to evaluate the logic and relative merits of **various** morality systems, especially those that have been involuntarily imposed upon him. Eventually, each individual should form his **own** morality system, in an **eclectic** fashion, by adopting and creatively enhancing the best precepts of various morality systems.

SUBJECT 10. What is Religion?

Often, in the course of Man's existence, he has found himself in need of important information about philosophical and natural phenomena, such as "when will it rain next?", "who will prevail in the next battle?", "what happens to an individual after he dies?", "why does Man exist?", et cetera. In some instances, Man's state of intellectual evolution has limited his ability to **accurately** discern such knowledge; in other instances, the *scientific process* has simply **lagged** Man's informational needs. In the absence of actual **facts**, Man has often approached such pressing information needs by venturing his **best guess** answers.

If Man's best guess answers functionally assisted him in the fulfillment of his needs, such answers then gained popular acceptance and utilization. Eventually, such best guess information becomes formalized in its organization and presentation, and endures generations of usage, until replaced by information of greater accuracy. This book speculates that religion is **categorically representative** of such best guess information systems.

Religions are formatted to provide their **followers** with information that assists them in meeting their **specific** survival needs, the most common being:

> a. **Man's need to secure food.** Religions offer rituals purportedly to influence the hunt, farming, fishing, et cetera.

> b. **Man's need to reproduce.** Religions offer rituals purportedly to influence fertility and control reproduction-related behavioral activity.

> c. **Man's inherent need to survive (and related fear of death).** Religions offer death avoidance *(afterlife)* scenarios.

> d. **Safety.** Religions offer rituals that purportedly protect followers from the injuries of battle or natural phenomena; more importantly, most religions motivate their followers to practice a common moral code.   Such conformity is usually enforced through **intimidation**, based upon Man's need to continue to exist; that is, if a follower violates the religion's moral codes, the follower might be threatened with deprivation of *eternal life.*

The common structure of most religions includes:

> - The designation of **a supreme being** or the **deification** of humans, other animals, or inanimate objects. Such **gods** are then purportedly embodied with **supernatural** powers that can be

evoked to the benefit or detriment of mortal Man. Certain associated **worship rituals** are typically established, to **influence** the designated deities and natural phenomena.

- A formalized presentation of philosophical subject matter (such as Existence), and the creation of an associated **moral code**.

- A hierarchy of **priests**, to speak to or for the gods, to perform rituals, to **interpret** religious writings, to **enforce** the moral codes, and to maintain and perpetuate the religion.

Religions vary in complexity, depending upon the nature of the civilization that they serve. On the lower end of the scale, simple tribal religions may employ *witch doctors*, bone tossing rituals, crude temples, and plant, animal, or natural phenomenon deities. On the other end of the scale, advanced societal religions may employ a hierarchy of gilt-robed priests, sophisticated worship rituals, ornate temples, and human or celestial deities.

Religions were and continue to be functional as problem solving aids, if their dogma is not **too** inaccurate, and if they permit the replacement of dogma with fact, when or if relevant fact becomes available.

SUBJECT 11. The Judeo/Christian *God*

The God of Western religions, like all religious deities, was devised by Man to assist himself in understanding the universe.

To better understand why and how Man devised God, one might consider the probable surrounding circumstances: Primitive Man had a very limited understanding of physical laws governing natural phenomena. The only manner in which Man could comprehend *Existence* was to consider it from his own limited perspective. To this end, Man most likely concluded the following **logical fallacy**: "since Man made tools, and since Man fathered his children, then **something** must have made the universe and fathered Man."

In devising a deity **image** to accommodate this best guess religious scenario, Man simply (and understandably) employed **familiar** human-like characteristics, including flaws; consistent therewith, the Judeo-Christian God has been traditionally envisioned in human-like form.

Personality-wise, Man embodied God with a generally benevolent nature; however, as evidenced in various religious scriptures, God also received the typically human character flaws of indecisiveness and irrationality. Certain biblical incidents are described, in which God **tests** the behavior of His earthly subjects. When they fail to perform to His liking, He either wreaks havoc upon the planet or simply kills specific individuals. The obvious irrationality of such actions lies in the fact that God was supposedly **prophetic and all knowing.** In this case, there would be no rationality to testing the behavior of His subjects, as the eventual outcome of any such test would be **implicitly** known to Him.

The Judeo/Christian God concept has remained popular for two primary reasons:

> a. Many individuals, due to their limited education or psychological mind-set, still **prefer** simplistic explanations regarding the physical nature of the universe.

> b. When a concept is commonly accepted by a large portion of society and practiced for a long period of time, it necessarily develops **institutional inertia.** An analogous phenomenon is that of a massive ship in motion; it might take several hundred yards to effect a change in course or to stop. Similarly, obsolete or inaccurate religious concepts may enjoy centuries of popular acceptance before giving way to fact and rational thinking.

SUBJECT 12. What is Perfection?

As individuals experience life, they form **expectations**, against which they judge their future experiences. When a new experience conforms to one's expectations, particularly in a beneficial manner, it is commonly **described** as *perfect.*

Each individual perceives the universe based upon his **unique** physical senses and relative to his **personal** needs. Consequently, the perfection of an occurrence is dependent upon the **subjective perception** of the individual rendering the description.

SECTION B. Problem Solving Skills

The fulfillment of any human need requires the **solving of problems**. Getting *good grades in school*, or having a *happy marriage*, or making *enough money* all require the solving of problems. Consequently, the quality of one's life is **directly** dependent upon his **problem solving skills**.

Although some problem solving skills are **instinctual**, many must be **acquired**. Of those that must be acquired, the most important are:

1. **Communication Techniques**   5. **Attention to Detail**

2. **Organization**   6. **Learning**

3. **The Problem Solving Process** 7. **Habit**

4. **Timeliness**

The primary benefits of practicing such skills are twofold:

- **First**, effective problem solving skills **save time** and **energy** that might be used to **enhance** one's overall **quality of life**.

- **Second,** effective problem solving skills **help** one to **survive in a competitive world**. Often, individuals must compete against one another, in the fulfillment of their respective needs. Such competition might include hunting, fishing, or foraging in a defined territory, vying for the affections of a mate, sparring in physical battle, contending in business endeavors, et cetera.

On occasion, an individual might have to compete with a smarter, stronger, or faster opponent. In such instances, it is possible to **prevail** through the use of **superior** problem solving skills.

Ideally, people should learn effective problem solving skills from their **parents**, or while in **school**. Unfortunately, many parents lack effective problem solving skills **themselves**, and the formal education process often fails to define and impart **practical** problem solving methods.

The following subject presentations will assist the reader to acquire problem solving skills that are minimally necessary to live a successful life.

SUBJECT 1. Communication Techniques

Most **problem solving** and **social** situations require interpersonal **communication**. Consequently, the success of one's problem solving approaches and social relationships is **directly** affected by his ability to communicate.

a. Problem Solving Communication.

Many **problem situations** result from the **conflicting needs** of the involved parties. Through communication, the parties can **define** their relative positions, and move towards **compromised** solutions.

Family arguments or **business** disagreements are representative of such problem situations. The following **communication technique** is effective in most such problem solving scenarios:

Step 1. In a problem solving situation involving at least **two** adversarial individuals, one individual should **first** state his **position** (problem, grievance, et cetera). He should state his position, as **clearly** and **unemotionally** as possible. If the involved parties are particularly emotional (angered or crying), they should agree on a **mutually** convenient time to **calmly** reapproach the subject.

Step 2. As the first party states his position, his adversary should attentively **listen** to what is being said. It is necessary to **understand** an adversary's position, in order to **respond** to it intelligently. If the subject is complex, or if a position statement is lengthy, one might take notes on primary points. While one party is stating his position, the listening adversary should make a conscious effort to avoid **thinking about what he is going to say next**.

Step 3. The first party should be permitted to finish his statement in its **entirety** and **without interruption**. The listening adversary may **politely** interrupt, if he has missed a word or did not understand a point; however, such interruptions should be limited to "would you please repeat or restate that."

Before progressing to the next step, the listening adversary should ask the speaking adversary if he has completed his **entire position statement**.

Step 4. After the speaking adversary has completed his position statement, the listening adversary should take a moment to mentally review what he understood the other party to have said. Upon doing so, the listening adversary should now orally **recount** what he understood his adversary to have said.

While making this reiteration, the speaker should **refrain from any hostile voice inflections or argumentative side comments**; this opportunity will come later. The function of this reiteration is to make one's adversary feel **understood**.

Upon completing the reiteration, one should ask his adversary if the reiteration **clearly** represented the adversary's stated position; if it did not, the adversary should then clarify any misunderstood point.

Step 5. After one has accurately reiterated his adversary's position, one should next determine if he can **agree** with any part of his adversary's position. If one can agree with some part of his adversary's position, he should state those areas of **common** agreement. If one cannot agree with any part of his adversary's position, one should at least express **empathy** for the sincerity of his adversary's feelings.

For example, one might say "although I do not agree with your point of view, I do understand that you are sincere in your belief that"...or, "I do understand that you are feeling anger"...or, "I do understand that you are feeling pain"...et cetera.

The object of steps *four* and *five*, in addition to understanding an adversary's position, is to **lower** the adversary's psychological **defenses**; thereby, encouraging his **receptiveness** to an alternate point of view.

Step 6. After reiterating his adversary's position, the individual (who has been listening) **should now have his turn to respond** to his adversary's position and to **state his own position**.

This second speaker should enjoy the **same opportunity** as that enjoyed by the first adversarial speaker; that is, the second adversary should be permitted to state his position **in its entirety** and **uninterrupted**.

Now, the second speaker should clearly express his position, and where appropriate, he might **politely** rebut his adversary's previously stated facts or logic.   One should **avoid** using facial expressions, voice inflections, or words that are **punitive or hostile** in nature. Remember, the object of the conversation is to win the adversary's **cooperation**, not to **beat them up**.

Step 7. All adversarial parties should take equal turns in the above manner, until their respective positions are understood and their mutual problems are resolved or compromised.

b. Social Communication.

One can create and maintain **enjoyable** social relationships by employing two basic communication guidelines:

> 1. **Be courteous**; that is, use social niceties such as *please, thank you, you are welcome*, et cetera.

> 2. Maintain a **balanced conversation** with regard to **reciprocal ego appeasement**.

It is necessary, in a balanced conversation, for **all** participants to feel that they are being **heard** and **appreciated**.

In a balanced conversation, one person talks about something and the other person **listens**, looking at the speaker (maintaining eye contact), nodding, and showing **interest**. Then the listener is given his turn (**equal time**) to talk about something and the first speaker listens, looking at the second speaker, nodding, and showing interest.   In this manner, each person takes an alternate turn at having his ego **appeased** by a listener, and then becoming *ego food* for the next speaker.

A conversation can become very uncomfortable if it is imbalanced *ego food* wise.   That is, one person might feel **slighted** if the other person does most of the talking; the listener might begin to feel devoured, *ego food* wise.   Equally, a speaker might feel slighted if the listener is constantly **looking around the room, thinking about what he is going to say next** or **interrupting.**

One should make a conscious effort to structure and maintain balanced conversations. For example, if one is conversing with an individual who is introverted, it may be necessary to **draw** them into the conversation by **asking sincere questions. On the other hand**, if one is conversing with an extreme extrovert, it may be necessary to tactfully ask them to **"take a breath and listen for a moment."**

By maintaining balanced social conversations, one helps to **ensure** the **success** of his marital, friendship, business, and casual relationships.

SUBJECT 2. Organization

An individual can **better** meet his needs if he knows the **quantity** and **location** of his **possessions.** Organization is the physical process of arranging one's possessions in a manner that makes them easily **identifiable** and **accessible.**

Organization, once achieved, is relatively easy to maintain. Furthermore, the time and effort that one spends organizing is like money in the bank, in that the organization is "in place" and ready to help him when he needs it. **Disorganization**, on the other hand, is **very wasteful**, because it typically prompts one to **redundantly** organize his possessions, in response to each new problem situation.

Of the personal possessions most commonly used in the fulfillment of one's daily needs, **money, tools, materials, information files**, and **clothing** are ideal candidates for organization. With regard to money, one might organize his finances by:

- **Balancing** his checkbook after each check or deposit.

- **Reconciling** his checkbook with his monthly bank statement.

- Maintaining an **in-basket** of monthly bills and obligations.

- Paying obligations, in a timely manner.

- Maintaining a **year-to-date** file of all paid bills/receipts for tax and legal audit trail.

The potential **benefits** of such organization are multiple:

- One better knows where he stands financially, permitting intelligent **planning** (for new acquisitions, et cetera).

- By paying bills on time, credit problems are **avoided**.

- Income tax filings will be far **easier** to prepare.

With regard to tools, homemakers might organize their cooking utensils by size and function; likewise, garage tools might be grouped by type (screwdrivers, wrenches, files, et cetera) and suspended from the wall, for quick access.

Personal or business records might be placed into file folders, labeled, and filed in alphabetic order.

With regard to clothing, individuals might:

- Segregate closets and drawers by type of garment.

- Create a written list of various combinations (outfits) that can be arranged from one's clothing.

- Designate certain outfits for certain days or activities.

Such simple clothing organization permits individuals to **minimize** the time that they spend dressing and **maximize** the economic use of their clothing expenditures.

An individual's **organization habits** regarding his personal possessions tend to be **reflective** of his **overall lifestyle**; that is, if one's desk, kitchen, garage, et cetera are disorganized, his overall life tends to be disorganized and **out of control**. Lives that are disorganized and out of control tend to be **problematic** and **unfulfilling**. Logically then, individuals might **best begin** improving their lives by organizing their personal possessions.

SUBJECT 3. The Problem Solving Process

Every individual must resolve a variety of **daily** problems, including *doing well in school, supporting himself, finding a spouse, maintaining good health,* et cetera. Consequently, one's quality of life is **directly** dependent upon his **general ability** to solve problems.

Regardless of the exact nature of one's problems, there exists a **problem solving process** that is commonly applicable to all problem situations. This problem solving process is a **formally-structured approach** that helps an individual to solve his problems in a logical, consistent, and efficient manner. By learning and employing the problem solving process, one **minimizes** the **time** and **effort** that is required to accomplish his desired goals and to fulfill his needs. These time and energy savings can then be used to improve one's overall quality of life.

To effectively solve any problem, one should:

- First **identify** and **analyze** the problem.

- Then **determine a plan of corrective action** (a solution).

- Finally, **implement** his **solution**.

The following presentation offers the reader a functional *step-by-step* **process**, that may be used in solving any problem.

Step 1. Identify the problem.

Before an individual can solve a problem, he must identify the problem; that is, he must clearly discern "what is bothering him" or "what he wishes to accomplish" or "what he needs," et cetera.

The identification of personal behavior problems, as compared to technical (financial, mechanical, et cetera) problems, can be quite difficult. The reason is twofold:

> **- First,** identifying one's personal behavior problems might involve the **acknowledgement** of **unpleasant realities**. Examples of such realities might include the acknowledgement of a *failing marriage,* of a *failing business,* or of

failing health, et cetera. Such acknowledgements might **threaten** one's ego, financial security, or very existence; consequently, they might be difficult to approach.

Representative of such acknowledgment difficulty is the individual who has a persistent *pain*, but avoids going to the doctor, because he **fears** that the pain is indicative of a serious health problem.

Although such acknowledgments are difficult, one should be comforted by the fact that problem situations are seldom, if ever, worsened by acknowledgement. **On the contrary**, acknowledgment usually leads to the **alleviation** of the problem, or the accomplishment of the desired goal.

- The second difficulty in such problem identification is **isolating the problem**. Quite often, one's problems are subtly intertwined with, or hidden by, other problems. For example, one might be subject to physical abuse by a hostile spouse, or to psychological abuse by a disloyal spouse. In such instances, the victim spouse might focus on the **obvious** behavioral problems of the offending spouse, thereby neglecting to address his own behavioral problems (for example, those that prompted/permitted the individual to **initially** enter into the relationship with the offending spouse).

To assist in identifying a problem, one should attempt to **isolate** the problem situation; that is, one should try to minimize the obscuring or frustrating cross-effects of other influences. As an example of minimizing an exacerbating cross-effect, imagine a situation in which a couple are on a ski trip, and have been skiing all day. They are hungry, tired, and cold. While riding on a chairlift they get into a discussion about *why they have not been getting along lately*, and the discussion turns into a heated argument.

In this example, it would be in the couple's best interest to **stop** the argument, return to their cabin, get warm, have a meal, rest, and later reapproach the relationship problem. By doing so, they would **separate** the problematic effects of cold, fatigue and hunger from the process of solving the relationship problem.

Two or more problems, when **intertwined**, may appear to be insurmountable; however, when separated, each problem might be **comfortably** identified and resolved.

In reiteration, do not permit **fear or ego sensitivity** to cloud problem identification, and, when identifying problems, try to **isolate** the problem from other exacerbating and interacting influences.

Step 2. Analyze the problem.

Before one can devise a practical plan for solving a problem or fulfilling a need, one must **understand** his problem or need; **analysis** serves this function. To analyze a problem, one should **disassemble** the problem into its basic functional **components**.

Once a problem situation has been disassembled, one should contemplate the component parts in a **general to specific** progression. By doing so, one creates a practical overall perspective for solving the problem. As a simplistic example, imagine that an individual is unhappy in his job, but unsure of the cause. Using a general to specific approach in his analysis of the problem, the individual might ask himself the following sequence of questions:

a. Do I like my profession?

b. Do I like my specific work duties?

c. Do I like my specific employer?

d. Do I like the people with whom I work?

Asking oneself questions, in the above listed **general to specific** sequence, better enables the individual to avoid erroneous or inefficient solutions.

The subject individual, in this simple example might answer questions *a*, *b*, and *c*, affirmatively; when answering question *d*, he might realize that he does not like his office mate, or work partner, et cetera.

Very possibly, the individual's job dissatisfaction might be resolved by simply changing office quarters or by changing work partners. **Most importantly,** by doing a general to specific analysis, the individual might **avoid** the **less efficient** solutions of changing employers or changing professions.

Step 3. Develop a plan of action.

The **first step** in developing a plan of action is to **realistically** determine what action must be taken to solve the problem or fulfill the need. This is accomplished through **personal creativity** or by seeking **expert advice.**

After an individual determines the actions that must be taken to accomplish his desired goal (such as *dieting, better study habits, quitting smoking,* et cetera), he should next determine a schedule for the completion of his planned action. Such a schedule should be detailed to the point of coordinating the component parts of the planned actions.

Effective planning **minimizes** one's expenditure of time, materials, and energy. To plan effectively, one should first consider the final configuration and timing of the desired **goal;** as examples, one might wish to be *at the theater by eight o'clock,* or one might wish to *lose twenty-five pounds in six months.*

With one's ultimate objective in mind, one should then **back-schedule** the timing of each **subordinate** task that must be performed to complete the desired **end event.** While doing so, individuals should be **realistic** in the time that they allocate to accomplish each component task, and they should give consideration to potential **variables** that might influence their planned actions. As an example, an individual might have a business appointment in another city. He knows that it will take one hour to drive there and that the appointment is at 2:00 p.m. Using effective planning, one should leave at 12:45 p.m. (allowing 15 minutes as a margin for error), and one should make sure that he has enough gasoline and that he has brought all materials that are necessary for the meeting.

As another example, an individual might wish to entertain friends for dinner. If the guests have been asked to arrive at 7:00 p.m., and if it will take two hours to ready the house, one hour to shop for food, one hour to bathe and dress, and one hour to prepare the food, then it would be wise to start cleaning house by 1:30 p.m. (allowing 30 minutes as a margin for error).

As another example, an individual might wish to purchase a new car in two years. If he estimates that the car will cost about $20,000 and if wishes to pay cash, then effective planning would dictate that he should save $850 each month. In the above manner, one would accumulate $20,400 over two years, providing a $400 margin for error.

In planning, one should also go from **general to specific** in task **scheduling**. The largest items should take precedence in consideration, because they will have the greatest overall and eventual influence. For example, if one were decorating a new house, it might be most efficient to sequence the work as follows:

    a. **Apply the interior wall paint.** By performing this task first, one might avoid getting paint on his new carpet, drapes, and furniture.

    b. **Apply the wallpaper.** By applying it in this order, there will be no furniture to work around, and it will be unnecessary to *cut-in* the paint around the edges of the wall paper.

    c. **Install the carpet.** Now there is no risk of getting paint on it, and there is no furniture to interfere with the installation.

    d. **Install the drapes.** With the carpet in, the length of the drapes can be accurately determined, and with the painting completed, there will be little risk of paint damage to the drapes, nor the need to cut-in paint around the drape mounting fixtures.

e. Place the **major pieces** of furniture in balanced room positions. There is now no risk of getting paint on them, and they will not interfere with the carpet installation.

f. Place the lamps, plants, and minor pieces of furniture to decorate in between the major pieces.

g. Hang the paintings, to balance color and to decorate wall spaces between the furniture, lamps, plants, and windows.

h. Finally, place the **trim items**, such as vases, knickknacks, et cetera.

The above sequence of actions is representative of **general to specific** planning; that is, it starts with the largest items (the walls), and ends with the smallest items (knickknacks). This approach eliminates having to re-position objects to accommodate the next step, thereby saving time and energy. Of course, occasional circumstances might dictate that a minor task take precedence over a major task; however, **the importance of the** *general to specific* **planning concept cannot be overstated.**

Planning is a definite and necessary step in the solving of **specific** problems; however, effective planning habits are **equally beneficial** in one's **daily life routine.** To this end, one might consider the following minimal daily planning activity:

a. Maintain a planning schedule, listing the daily activities that one wishes to accomplish.

b. Each day's planned activities should be prioritized by **importance** and respectively numbered, the number one being assigned to the most important activity, and so on.

c. Each morning, one should begin with his first scheduled activity and stay with it until it is finished, then go on to activity number two, and so on. Granted, there will always be exceptions to any planned sequence, prompting one to jump priorities or work simultaneously on multiple activities; however, one should try to stay within, or return to, his planned schedule.

d. At the end of each day, an individual should review his schedule and transfer that day's unfinished activities to the top of the next day's schedule, assigning them first priority.

It is wise to be conservative in one's planning approach; in particular, one should anticipate that it will typically take longer (or cost more) than planned, to accomplish a desired goal.

Step 4. Implement the plan of action (the solution).

Each of the previous steps are **analytical** in nature; in contrast, this final step typically requires **assertive physical action**.

Identifying a problem, analyzing it, and developing a plan of action can all be futile if individuals fail to **implement** their plans of action. The **key** factor in implementing a plan of action is **self-discipline**.

Often, individual actions result in obvious and immediate personal rewards. Some actions, however, do not have an **apparent** or **immediate** personal benefit. Such actions require **vision** and **self-discipline** to enable their completion.

Self-discipline is the mental process by which one convinces himself to expend **immediate** time and energy for the purpose of creating a personal benefit that will materialize at some **future** date. As examples, consider *chopping firewood*, or the *farming of a food crop*. Both activities require immediate effort to produce an eventual benefit.

The required **intensity** of self-discipline is **directly** related to the **complexity** of one's goal and the **length of time** that it will take to realize personal benefit. An individual must **envision** the anticipated benefit of his eventual goal, in order to create and maintain the self-discipline that is necessary to complete it.

Some benefits of self-disciplined acts are **quantitative** in nature and are relatively easy to visualize - for example, the self-disciplined act of saving money. Obviously, if one puts $1,000 into the bank at ten percent annual interest, one can easily visualize that he will have earned $100 after one year.

The GUIDE

The benefits of certain quantitative goals may be of greater complexity, making them difficult to visualize. For example, the potential benefits of working four years to obtain a college education may be difficult to discern. Consequently, such an act might require considerable vision and self-discipline.

To create and maintain the self-discipline that is necessary for such a goal, one should envision the potential benefits of the accomplishment, such as **financial earnings, prestige, job satisfaction,** et cetera.

Visualizing the **potential benefits** of a goal is the **key** to self-discipline. When the goal is quantitative in nature it is very helpful to structure a realistic **model** or **scenario.** For example, one might make the following assumptions:

- **Without** a college education, an individual might earn an average annual income of $25,000.

- **With** a college degree, he might earn an average annual salary of $45,000.

- The typical individual will work an average of forty years before retiring.

Based upon the above assumptions, an individual's college education could yield him $700,000 **more income** than he would have earned without it.

The supporting mathematics are relatively simple: if one might earn $45,000 per year with a college education, or $25,000 per year without a degree, the potential annual economic benefit of the education is equal to the difference, that being $20,000 per year.

Extending this $20,000 per year potential benefit, over an estimated career of forty working years, the result is an overall career benefit of $800,000 ($20,000 per yr. times 40 yrs).

To be fair in the comparison, one should consider the **cost** of obtaining a four year college degree. Such costs might include the **loss of earned income** while attending school and the cost of tuition. If one estimates this cost at $100,000, the resulting **net** benefit would be $700,000 ($800,000 from above, minus the $100,000 cost).

Based on the above assumptions and mathematical results, one would have to work **sixty-eight years** without a college degree to earn the same money that one would earn in **forty years** with a college degree - that is **twenty-eight years more!**

Obviously, if four years of college work can save twenty-eight years of extra labor, it is certainly worth the self-discipline!

Some self-disciplined problem solving actions yield **qualitative benefits** as compared to quantitative benefits, for example, the achievement of **better health**, of a **happier marriage**, or of a **creatively fulfilling job**, et cetera.

Often, such qualitative benefits are **more** difficult to visualize than quantitative ones; consequently, their achievement might **require a greater degree of self-discipline**. For example, an individual might be able to exercise the self-discipline necessary for vocational success because he can comfortably visualize the relative financial (quantitative) benefits; the same individual may be unable to exercise the self-discipline necessary to maintain a healthy marriage, because he **cannot** comfortably visualize the related qualitative benefits.

Creative visualization is often required in the attainment of qualitative benefits. For example, consider the *quitting of cigarette smoking*. To develop and maintain the necessary self-discipline, one might envision himself (in his *mind's eye*) doing his favorite activities, such as fishing, cooking, eating, making love, et cetera. Next, one might envision himself doing the same activities when he is sixty, sixty-five, seventy, and seventy-one years of age and so on. Next, one might consider the reality that cigarette smoking increases the risk of cancer, heart disease, emphysema or stroke, any of which might rob an individual of years or months of healthy life. Finally, the individual might ask himself, "is the pleasure of smoking cigarettes worth giving up years of potentially enjoyable life?"

Another form of helpful visualization, in this particular instance, is to imagine oneself sitting in a doctor's office, with the doctor looking him in the eye and sadly saying, "you have six more months to live, because you have lung cancer," and further stating that "you could have lived and enjoyed many more fruitful years, had you quit smoking." Additionally, one might go to the cancer ward of a local hospital and see the patients, look at their **faces**, and ask them how they **feel**. This is similar to a race-car driver walking a race course before driving it; it permits an individual to clearly see and avoid the hazards before a damaging encounter.

Such visual aids can be a motivating tool in the stimulation of all self-disciplined acts; for example, if one wants a new car, he might keep a *picture* of the desired car in his briefcase or on his closet door. Likewise, if one wishes to be slimmer, he might write his desired weight across a picture of a slim body, and then keep that picture on his refrigerator door, or in his lunch box. Such pictorial visualization aids serve as a constant stimulant to the **subconscious mind**.

In reiteration, individuals can simplify problem solving by:

Step 1. Identifying the problem.

Step 2. Analyzing the problem.

Step 3. Developing a plan of action.

Step 4. Implementing the plan of action.

SUBJECT 4. Timeliness

The **timely** performance of an individual's personal and business activities can **assure** the accomplishment of his desired objectives with **minimal** waste of labor and materials.

As part of the planning process, individuals establish **time schedules** according to which certain desired events should occur. The object of such time scheduling is twofold:

a. Physical necessity. Most desired events (accomplishments, goals, problem solutions, et cetera) are preceded by the completion of certain related tasks. By their very nature, such tasks must normally be completed in a specific sequence; that is, one task usually cannot begin until the previous one has been completed. **Time scheduling** is used to plan and control the sequenced completion of such tasks; this process is obvious in such activities as *cooking, manufacturing, construction, business transactions,* and *life* in general.

b. Efficiency. Aside from assuring that certain events will occur in some desired sequence, time scheduling **diminishes** labor and material waste. To this end, individuals establish mutually convenient meeting times for the accomplishment of common objectives, such as *business meetings, school classes, weddings, lunches,* et cetera. By adhering to such mutually established time schedules, no party is forced to **waste his time** by having to wait for the arrival or performance of another party.

Many problem solving scenarios require the use of certain **materials**, such as money, food, chemicals, manufactured components, et cetera. Such materials might possess a variety of **time related** economic characteristics, including *perishability, storage costs, obsolescence, earning potential,* et cetera.

If an individual fails to exercise effective time scheduling in his use of such materials, he might experience considerable (and unnecessary) **expense.** For example, receiving materials too soon might result in spoilage or unnecessary storage expense, and receiving materials too late might result in wasted idle labor expense.

Effective time management saves labor and materials. Such labor and materials can be used to enhance the quality of one's life; consequently, effective time scheduling, and the timely performance of such schedules, can substantially improve the quality of one's life.

SUBJECT 5. Attention to Detail

Attention to detail is an **ancillary** problem solving skill. One can certainly live a successful life without it; however, successful living **favors** those who practice it.

Attention to detail is simply a matter of **refinement** in one's organization and planning techniques. The more detailed that one is in his organization and planning, the more variables one can anticipate and control. Anticipating and controlling variables results in a **higher probability of success** with regard to one's problem solving, task accomplishments, and overall life achievements.

Attention to detail, though generally beneficial, can also reach a point of diminishing returns. **One should not allow himself to become so immersed in organization and planning that he loses sight of his overall objectives, or fails to enact his plans.**

SUBJECT 6. Learning

Some problem solving methods are **reflexive** or **instinctual**, such as a *child's sucking of a mother's breast*, or the *blinking of one's eye*, however, **most** problem solving techniques must be **learned**.

One learns problem solving by two methods: through personal **trial and error**, or through expert **guidance**.

a. Trial and Error.

When one does not know how to solve a particular problem, he assesses the situation, compares it to his previous problem solving experiences, and then formulates a **best guess solution**.

Depending upon the extent of one's **previous** problem solving experiences (often referred to as one's *maturity*), and the efficiency of one's mental processes (often referred to as one's *intelligence*), his chosen solution might be a **success** or a **failure**.

The prospect of failure is an integral part of every problem solving approach; consequently, failure should not be irrationally feared.

The **irrational** fear of failure can assure **eventual** failure. That is, if one hesitates to try a problem solving approach for fear of failure, he absolutely precludes himself from any chance of ever solving the subject problem, and in effect **"he fails!"** As an example of such self-induced failure, an individual might have a constant pain, but does not want to go to the doctor for fear of detecting a serious ailment; consequently, the individual might prematurely die from a condition that may have been treatable. In such an instance, the individual's fear of facing an ailment (a limited physical failure) results in his death (the **ultimate** physical **failure**).

One should neither fear nor invite failure. There are two effective methods of avoiding unnecessary failure: the **first** is to **learn from, and not repeat**, one's previous **failures**; the **second** is to **seek and follow expert guidance**.

b. Guidance.

Guidance, like a good road map, indicates the most efficient path to a desired destination.

Seeking **expert guidance** for health, family, financial, or other problems, is an effective form of **failure avoidance**.

Obtaining a basic education, enhanced by university study or trade school, is a form of failure avoidance.

Problem solving through personal *trial and error* can be very **inefficient**; guidance (through education) can save an individual countless hours (or years) of trial and error experimentation.

Through formal education, an individual can learn effective problem solving methods. Most established problem solving methods have come about from the **cumulative** trial and error efforts of millions of individuals which have taken place over thousands of years.

Guidance allows one to avoid the impracticality of having to **reinvent** the *wheel, bronze tools, farming techniques, scientific theories*, the *radio, television*, the *internal combustion engine, atomic energy*, et cetera.

Granted, some problem solving scenarios are **subjective** in nature, necessarily requiring a personal trial and error approach. For example, one might be advised by his parents or friends that he should enter a "particular" profession. But only the individual, himself, can answer the subjective question, "is this the **right** profession?"

The wise individual soon learns to **discern** between those decisions that are personal/subjective in nature and those that are not. It is far more efficient to employ the successful problem solving approaches of others, rather than constantly experimenting with one's own time and life.

In reiteration, individuals can improve their problem solving abilities by **learning** effective methods. Failure is an integral part of the learning process, and should not frighten or deter an individual from self-improvement.

SUBJECT 7. Habit

Habit is a subtle, effective, and necessary problem solving skill. It is the simple act of doing the same thing over and over until it becomes a conditioned response, requiring no preplanned or controlled effort.

Initially, some acts of self-discipline can be very **uncomfortable**, such as dieting, exercising, studying, saving money, et cetera. Through habit, such actions can progress from being discomforts to being both **comfortable and behavioral necessities.** For example, an individual might go for a walk or run in the morning. When his actions reach the point of habit, the individual will eventually feel discomfort, if he fails to take his morning exercise.

Through habit, a clumsy and struggling problem solving attempt can mature into a simple and effective routine. For example, a master craftsman can produce a product much faster than an apprentice; the apprentice must slowly consider each move, while the craftsman can rely upon habit reinforced skills. Likewise, an accomplished musician can play a complex musical arrangement while casually talking to someone. This is possible because the musician's brain/finger coordination has been conditioned through habit.

One must also remember that individuals progress through **change**. Although habit is a necessary and valuable skill, it should not be embraced to the point of **detriment; established habits should give way to self-improvement.**

In summary, individuals should use their problem solving skills just as craftsmen use their tools. An individual's toolbox of personal problem solving skills should include:

1. Communication

2. Organization

3. The Problem Solving Process

4. Timeliness

5. Attention to Detail

6. Learning

7. Habit

Craftsmen, through the skillful use of their tools, create beautiful products; likewise, all individuals can create a *successful life* through the effective use of their personal problem solving skills.

PART TWO: Health Considerations

- Contents -

[Note - The words *Man*, *him*, *he*, *his*, and *himself* herein refer to the species in general, with **no sexist connotation intended**.]

PART TWO: Health Considerations

Successful living consists of **four life elements:**

- **Good Health**

- **Loving Family Relationships**

- **Financial Security**

- **Fulfilling Play**

These four life elements are interactive. A problem with any one element might negatively impact the others.

Of the four, one's health is **most influential**, in that **good health** is necessary to create and enjoy the other three elements of successful living. More so, **one's very existence is dependent upon his good health**.

SECTION A. How to Attain Good Health

Good health is not an accident, nor is it luck or simply a genetic blessing; it is acquired and maintained through **good health habits**. Good health habits can be divided into four areas:

1. **Cleanliness**   3. **Rest**

2. **Diet**   4. **Exercise**

SUBJECT 1. Cleanliness

Cleanliness is the simple act of avoiding things and conditions that are potentially harmful.

Cleanliness should be practiced in four areas:

    a. **Personal Hygiene**   c. **In the Workplace**

    b. **In the Home**   d. **In the General Environment**

a. Personal Hygiene.

Personal hygiene is one's first line of defense against bacterial infection, poisons, and other harmful materials.

The following hygiene habits minimize one's exposure to potentially damaging substances:

- Wash the hands, with soap and warm water, before eating. By doing so, one minimizes the possibility of contaminating food with harmful bacteria or toxins.

- Wash the hands and mouth area (men should also wash their moustache) with soap and warm water after meals. By doing so, one removes organic material that might promote infectious bacterial growth.

- Brush and dental floss the teeth after each meal. By doing so, one removes organic materials which might promote gum disease and tooth decay.

- Shower each morning, washing the body and hair with soap, and put on clean clothing. By doing so, one removes organic substances that might support bacteria growth and toxins that might cause skin irritations.

- Wear a different pair of shoes on alternate days, and use foot powder. By doing so, one minimizes the accumulation of foot perspiration, thereby reducing the opportunity for the growth of tissue-damaging bacteria.

- Wash the hands, face, and genitals with soap and water before each sexual encounter. By doing so, one minimizes the possibility of introducing harmful bacteria into or onto the genitals.

- Wash the hands, face, and genitals with soap and warm water after each sexual encounter. By doing so, one removes organic substances that might support bacterial growth and reduces the probability of spreading contagious diseases.

- Wash the hands with soap and warm water before and after using the toilet/urinal (particularly in public restrooms). By doing so, one minimizes the possibility of infecting one's genitals with harmful bacteria or spreading contagious skin diseases.

- Wipe (clean) the anus after defecating. By doing so, one removes organic material that might infect the urinary tract or support the growth of harmful bacteria.

b. Cleanliness at Home.

The following actions are suggested to minimize one's exposure to illness-causing bacteria and toxins in the home:

- Clean sinks, tubs, toilets, bath and bed linens weekly.

- Clean/vacuum floors bimonthly.

- Keep food preparation, cooking, storage, and eating areas clean at all times.

- Keep food preparation and eating utensils clean at all times.

- Open windows regularly, for sun and fresh air circulation, depending upon the season.

- Clean garage areas semiannually. Use safety goggles when working on garage projects. Wear heavy gloves when handling plants, rough wood, and metals. Wear safety goggles, fume mask and plastic gloves when using insecticides, cleaning chemicals, and other hazardous chemicals.

- Avoid exposure to hazardous automotive, household cleaning, and pest control materials. Wear plastic gloves and safety goggles when using such materials. Do not store such materials near food, or within the reach of children or pets.

c. Cleanliness in the Workplace.

Individuals should avoid potentially harmful substances and conditions in their workplaces. In particular, one should avoid exposure to **excessive radiation, carcinogenic/toxic substances** and **fumes, organic contaminants**, et cetera.

Furthermore, one should endeavor to protect fellow employees, and the general public, from exposure to such hazardous substances and conditions.

If one's employer is knowingly permitting such exposures, and if one cannot reasonably convince his employer of the immorality of such actions, then one should be prepared to terminate his employment relationship and report the employer's actions to the appropriate regulating authorities.

d. Cleanliness in One's General Environment.

One's environment should provide clean air, clean water, and a functional sanitation system. Most municipalities, in Western societies, effectively accomplish this task.

If one lives in a rural community and relies upon a well water system and a cesspool/leach-line sanitary system, he should periodically check his water quality for organic/chemical pollutants.

With regard to the air that one must breath, if the air looks dirty, smells acrid, or hurts the eyes and lungs, obviously it should be avoided.

Commercial industry and private transportation have created valuable societal benefits; unfortunately, they have also created substantial environmental pollution.

The human body has a limited ability to *filter out* consumed pollutants. If one's body regularly consumes excessive pollutants, cancers and internal organ failures are probable. **Although transportation and industry provide jobs, money, mobility, material possessions, and more, such benefits can only be enjoyed if society is healthy.**

SUBJECT 2. Diet

a. Healthy Foods.

As primitive Man evolved, he developed certain bodily and metabolic characteristics to accommodate the ingestion of foods that were present in his **natural** environment.

Later in Man's evolution, he developed the use of tools, such as fire and hunting weapons.

Man's tool usage altered his eating habits. Weapons permitted the efficient taking of game, thereby increasing meat consumption. Fire could be used to prepare foods, thereby killing parasites, tenderizing the foods, and releasing nutrients.

The physical rigors of Man's hunting lifestyle, combined with the **low fat** content of *wild game*, minimized Man's susceptibility to fat-related cardiovascular maladies.

Primitive Man's natural food and lifestyle worked in metabolic harmony to create and maintain good health.

Over the past few thousand years, Man has altered his natural survival activities; instead of **hunting wild game**, he turned to the domestication of **livestock**. His diet of lean meats (from wild game) was replaced with the fat marbled meats of domesticated animals.

As Man progressed from a **forager/hunter** to an **urban tool user**, his lifestyle progressed from one of **action orientation** to one of **sedentary orientation**.

Man's modern combination of a **high fat** diet, and a **sedentary** lifestyle is dissimilar to the conditions that supported Man's evolutionary development. This book speculates that it is in one's best health interest to practice diet and exercise habits (see *Exercise*) that are reminiscent of the **natural conditions** that supported Man's evolutionary development, while at the same time enjoying the health benefits afforded by modern technology.

Foods that are naturally beneficial include **clean water, mother's milk (for infants), low fat dairy products, berries, fruits, nuts, certain** roots, legumes, grains, certain leaves and stalks, eggs, honey, certain saltwater plants, fresh and saltwater fish and crustaceans, limited lean meats, and certain minerals.

b. Food Preparation.

Foods should be **fresh, clean,** and particularly free of harmful chemical substances.

Steaming and **boiling** are excellent cooking methods; such methods enhance digestibility, release flavors, and make nutrients accessible. The resulting broths should also be consumed, if possible. One should avoid frying foods, except in a small quantity of polyunsaturated vegetable oil, as frying tends to add fat content to foods, and it can produce carcinogens.

c. Problem Foods and Substances.

1. Sugar. Primitive Man's primary source of sugar was ripe fruits, certain vegetables, and limited honey. The human body evolved the ability to metabolize sugar, relative to the quantities that were consumed in prehistoric times. This book speculates that when one eats a candy bar, or a piece of cake, or pie, or pastry, or drinks a cola, or alcohol, the potential exists for consuming far more sugar than one naturally needs or is able to properly metabolize. In rough approximation, an individual would have to eat **seven** apples, **five** banana's or **six** oranges to equal (in natural sugar) the sugar that is ingested by eating **a typical** three ounce *candy bar.*

Excessive quantities of processed sugar can promote tooth decay, obesity, and other physiological disorders.

2. Caffeine. Caffeine can cause constriction of the blood vessels (and primary arteries) and stimulation of the nervous system; consequently, coffee, tea, and caffeinated softdrinks should be consumed in moderation.

3. Nicotine (and related *tars*). Nicotine is potentially **addictive** and **toxic.** It is suspect of causing cancer, heart disease, birth defects, and emphysema. Tobacco use is the primary source of nicotine consumption; consequently, one would be wise to avoid or moderate tobacco use.

4. Alcohol. Alcohol is addictive and potentially damaging to human tissue. If consumed at all, it should be taken in moderation. Some research suggests that alcohol consumption should not exceed two onces per day, and that **distilled spirits** cause blood alcohol levels to rise much faster and decline slower than alcohol consumed in the form of **wine**. Alcohol consumed with meals, in the form of wine, might beneficially stimulate the production of digestive hormones; distilled alcohol, consumed with meals, does not appear to have a similar beneficial effect.

5. Commercially manufactured foods, enhancer, and medicines.

Many such substances are well tested by their manufacturers and controlling government agencies, and have truly bettered Man's quality of life. However, individuals should consider that the human body evolved to accommodate the metabolizing of substances and foods that **naturally** occurred in Man's primitive environment.

This book does not suggest that individuals should disobey their doctor's medication advice, or forego enjoying the benefits of manufactured foods; however, one would be wise to question and understand the relative risks/benefits of ingesting such substances.

Again, many problem foods and substances can be safely consumed when done so in moderation. An occasional *French pastry*, *Mexican meal*, or *Champagne celebration* does no permanent damage. **Moderation is the key word!**

SUBJECT 3. Rest

One's *general health*, *appearance*, and *longevity*, are dependent upon **good rest habits**.

To better understand the necessity for good rest habits, one might consider the nature of Man's evolutionary development.

Primate evolution began more than three million years ago. Man specifically developed as a forager and plains hunter. In that such survival activities were best conducted in daylight, the twelve evening (dark) hours were probably used to rest. During sleep, the body's metabolism slowed and the body was relatively free of physical motion and intellectual problem solving demands. This book speculates that Man's body evolved to optimize its use of this rest period.

About two million years into Man's evolution, he developed the ability to control *fire*. The tool of fire provided evening light, heat, and safety, thereby permitting Man to extend and enhance his daytime (waking) activities. By doing so, however, he necessarily shortened his natural rest period, possibly frustrating the fulfillment of his physiological rest needs.

Modern Man's cultural advances have certainly enhanced his quality of life; however, the related stress and noise pollution has also created the opportunity for further frustration of evening rest needs.

It has become impractical for Man to enjoy his *primitive* twelve hour *rest/sleep period*, consequently, eight to nine hours have become an optimum rest period.

Although individuals can survive with less than eight to nine hours of sleep, this book speculates that doing so diminishes one's overall well-being.

Consider what happens when individuals shorten their sleeping hours:

- When one is awake, his heart beats about 72 times per minute (or faster). In deep sleep, the heart slows to about 60 beats (or less) per minute; **in other words, the heart beats about twelve extra beats for each minute that one is awake, as compared to being asleep.**

Potentially, lost sleep equals extra heart beats. If individuals sleep six hours per night instead of eight, they potentially expend twelve extra beats per waking minute for two hours (one hundred and twenty extra waking minutes); that is 1,440 extra heart beats per evening, or 525,600 additional beats each year. One might question the health consequences of this extra heart action.

- When individuals sleep, their overall **metabolisms slow;** their **body temperature**s, pulse rates, and rates of breathing all **drop.** Because chemical reactions slow as ambient temperatures drop, and considering that the aging process is a chemical action, this book hypothesizes that **the body's aging process might be slowed during sleep.**

▫ When awake, one's physical processes are dedicated to keeping the body warm, digesting food, and supporting muscle movement. When asleep, less energy is required to keep the body warm and little energy is expended on muscle movement. This book speculates that the body uses sleep time to facilitate tissue repair, the expulsion of waste materials, and other body maintenance functions; and furthermore that individuals deprive themselves of such necessary body maintenance time through insufficient sleep.

▫ This book also speculates that sleep permits the brain to perform beneficial **non-conscious** processing tasks. Such tasks might include the coordinating of body maintenance, experimental problem solving scenarios (**dreams**), and database maintenance routines. If these assumptions are accurate, one might question the mental and physical health consequences of inadequate sleep.

▫ Insufficient sleep can result in **bags** or **dark circles** under the eyes.

Granted, shorter sleeping hours might allow one to accomplish more problem solving tasks, potentially bettering one's quality of life. **On the other hand**, shorter sleeping hours might equally diminish one's quality of life by depriving him of adequate health, or worse yet, **by shortening his life**.

The following conditions are conducive to good rest:

▫ A comfortable bed.

▫ A quiet and dark sleeping area; one might use an eye cover in the morning to diminish the stimulating effect of sunlight.

▫ Avoid the excessive consumption of sugar or alcohol. Although alcohol initially dulls the senses, this book speculates that the eventual metabolizing of such sugar based substances actually stimulates consciousness.

▫ Refrain from active thought. Once the lights have been turned off, one should say to oneself, "this is a **sleeping time**, **not** a **problem solving time**."

- One might do some light reading prior to sleep, to clear his mind of heavier subjects, and to break intense problem solving thought routines.

- It is normal to periodically awaken during the night, due to noise, dreams, or to use the toilet. In such instances, one should take care not to permit his mind to go into an active problem solving mode. Once the mind begins to consciously work on problem solving, it becomes difficult to go back to sleep.

- If awakened by a vivid dream, or if one is having difficulty going to sleep, one might go to the kitchen, and **heat a half cup of milk**. The physical act of going to the kitchen tends to divert the mind from complex thoughts, and the drinking of the warm milk begins a calming *digestive process*.

SUBJECT 4. Exercise

Having a good life is dependent upon one's ability to solve problems. Many problem solutions require **physical action**, such as *walking to the store*, *making love*, *working in the garden*, *self-defense*, et cetera.

The body's ability to physically respond as desired is primarily dependent upon one's muscle tone, strength, flexibility, and the capacity of his cardiovascular and pulmonary systems.

The condition of one's muscles, heart, and lungs is directly dependent upon his exercise habits; consequently, one's overall problem solving ability (and his resulting quality of life) is directly influenced by his exercise habits.

a. The Nature of Exercise.

To best understand the underlying function of exercise, one might again consider Man's evolutionary development.

As primitive Man adapted to his particular environment, his body evolved to accommodate his survival activities. Such activities included:

- **Stooping**, to pick roots and berries and to drink.

- **Reaching**, to pick fruits and leaves.

- **Climbing**, to reach fruit and leaves and for self-defense.

- **Jumping**, to reach foods or traverse obstacles.

- **Walking**, to forage large areas.

- **Carrying**, to transport food and materials.

- **Running**, to chase game and escape predators.

- **Fighting**, to defend himself, family, and territory.

Primitive Man's performance of the above listed activities also contributed to the healthy functioning of his other bodily processes:

- **Blood circulation** (the distribution of oxygen and nutrients to all extremities of the body) was enhanced by physical activity.

- **Digestion** was assisted by physical activity. Once the initial digestive process was underway, physical activity helped to move food and waste through the digestive track.

- **Breathing** was stimulated by physical activity, thereby increasing the intake and distribution of oxygen to all parts of the body.

- **Muscle tone** was maintained through physical activity. Healthy appearance was certainly a benefit, but of greater importance was the structural support of internal organs. Infirm muscles cannot properly support and protect (from trauma) organs like the heart, kidneys, liver, and intestines. Good muscle tone was needed to hold the spinal column (upper body and head) upright.

- **Reproduction** was assisted by muscular strength, which was used to fend off unwanted suitors, to spar for a desired mate, to comfortably engage in intercourse, to carry, bear, and raise a child, et cetera.

- **Flexibility** of the joints was maintained through physical activity.

As Man intellectually evolved, he changed the ways in which he fulfilled his daily hunting, foraging, and tool making needs.

As social structures grew in complexity, individuals became **specialized** in one survival task, rather than performing an array of general survival tasks (see *What is Money?*).

Some individuals specialized in hunting, some in foraging or agriculture, some in tool making, et cetera. Presently, such task specializations are referred to as **jobs**.

In primitive times, individuals bartered their specialized services and products for needed services and products.

Eventually, **money economies** developed, permitting goods and services to be exchanged in commercial marketplaces (stores, offices, et cetera).

Modern societies have grown increasingly sophisticated in tool usage and task specialization; consequently, most modern **jobs** are **sedentary** in nature. Representative of such jobs are: lawyers, scientists, businessmen, doctors, teachers, et cetera.

The evolution of the body's **digestive, nervous, muscular, skeletal, cardiovascular, pulmonary**, and other systems was shaped by Man's environment, foods, and survival activities; that is, the digestive track developed to metabolize certain natural foods, the nervous system evolved to accommodate certain natural stimuli, **the muscular and skeletal systems evolved to facilitate certain natural movement needs**, et cetera.

Furthermore, each such body system evolved to **complementally interact** with the other body systems. Logically, then, this book speculates that if one of the body's systems is substantially altered in its natural functioning, then all of the body's interactive systems will be affected.

Modern Man's sedentary lifestyle substantially alters the natural functioning of his muscular, cardiovascular, and pulmonary systems. This fact, in combination with a typically **high-fat-diet**, has placed modern Man in a **health risk** position.

Exercise is an effective method of compensating for the natural physical activities that have become culturally impractical. Through exercise, one permits his heart, lungs, and muscles to naturally complement and assist his digestive processes.

b. Exercise Methods.

This book suggests that exercise should be reflective of Man's natural primitive activities. Such activities might include stooping, reaching, climbing, jumping, carrying objects, walking, running, and fighting.

There are a variety of methods by which one might exercise: interactive sports, bicycling, swimming, and gymnasiums are all effective approaches.

Exercise is not necessarily enjoyable; consequently, it requires **self-discipline**. If one's chosen form of exercise involves the use of special facilities or special equipment, or if it is dependent upon sport interaction with others, then **exercise avoidance opportunities** are created, such as "I did not have time to go to the gym", or "I could not find a tennis partner", or the "pool heater was broken", or "my bike had a flat tire", et cetera.

A simple personal exercise routine, in and around the home, is conducive to consistency.

The **morning** is a good time to perform an exercise routine. It helps one to awaken and prepare one for the day's activities.

Morning exercise **limbers** the body and **invigorates** it with oxygen, **primes** the **appetite**, and **sets the metabolism** at a rate that will discourage fat storage.

Warning: The suggested exercises in the following paragraphs assume that the reader is safely capable of exercising. One's exercise ability may be limited by his age or state of health; consequently, individuals should consult their physicians before beginning the exercises herein suggested.

Consider the following exercise routine to fulfill one's natural **walking and running** needs:

- Upon arising in the morning, put on good jogging shoes and a warm-up outfit.

- Select a relatively flat running area, about one-half mile from one's home. Preferably the running area will have a **grass or dirt surface**, such as a grass-lined street, a ball park, a country lane, or a beach, et cetera. One should avoid running on asphalt or cement. Such surfaces are relatively inflexible; consequently, they stress the bones and tendons, and fatigue the cartilage. Also avoid uneven surfaces that might prompt ankle sprains; one might also wear high-top athletic shoes to avoid ankle sprains.

- Each morning, warm-up the body by walking to the running area. Then run the one-half mile stretch, then walk for a moment (enjoy the air and scenery), and then run back to the starting point of one's running area, for a total run of one mile. One should try to make sure that his pulse rate gets up to at least one-hundred twenty beats per minute (**individuals should consult with their physician prior to commencing this or any suggested exercise routines**).

- Now, by walking home from the running area, one permits his heart and breathing rate to gradually calm, and muscles to relax without cramping.

The above daily routine (one mile of walking and one mile of running) permits the individual to:

- Develop and maintain the lungs' capacity.

- Maintain muscle tone and strength.

- Maintain joint flexibility.

- Stimulate blood flow, thereby clearing cholesterol plaque build-up, and invigorating body extremities.

- Stimulate the appetite and digestive process.

- Divert one's thought to a naturally calming activity.

- Maintain the body's general motor skills.

Such an exercise regimen might be enhanced by the company of a dog; they are good natural running partners, dating back to their primitive hunting relationship with Man. If one enjoys the company of a dog in this capacity, be sure to carry a plastic bag to *clea nup* after the dog.

Upon returning home, while the body is still warm, one might do **calisthenics** to exercise the body's stooping, reaching, climbing, jumping, and carrying abilities.

- One does not need a formal gymnasium to do such calisthenics; the center of the living room will do.

- Structure a personal routine of **sit-ups, push-ups, bending, stretching, jumping,** and **lifting exercises,** starting with a few of each and increasing the numbers, as one's conditioning improves.

- One can use books or stones for weights.

- Try to eventually do about fifty sit-ups, twenty push-ups, ten or fifteen alternate toe touching bends, fifteen jumping-jacks, and two repetitions each of ten biceps, triceps, and pectoral lifting routines.

The above suggested running routine need not take more than **twenty minutes**, and the calisthenics routine need not take more than **fifteen minutes** daily, for a total of thirty-five minutes.

Granted, one may not be able to start these exercise routines at full pace. Individuals might start by walking only, and doing a few simple stretching exercises. **Again, individuals should consult with their physicians before commencing any exercise program suggested in this book.**

The key to building an effective exercise routine is to **do something every day**. Eventually, one's daily routine will turn into a habit, and the intensity of the routine will increase naturally, as one's condition betters.

The maintenance of one's **fighting** (self-defense) skills can be accomplished through sports activities such as Judo, Karate, or boxing classes. One might consider a three or four month training series, spending one or two evenings a week. Individuals might consider refreshing their self-defense skills every five years or so.

c. Bodybuilding.

Bodybuilding is the intentional enlargement of one's muscles through the act of lifting weights or by using special exercise equipment/methods.

Certain bodybuilding approaches may be beneficial; however, one might question the propriety of enlarging one's muscles beyond their genetically intended size, and beyond the practical capacity that is required for typical daily living.

Some individuals use *anabolic steroids* (synthetic hormones) to enhance muscle development. If improperly used, such steroids can cause physical and behavioral problems. In particular, the mass of one's muscle tissue, the density of one's bones, the thickness of one's cartilage, and the tensile strengths of one's ligaments and tendons are all genetically predetermined to harmoniously counter-support one another. This book speculates that the improper use of steroids might cause abnormal muscle development, thereby disrupting the body's natural structural interrelationship, resulting in potential **trauma** to bones, cartilage, tendons, and ligaments.

Under professional medical supervision steroid use might be appropriate, for example when the body's normal hormone production has been retarded because of illness, trauma, or genetic defect. However, one might question the morality of using steroids to gain unfair competitive athletic advantage, or for purposes of vanity.

The problem solving approaches of civilized peoples are **intellect/tool** oriented, rather than **brute force** oriented; consequently, one might consider the benefits of developing his intellectual problem solving skills, rather than his muscular appearance.

d. Making Time for Exercise.

One might ask, **"how can I afford thirty-five minutes to perform a morning exercise routine, when I have work that must be done and a family to support?"** The answer is that **"one's health is of first concern; it takes priority over all other life considerations."** Unless one maintains good physical health, one cannot be a good spouse, parent, or worker. **Unless one feels good, life is not worth living.**

Health first is not an option; it is a necessity! Unless individuals accept this reality, the quality and length of one's life will be diminished. To this end, individuals should establish working hours that will accommodate their exercise needs. Moral employers are considerate of employee health needs, and some professions are conducive to flexible hours. One should seek out such supportive conditions.

An occasional work task may arise, that conflicts with one's morning exercise schedule; however, such interruptions should be the exception. Granted, one might earn **more money** if he worked the **extra hour** instead of exercising. Individuals should guard against such **short-sighted logic**; the additional net worth that one could earn by disregarding one's daily health needs is never worth the **negative health trade-off.** Additional net worth does little good, if one does not live to enjoy it.

In summary, a daily exercise regimen can provide many potential benefits:

- A healthy appearance.

- A general feeling of well-being.

- An enhanced appetite and improved digestion.

- Restful sleep.

- Illness avoidance.

- Clearer thought.

- A better overall physical relationship with one's spouse.

- An improved probability of surviving illness, accident, natural disaster, or physical assault.

SECTION B. The Nature and Avoidance of Illness

People use their thought processes and motor skills to solve problems and accomplish goals. They then use their physical senses to enjoy the benefits of such actions.

When a body is ill, its thought process, motor skills, and senses are typically diminished, thereby inhibiting the individual's ability to live a fulfilling life.

With the above reality in mind, it is in one's best interest to **avoid illness**. The following is a discussion of the most common, and severe, forms of illness, and how they might be avoided.

The following medical subject presentations are general in nature and should not be relied upon for self-diagnosis or treatment of illness. All individuals should practice a regular health mainte-nance routine, as directed by their physician.

SUBJECT 1. Heart Disease

There are many cardiovascular related maladies, such as genetic valve or muscle defects, collapsed, ballooned, or ruptured arteries, or rhythm abnormalities, et cetera. Of the many such maladies, **atherosclerosis** (a form of *arteriosclerosis*) claims the **most** lives, and is probably the one **most easily avoided**.

Granted, one might have a genetic predisposition towards athero-sclerosis, a condition in which the body produces excessive complex fatty plaques. Typically though, atherosclerosis is self-induced by the **victim's poor health habits**. Such habits might include:

- **The ingestion of meats, produce, and dairy products** that have high cholesterol and fat contents, causing the deposit of complex fat plaques on the inside walls of the arteries.

- **Inadequate exercise**. Exercise creates energy demands, permitting extra cholesterol and fats to be metabolized. Additionally, exercise increases the velocity of blood flow, expanding the walls of the veins and arteries, thereby breaking loose and clearing plaque deposits.

- **Cigarette smoking**. Cigarette smoking appears to contribute to atherosclerosis. This book hypothesizes that chemical agents in cigarette smoke **inhibit** the body's normal metabolizing of fats, thereby permitting smokers to consume **greater** quantities of fatty foods without resulting in weight gain. If this assumption is accurate, the smoker is probably exposed to higher blood levels of atherosclerosis causing **fatty plaques**.

Arteries, constricted by atherosclerotic plaque, eventually **restrict** the flow of blood. When the blood flow is slowed, a **clot** can form at the point of constriction, completely blocking the artery. If the artery is feeding a heart muscle, a **"heart attack"** occurs; that is, the heart muscle is damaged due to lack of oxygen. If the muscle damage is severe enough, death may occur.

Death by heart attack is painful, and typically premature. Such a death is particularly unfortunate, considering the ease with which it might be avoided!

The following steps help to prevent atherosclerosis:

1. **Avoid** cigarette smoking.

2. **Avoid** fat-laden foods.

3. **Have** regular health check-ups, including cholesterol-related **blood analysis, electrocardiogram**, and **cardio-stress tests** (as directed by your physician).

Practical **remediation** for atherosclerosis includes:

- The use of cholesterol-reducing **drugs**.

- **Angioplasty**. In this procedure, a balloon tipped catheter is inserted into an artery incision. The tip of the catheter is then snaked through the vascular system, until it is at the point of the arterial blockage. At that point, the balloon is inflated, forcing an opening in the plaque blockage.

- **Mechanical endarterectomy.** This procedure again involves the insertion of a catheter into the affected vessel, and the surgical/mechanical clearing of the atherosclerotic plaque blockage.

- **Bypass surgery.** This procedure involves the surgical bypassing of the atherosclerotic area, typically using a healthy vein from the patient's leg.

- Blockage clearing **laser surgery** is in development.

Maintaining a healthy diet, exercising, and not smoking, are surely easier than remediating heart disease or suffering a painful, premature death.

SUBJECT 2. Cancer

Cancer is the occurrence of autonomous, **excessive tissue growth, due to spontaneous and uncontrolled cell reproduction.** Cancer appears to be induced by one of two malfunctions in internal cell chemistry:

- The cellular control element which prompts cell reproduction becomes **permanently** locked into an **"on"** condition; telling the cell to continuously reproduce...or...

- The cellular control element which inhibits cell reproduction becomes **permanently** locked into an "off" condition, again encouraging the cell to continuously reproduce.

In either instance, the cancerous cell uncontrollably reproduces.

The exact nature of this cell reproduction malfunction is unclear; however, its incidence appears to be **triggered by,** or **associated with, certain conditions:**

- **Cigarette smoking (tobacco use).** The chemical agents in tobacco smoke (and juices) might irritate and damage the tissue linings of the mouth, nose, throat, lungs, digestive tract, skin, and eyes. Cancer might result from such continuous irritation.

- **Drinking alcohol**. The body can properly metabolize a limited daily quantity of alcohol. Excessive alcohol consumption might irritate human tissue, particularly the digestive tract, brain, heart, kidneys, liver, bladder, the circulatory system, and the tissue linings of the mouth. Such irritation might eventually induce cancer.

- **Exposure to the sun**. Sun radiation kills skin and eye cells. A nice suntan is certainly attractive, but one must realize that it is actually a visible layer of burnt skin tissue. Continuous exposure to sun radiation might lead to cancer.

- **The inhalation of, or skin exposure to, commercial toxins**, including certain agricultural and home insecticides, cleaning solvents, paints, fuels, et cetera. Such exposure might induce skin, lung, or liver cancers.

- **The ingestion of certain** *preservatives* which become carcinogenic at high temperatures. **The ingestion of produce containing certain carcinogenic agricultural chemicals**. Such carcinogens might cause intestinal, liver, or colon cancers.

- **Excessive exposure to atomic radiation**. Such exposure can induce a broad variety of cancers.

- **The repetitive damage of any body tissue**. The continuous irritation of any body tissue, regardless of the source of such irritation (heat, mechanical, toxins, et cetera), can potentially induce cancer.

Cancer, once experienced, can be quite difficult to eradicate. If its progress is unchecked, it might eventually enter the lymphatic system, and be spread throughout the body; this process is referred to as **metastasis**.

If a cancer has metastasized, it eventually interferes with the healthy functioning of various body organs, **typically resulting in death**.

If cancer is diagnosed in its early stages, it can often be successfully treated with **drugs**, **radiation**, and/or **surgery**.

One can substantially reduce his risk of contracting most forms of **cancer by:**

- Maintaining a **low-fat**, high-fiber **diet**, free of carcinogenic chemicals.

- **Avoiding tobacco** products.

- **Moderating alcohol** consumption (see *Problem Foods and Substances*).

- **Using** an ultraviolet **sun screen** lotion, **sun glasses**, and **hat** when in the sun.

- **Minimizing** one's exposure to commercial **toxins**, such as cleaning solvents, pesticides, hazardous waste, et cetera.

- Choosing to live in an area that has **minimal** air and water **pollution**.

- Following a physician-directed schedule of **breast, pelvic,** and **colon examination.**

- Periodically examining oneself for abnormal lumps, the color change or bleeding of moles, or any abnormal skin growths.

The above suggested avoidance practices are relatively simple, compared to the difficulty of curing cancer and its potential deadliness.

SUBJECT 3. A.I.D.S. (Acquired Immune Deficiency Syndrome)

AIDS is caused by a **virus.** When the virus enters the body, it is intercepted and engulfed by an immune system cell **(phagocyte).** This is the body's method of controlling foreign matter. Unlike other viruses, the AIDS virus kills the body's defensive phagocyte.

As the AIDS virus multiplies within the body, it kills a greater and greater number of phagocytes. Eventually, the body is stripped of its natural immune system; consequently, illnesses that are normally controlled by one's immune system are then allowed to run their course, unchecked. The AIDS sufferer may then fall victim to a variety of illnesses, and eventually die from a combination of such maladies (pneumonia, Karposi's sarcoma, et cetera).

Once contracted, there is no known cure for AIDS.

The provenance of AIDS is uncertain. There is medical speculation that AIDS originated as a mutated strain of an African monkey virus; however, the nature of AIDS transmission is **clearly understood**:

- In Western societies, the **primary source** of AIDS exposure is through participation in the act of **anal copulation**.

The human colon, aside from channeling waste digestive fluids, decaying organic material, and digestive bacteria, can harbor the AIDS virus (in an infected individual).

The penis has a surface network of capillaries and an extensive deeper network of blood channels and veins (for erection). When an individual's penis penetrates the rectum of an AIDS infected host, the AIDS virus is introduced into the blood system of the perpetrator.

In that anal sex is practiced almost exclusively by male homosexuals, one might presume that such individuals are the primary carriers and victims of the AIDS virus.

- **Intravenous drug use** is the next most prevalent method of AIDS transmission.

When an AIDS-infected drug user shares an uncleaned hypodermic needle, the victim co-user becomes **infected by** the AIDS contaminated blood residue on the **shared needle**.

- One of the **most heinous** sources of exposure is through medical **blood transfusion**. The victim is typically a hemophiliac or trauma patient who innocently receives AIDS contaminated blood.

- Heterosexual intercourse is a minor source of AIDS transmission; the primary carriers being infected prostitutes, bisexual males, and intravenous drug users.

- Infants can contract AIDS, through prenatal exposure. The children of drug users and prostitutes are typical victims.

- Other sources of exposure, such as casual contact, are rare.

AIDS can be effectively avoided, with the following precautions:

1. **Use a condom** when unsure of the health status of a sex partner.

2. **Do not share** or use uncleaned hypodermic **needles**.

3. If one is scheduled for a medical operation, he should consider stockpiling his own blood, in the event that a transfusion is required; otherwise, one should prefer blood transfusions from medical sources which have *state-of-the-art* **blood screening** equipment.

This book speculates that the AIDS virus has probably existed, and taken some lives, for many years. Because AIDS strips the body of its immune system, the occasional AIDS-caused death was most likely **misdiagnosed** as being attributable to the final **recognizable malady** that ran its fatal course.

The disease was not specifically identified until an abnormally disproportionate number of male homosexuals started dying from certain similar maladies (pneumonia, Karposi's sarcoma, and others).

The incident of AIDS had to reach a certain mathematical **threshold level** before it could be diagnosed **as a disease** and become generally threatening. The proper (or **morally improper**) set of conditions have not previously existed to support such a critical **threshold level**.

The above listed methods of AIDS avoidance are certainly effective; however, it is of **sad social commentary** that one must practice such precautions. Using condoms and clean needles are only quick fix

palliations to the deeper-rooted social problems of homosexuality, drug addiction, and prostitution.

SUBJECT 4. Substance Abuse

Understanding the **addiction process** is the first step towards its avoidance and cure.

Be it *alcohol, heroin, cocaine, marijuana,* or any other mind-altering substance, the physiological **addiction process** is similar.

The addiction process begins long **before** the first drink, snort, toke, injection, or pill; that is, it begins when an individual is **unable** to effectively fulfill his life needs.

Having one's life *in order* means having good health, a loving relationship with one's family and friends, financial security, and the fulfillment of one's play needs.

One experiences a sense of general **well being** (happiness, wholeness, pleasure, euphoria), when his life is in order.

One gets his life in order, and fulfills his needs, through effective problem solving skills.

Some individuals, due to **deprivation** or **ignorance** of effective problem solving skills, are unable to fulfill their life needs. When important needs, such as those for *companionship,* a *home,* a *job,* or *good health,* go unfulfilled, the individual might suffer a sense of emptiness, longing, and emotional pain.

The natural and healthy way to resolve any state of need (and associated discomfort) is to employ one's problem solving skills in its fulfillment.

If individuals lack the **materials** or **techniques** to solve their problems, they often seek a method of minimizing the discomfort that is associated with their unresolved need.

Towards this end, many individuals use alcohol, marijuana, cocaine, heroin, or other substances. By using such substances, the individual experiences a state of **euphoria** which **mimics** the mental sensation of

having one's life in order, or the mind altering substance might simply create a mental state that **diverts** the individual from conscious awareness of the discomfort of his unresolved needs.

In either case, the individual has employed a relatively quick and easy **pseudo-solution.**

Each such mind-altering substance, regardless of its unique effect, leads the individual into a similar addiction cycle:

a) The individual begins the cycle by suffering **mental anguish,** because of an unresolved life need.

b) The sufferer uses a **mind-altering substance** to **palliate** the problem associated mental anguish.

c) When the euphoric or diversionary effect of the substance has dissipated:

> - The sufferer still has the **original** unresolved need and related anguish.

> - The individual, by using the mind-altering substance, has most likely created **additional** material or relationship problems, with his parents, spouse, children, friends, employers, strangers, the police, et cetera.

> - The individual, by using the mind-altering substance, has most likely created **physical** problems, such as damage to body tissues (liver, nostrils, nerve and brain cells), trauma from falling or auto accidents, sleep disorders, eating disorders, sexual disorders, AIDS, et cetera.

d) The individual now suffers from the **cumulative** effects of the mental anguish induced by his original unresolved need, and the anguish induced by his new substance abuse-related problems.

e) This growing **discomfort level** increases the individual's desire for the palliating effect of the mind-altering substance.

f) **This self-feeding cycle continues, until the individual is institutionalized or dies.**

Avoiding the of use mind-altering substances is best accomplished by learning and employing effective problem solving skills. If such skills are not practiced, or taught in one's home, one **must** seek other sources of proper education. In the absence of a good home environment, **the involvement in and completion of one's formal schooling becomes very important.** Additionally, one must **avoid** personal or geographical associations that invite the opportunity for substance abuse. To this end, one must exercise **self-discipline** in his peer group associations and remove himself from neighborhoods or environments which are substance abuse conducive.

If one is already addicted to the use of a mind-altering substance, he should:

a) Seek medical supervision in the physical **curtailing** of his **substance dosages.**

b) Study and **understand** how the **addiction cycle** works.

c) **Remove** himself from any **environment** that is conducive to substance abuse, such as his neighborhood, place of employment, et cetera.

d) **Learn** effective **problem solving skills,** for the fulfillment of his health, family, money, and play needs.

SUBJECT 5. Teenage Substance Abuse

Teenage substance abusers experience the same **addiction cycle** as described above. Because a teenager's sense of **reality** is still in formation, his use of mind-altering drugs might result in psychological damage.

An individual's sense of *reality* is his understanding of *how life works.* It becomes his general guide for interpreting his experiences and motivating his actions.

One's *reality* is formed through his **perception** of the world around him, and his perception is dependent upon his thought process and physical senses.

Teenagers have a relatively **limited** pool of personal experiences; consequently, their sense of *reality* is **particularly** sensitive to each new experience and perception.

If one's senses are **distorted by mind-altering substances**, his perception of information and experiences (the facts) might be **inaccurate**; furthermore, his **deductive reasoning** (his logic) might become **flawed**. When individuals use **irrational logic**, to process **distorted facts**, they necessarily create a **dysfunctional** *reality*.

The following example, although simplistic, demonstrates how a teenager might develop a dysfunctional response if the teenager is under the influence of a mind-altering substance:

> Under the influence of a mind-altering substance, and in a socially **inappropriate** setting, a teenager might smile at a stranger. The stranger might then respond with a look of **fear** or **anger**.

> The teenager, due to the effects of the mind-altering substance, may fail to realize the actual cause of the stranger's response; consequently, the teenager might **misperceive** the stranger's response as **a personal rejection**.

> This misperceived experience might then prompt the teenager to avoid smiling at strangers, in socially **appropriate** situations.

A special responsibility lies with parents, to provide their children with effective problem solving skills thereby minimizing the child's potential need to use mind-altering substances. Furthermore, parents should not allow their children to be subjected to geographic or peer group environments that are conducive to substance abuse.

Granted, every child has a personal responsibility to act in a **healthy** manner; however, by the very fact that **they are children**, the parents are **ultimately responsible** for their guidance and protection.

SUBJECT 6. Tobacco Use

Tobacco use may be **addictive** and **might contribute to cancer, heart and lung disease**, and **birth defects**. **Nicotine**, a principal drug in tobacco, is a **poisonous** alkaloid in concentrated dosages.

Cigarette smoking is the most common form of tobacco addiction. Many people begin smoking in their youth, usually in response to **peer group pressure, social or family tradition**, or from the inducement of **commercial advertising**.

As people mature, their lives increase in complexity and responsibilities, and they experience associated **stress**. Such stresses are naturally alleviated through the process of solving one's stress associated problems.

If one is inefficient in his problem solving skills, he may seek **shortcuts** for dealing with his problem related daily stress. Cigarette smoking is one such **palliation**.

Individuals become addicted to smoking because:

- Smoking becomes inextricably mixed into the smoker's daily routine, forming a strong **habit pattern**.

- Smoking appears to relieve tension by introducing **carbon monoxide** into the blood system and **restricting blood flow**, therein **deadening** the **senses**.

- As previously hypothesized, smoking alters the body's metabolism, thereby permitting one to eat more food without gaining extra weight. The individual consequently, then uses the **food consumption pleasure**, to offset stress (see *Obesity*).

Although cigarette smoking **palliates** the smoker's stress symptoms, it also increases the probability for **general health problems**.

Quitting smoking is difficult, but it is well within the abilities of the average person. One should avoid **gimmick** or **fad** quitting techniques. The best method is simple and immediate **abstinence** (under the direction of one's physician). Granted, one might be very uncomfortable for a couple of weeks, but the process is not harmful; **on the contrary, it might save one's life**.

Cigarette withdrawal symptoms may include nervous tension, anxiety, headaches, insomnia, and weight gain. A physician can recommend medication, diet changes, and exercises to assist in dealing with the discomforts of such withdrawal symptoms.

If an addicted smoker wishes to quit, he might consider permanent abstinence, because smoking in moderation can be very difficult.

Individuals should endeavor to educate those that are ignorant of the potential dangers of smoking, particularly children, young women, and citizens of *third world* countries.

SUBJECT 7. Obesity

Obesity is physically and emotionally damaging.

Obesity contributes to many **maladies**, such as heart disease and high blood pressure.

Obesity places abnormal stress on the bones, joints, tendons, and ligaments.

Obesity limits physical mobility, thereby hindering healthful exercise, self-defense, and emergency responses.

Aside from being generally unhealthy and physically unattractive, many people perceive obesity as being indicative of unresolved **emotional problems**; consequently, obese individuals are often **rejected** by prospective mates, employers, and society in general.

a. **What causes obesity?**

- **Improper diet.** Consuming foods rich in fats and sugar, or consuming too much of any kind of food, can lead to obesity (see *Diet*).

- **Insufficient exercise** can lead to obesity (see *Exercise*).

- **Ineffective problem solving skills might encourage obesity. If individuals are ineffective at fulfilling their life needs, they may experience abnormal frustration and mental discomfort.** This book speculates that some such individuals seek sources of pleasure or diversion to ease such frustration and mental discomfort.

The need for nourishment is fulfilled through the act of **eating**; consequently, there is a natural pleasure associated with the act of eating.

Some individuals use this natural eating-associated pleasure response to ease the frustration and mental discomfort that has resulted from their unfulfilled life needs. In doing so, they typically eat far more food than is required for normal nourishment purposes; consequently, they become obese.

Their state of obesity adds to their unresolved personal problems and associated anguish, consequently driving them **further** into their food consumption/obesity cycle.

- **Family influence.** Individuals raised by obese parents may develop obesity prone lifestyles.

- **Physical disorders.** A propensity for obesity might result from a genetic defect, illness, or trauma.

b. Treating Obesity

Consideration should be given to the following areas in the treatment of obesity:

   1. **Diet**. A low-fat, low-sugar, nutritionally balanced diet should be established. A physician should determine the proper daily calorie consumption that is required to sustain an obese individual while he is losing weight.

   2. **Exercise**. Obese individuals should engage in a physician-directed exercise program.

   3. **General health**. A physician should diagnose and treat any physical conditions that have contributed to the obesity, or that have resulted from the obesity.

   4. **Psychological health**. A psychiatrist should diagnose and treat any psychological problems that have contributed to the obesity, or that have resulted from the obesity.

5. **Personal problem solving skills.** The individual should review the status of his unfulfilled life needs, and determine if his personal problem solving skills are lacking in effectiveness.

SUBJECT 8. Homosexuality

This book speculates that homosexuality is a **sexual disorder**, rather than an *alternative normal lifestyle*, and that it results in personal and societal problems.

To be remediated, or avoided, homosexuality must be understood. Towards this end, one might start by considering Man's basic sexual nature:

> The human species, for reproduction purposes, evolved into sexually complementary **male** and **female** counterparts, with reproduction requiring the cross-fertilization (intercourse) of the two parts.

> Man's need to engage in intercourse is genetic in nature. The natural intensity of this instinctual desire ensures the **perpetuation** of the species.

> Children require approximately sixteen years of nurturing, a lengthy period relative to most other species. Because nurturing (the physical support and training of children) requires the efforts of **both** parents, Man evolved an instinctual need to ***pair bond***.

Considering the above facts, it can be understood why **normal** individuals possess a strong instinctual desire to engage in sexual **intercourse**, and to **pair-bond** with a member of the **opposite sex** (see *How to Select a Spouse*).

This instinctual desire to mate with a member of the opposite sex is **disrupted** in some individuals by ***improper relationship conditioning*** or by ***organic causes***.

a. Improper Relationship Conditioning

- Child/parent relationships.

One's understanding and expectations of others is largely influenced by his childhood family relationships; that is, the individual learns (is conditioned) by **how he related to his individual parents**, and by **how he perceived his parents' interpersonal relationship.**

If an individual's parents were behaviorally imbalanced, the individual might develop *sexual role model* **misperceptions** and **confusion.** Such misperceptions might **interfere** with the individual's efforts to form healthy sexual relationships, thereby encouraging homosexuality.

- Adolescent sexual experimentation.

Adolescents have strong **sexual drives.** The natural fulfillment of such drives is often **frustrated** by parental and societal **taboos** against pre-marital sex. Additionally, adolescents might find it difficult to enter into heterosexual relationships, due to **immature fears** of personal rejection and **lack of opportunity**; consequently, an adolescent might find **homosexual experimentation** to be more opportune and less threatening than heterosexual encounters.

In such an event, the homosexual experimentation might lead to **sexual habit,** thereby **interfering** with normal heterosexual development.

- Lack of heterosexual opportunity.

Some individuals might be subject to **sexually segregated environments or conditions,** such as **religious sects, prisons, schools, military, employment,** et cetera. In such instances, an individual might misdirect his sexual drives into homosexual relationships.

b. Organic causes.

- Imbalanced hormone levels can alter normal sexual behavior and physical characteristics. Such imbalances might result from genetic defect, illness, or trauma.

- Unattractive physical appearances, such as obesity or disfigurement, might limit heterosexual development opportunity, thereby encouraging homosexuality.

This book also conjectures that homosexuality is **detrimental** to the individual and to the species, because:

- It **precludes selective breeding** and **produces no offspring**. In effect, it terminates the individual's genetic sequence and deprives the species of genetic betterment opportunity.

- The various body systems (digestive, nervous, immune, et cetera) evolved in mutual harmony to accommodate natural bodily functions. If the body is used in an **unnatural** manner, certain **detrimental** side effects might result. As an example, Man evolved to walk on his feet; however, it is possible to stand, and walk, on one's hands. If one made a habit of doing so, detrimental muscular, joint, circulation, digestion, and other internal problems might result, because the subject action is **inconsistent** with the evolutionary nature of the body.

Likewise, the penis evolved to be placed into the vagina, and the vagina evolved to receive a penis. It is possible to place the penis into other body orifices, and it is possible to place other objects into the vagina for the purpose of **simulating** intercourse; however, if one makes a habit of doing so, detrimental immune system, digestion, tissue damage, psychological, or other side effects might result.

- It subjects the individual to social **ostracism**, and the resulting **emotional damage**.

- It deprives the individual of a sense of normality and reproductive fulfillment.

Treating homosexuality:

The first step in treating homosexuality is for the homosexual individual to **acknowledge** that he is suffering from a **sexual disorder**, rather than living a normal *alternative lifestyle*. Next, the individual might **seek** the professional services of a **psychiatrist**, who should be able to determine the underlying causes of the disorder.

If the disorder has resulted from improper relationship conditioning, psychiatric counseling might assist the individual in exposing the initial source of the improper conditioning, and in the **reconditioning of heterosexual attitudes**.

If the disorder has been induced by organic causes, the psychiatrist might assist the individual in determining drug, surgical, or other therapy, and in reconditioning heterosexual attitudes.

Society might help to discourage and remediate homosexuality by practicing **healthy family values**, and by treating homosexuals in a **compassionate** manner.

SUBJECT 9. Selecting Qualified Medical Services

Professional medical services are necessary to diagnose and cure illnesses. Such services are provided by physicians, psychiatrists, psychologists, pharmacists, nurses, technicians, et cetera.

When ill, one's health becomes dependent upon the abilities of his attending medical professionals; consequently, selecting **qualified** professionals is of **paramount** importance.

One should try to select medical professionals that are **intelligent, well-trained, experienced,** and **aggressive** in their **problem solving approaches**.

Physicians, as an additional requisite, should appreciate and practice **good personal health habits**. One should seriously question employing any physician that **smokes** or is **overweight**.

Likewise, professionals dealing in behavioral medicine should appreciate and practice **good personal behavior and interpersonal relationship habits**. One should seriously question using a marriage counselor who has an **unstable** marriage, or a psychologist who is personally **imbalanced**.

Psychiatrists, because they treat both behavioral and organic illnesses, should be subject to the **highest** level of professional **scrutiny**, meeting all of the above stated requisites.

One should not hesitate to ask medical professionals direct and **pertinent** qualifying questions regarding their technical or personal backgrounds. Medical professionals should understand a patient's concern and not object to such inquiries.

If one's physician diagnoses a **major illness,** or suggests **major surgery,** it is wise to seek a **second** professional **opinion.**

PART THREE: Family Considerations
- Contents -

[Note - The words *Man*, *his*, *he*, *him*, and *himself* herein refer to the species in general, with **no sexist connotation intended.**]

PART THREE: Family Considerations

Man's need to reproduce is inherent and of the **highest priority**, second only to basic survival.

Family needs are those associated with reproduction:

a. **Selecting a Spouse**   c. **Marriage**

b. **Sexual Intercourse**   d. **Having Children**

The primary purpose for having children is to perpetuate one's genetic existence, and, through selective breeding, to combine one's genetics with those of another's, to (hopefully) better the human species.

Rearing children takes at least sixteen years, and requires the joint efforts of **both** parents, consequently individuals instinctively **pair bond** to ensure that both parents will be present throughout the child rearing period.

SECTION A. How to Select a Spouse

In pair bonding, individuals select spouses, based upon their **physical** and **behavioral** qualities. A prospective spouse's physical and behavioral qualities are indicative of his/her abilities to bear and rear healthy children, to defend and materially support the family, and to maintain a healthy marital relationship.

SUBJECT 1. Selecting a Spouse for *Physical* Traits

Most individuals are **initially** drawn to one another by their physical appearances. Certain physical traits are commonly acknowledged as being **attractive**, **pretty**, **handsome**, et cetera. The basis for such preferential assessment lies in the potential **benefits** that are traditionally associated with such genetic traits. In particular, *attractive* genetic traits are those that might benefit the **survival** of the family unit, and the species in general.

Evolution occurs when beneficial genetic characteristics are **selectively** inbred. Concurrently, beneficial genetic characteristics become **instinctual** in preference; in other words, an individual's **basic** concepts of beauty, handsomeness, attractiveness, et cetera, have resulted from millions of years of **selective breeding** and are instinctual in nature.

To exemplify this process, consider a speculative scenario in which primitive Man observed that a higher infant survival probability was enjoyed by the children of larger breasted mothers, possibly due to the comparative lactation characteristics of various sized breasts. Under such a scenario, larger breasted females may have become the object of **instinctual breeding preference**, due to the associated infant survival benefits.

As another example, some individual primates, due to **genetic mutation**, may have been born with slightly longer legs. These individuals may have been able to stand taller and run faster, enabling them to better see and escape stalking predators, or to see and pursue potential game. Such individuals, due to the relative benefits of their physical differences, may have become the object of instinctual breeding preference.

Man has been genetically progressing through selective breeding for several million years, Consequently, he has evolved many instinctual breeding preferences.

When observing a prospective mate, one describes such beneficial physical characteristics as being **attractive**; that is, when one says that he finds another (of the opposite sex) to be attractive (or pretty, handsome, et cetera), he is actually saying that the subject individual has desirable physical (genetic) traits for the purpose of breeding.

The following physical traits are traditionally identified as genetically beneficial and attractive:

- Good health.
- Good skin, hair, and teeth condition.
- Acute senses, particularly vision and hearing.
- Good height and musculature.

- Good physical coordination.
- Balanced/symmetric body and facial proportions.
- The absence of genetic defects or deformities.

Individuals possessing such characteristics enjoy **broader** mate selection opportunities, permitting them to preferentially select mates with similar and equally beneficial traits. In this manner, the species improves itself by pooling beneficial genetic traits and excluding detrimental traits.

Mate selections that inbreed genetically **disadvantageous** character-istics are naturally **avoided** by all species.

Cosmetic Surgery

Some individuals use cosmetic surgery to alter the appearance of their physical traits (genetics), for the specific purpose of becoming **more attractive** to prospective mates.

Considering the natural process and function of selective breeding, cosmetic surgery poses a **moral dilemma**.

The genetic betterment of the species is dependent upon selective breeding, and selective breeding is dependent upon an individual's ability to **accurately** assess the physical characteristics of a prospective mate.

An increasing number of individuals are currently using cosmetic sur-gery to alter their genetic body characteristics (facial, breast, fat dis-tribution, et cetera). Considering the fact that the children of such individuals will possibly **inherit** their parents' features (in pre-altered form), the question must be raised **"do such individuals have a moral obligation to inform prospective mates of the exact nature of their cosmetic alterations?"** and **"at what point in their courting relation-ship should they do so?"**

SUBJECT 2. Selecting a Spouse for *Behavioral* Traits

The successful rearing of children requires the long-term attention of both parents; consequently, instinctual **pair bonding** evolved. **Mar-riage** is society's formal recognition of a particular pair bond.

An individual's pre-marital behavioral characteristics are **indicative** of the way that they will act in marriage; consequently, it is necessary to look beyond a prospective mate's appearance to ensure a lasting relationship.

Individuals who possess the following behavioral qualities tend to make good spouses, creating stable, pleasurable marriages:

a. **Intelligence.** Intelligent individuals tend to be **superior** problem solvers; consequently, they typically enjoy an above average **quality of life,** and their spouse's quality of life is indirectly enhanced by marital association.

b. **Emotional security.** Emotionally secure individuals possess a high level of **self-esteem** and **self-reliance;** that is, they are confident in their abilities and desirability, and they are not overly dependent upon others for guidance, purpose, or fulfillment.

One should take care not to confuse **self-reliance** with **aloofness** or **introversion;** the former is an **attribute,** while the latter two are character **flaws.**

Emotionally insecure individuals often enter marital relationships in escape from other problems, or **to be taken care of.** Such marriages tend to be **fraught with problems** and **short-lived.**

c. **Financial security.** Financially self-secure prospective mates tend to make better marriage partners, particularly those who have **prepared** for their financial future through formal education or job training, and those who have been **independent** and self-supporting for at least **five** years.

An individual's financial self-reliance is indicative of good problem solving skills and good moral values.

Financially insecure individuals who lack the ability to support themselves often marry to escape an uncomfortable relationship with their parents or previous spouse.

Such individuals, being primarily motivated by their support needs, may fail to realistically judge the personal qualities of prospective spouses; consequently, the marriage may be **problematic.** If so, their financial insecurity might further limit their ability to face and resolve marital problems for fear of loosing their financial support.

d. **Philosophical/cultural compatibility.** A prospective mate should be physically attractive; however, one should also consider **intellectual compatibility.**

If the marriage partners are **too divergent** in their philosophical beliefs and problem solving approaches, the marriage will be fraught with disagreement and inefficiency.

Early in courting, one should question and qualify a prospective mate regarding his philosophical beliefs. **Is he religious?, what are his political beliefs?, what is the basis of his morality?,** et cetera.

e. **Social compatibility.** Prospective mates should equal or complement one another in **cultural experience,** social **etiquette,** and general knowledge. Marital partners must be able to **respect** one another's **social image.**

Regardless of the individuals' physical attractiveness, the marriage will be **short-lived** if one is **embarrassed** by the other's lack of dining/social etiquette or general knowledge.

f. **Good parental relationships.** The way that a prospective mate relates to his mother and father, and the manner in which his mother and father interrelate are **indicative** of the prospective mate's **family concepts and conditioning,** and therefore, **precursor to** how he/she will relate to his/her own spouse and children.

An individual's parents continue to **influence** him until his death; consequently, it is **very important** that each marital partner **get along well** with the parents of his prospective mate, and that the two sets of parents relate well to one another.

Any problems in these cross-parental relationships can create allegiance conflicts and added marital stress, therein **decreasing** the probability of a successful marriage.

In addition to the above, an individual that is **presently married** should **not** be considered as a prospective spouse, regardless of his apparent behavioral or physical qualities. Such individuals, by participating in an extramarital romantic relationship, are **clearly demonstrating their moral attitudes**. It is highly probable that such individuals will **repeat** their immoral behavior in their subsequent marriages.

SUBJECT 3. What is Love?

Marital love is an emotional feeling about a prospective mate that is **prerequisite** and **precursor** to a successful marriage.

An individual is *in love*, when he concurrently experiences the following three realizations, relative to a prospective spouse:

> a. He perceives his prospective spouse to be **physically attractive** (per the above suggested criteria).

> b. He perceives his prospective spouse to be **behaviorally attractive** (per the above suggested criteria).

> c. He feels **unquestionable willingness to commit** to a **permanent** and **monogamous** relationship with the subject individual.

It may be necessary to interact with and court **many** prospective spouses, to eventually experience love.

One might find some prospective spouses to be physically attractive and others to be behaviorally attractive. And still others might be found to be both physically and behaviorally attractive, but the individuals might not be ready for a permanent commitment.

Selecting the proper spouse is a matter of **planning, mathematics,** and **timing. One must know what he is looking for, and then he must interact with as many prospects as is necessary to find it.**

There is no **one perfect spouse**; in reality, any individual can have a successful marriage with any one of **many** prospective spouses. Each prospective spouse has certain beneficial and disadvantageous characteristics; one must simply weigh the alternatives and try to make the **optimum** choice.

SUBJECT 4. At What Age Should Marriage be Considered?

To intelligently judge the behavioral traits of a prospective spouse, and to be personally capable of maintaining a successful marriage, an individual should possess the behavioral qualities that were outlined in *Subject 2*, above. The time required to attain and refine such behavioral traits varies with each individual; consequently, there is no universal **right age** for marriage.

As one interacts with each additional prospective spouse, he develops a **mature perspective** for judging human nature, thereby increasing the probability that he will make an intelligent spousal selection.

If one fails to interact with an adequate number of prospective spouses, he might **forever doubt** the propriety of his spousal choice. He might **eventually** wonder **"what it would have been like with this one or that one"**, thereby creating opportunity for **temptation**.

Certainly the spouse that one would have chosen at eighteen years of age is not the same individual that he would choose at twenty-one, and the individual that one might choose at twenty-one is not typically the one that he would choose at twenty-five years of age.

The probability of a pleasureful and long lasting marriage is increased if the partners share a similar sense of **reality**; that is, their personal concepts of existence, how the universe works, what is right or wrong, their expectations, et cetera.

An individual's reality forms from the intellectualization of his physical and informational experiences. It is eventually shaped by the **cumulative** effect of his perceptions.

In one's **youth**, his reservoir of experiences is relatively **limited**; consequently, his developing reality is very sensitive to each new experience. As one ages, his pool of experience grows; consequently, each new experience has a lesser affect on his overall sense of reality.

Individuals who enter marriage in their youth may initially share similar realities; however, it is highly probable that their realities will mature at different rates and in different directions.

As their realities **diverge**, conflicts can develop over values, expectations, et cetera. Such conflicts can degrade the quality of the marriage and lead to its demise.

Most individuals have developed a relatively stable reality by the time they have reached their **middle to late twenties** (in Western societies); this age bracket tends to be appropriate for marriage consideration.

Generally speaking, the longer one waits to marry, the higher the probability that the marriage will be successful. There is, of course, a diminishing point of return; that is, individuals should marry while they are still of **child bearing** age.

SECTION B. Reproduction and Sexual Intercourse

Reproduction is an inherent survival mechanism, common to all life forms. Through reproduction, an individual's genetic essence can continue to live, long after the death of his body.

SUBJECT 1. How does Man Reproduce?

The human species, like most others, evolved into male and female reproductive counterparts, requiring cross-fertilization to produce off-spring.

The human reproductive process consists of the following sequential occurrences:

a. An individual reproductive cell, called an **ovum** is released from the female's **ovary** (the female reproduction organ), and remains alive in the female for about two days (awaiting fertilization).

b. Many single reproductive cells, called spermatozoa (**sperm**), are produced in the male's **testicles** (the male reproduction organs), and are held in his **seminal vesicles**, awaiting **ejaculation**.

c. The sperm cross-fertilizes the ovum through the act of **intercourse**. It does so by the insertion of the male's **penis** into the female's **vagina** and the subsequent ejaculation of millions of sperm cells into it.

d. When a sperm cell comes into contact with the fertile ovum, it joins the ovum, forming a new cellular entity, referred to as a **zygote**. The zygote immediately begins cellular division and growth.

e. The zygote then attaches itself to the inner wall of the female's **uterus**. At this point, the cellular entity becomes referred to as an **embryo**.

f. The embryo remains in this attached position, being nourished by the female's body, as it develops into a mature **fetus** (an unborn child).

g. After approximately nine months of development, the fetus is passed through the mother's birth canal and emerges as a newborn child.

SUBJECT 2. Why and How is Intercourse Performed?

Because the survival of the species depends upon sexual reproduction, primitive Man evolved physiological **mechanisms** to ensure his desire to perform intercourse:

> - **Hormone secretions.** The human sex organs secrete chemical agents, called hormones, that physiologically **trigger** sexual **receptiveness in females** and sexual **aggressiveness in males**.

> - **Pleasure/response stimulus.** The human **genitals** (the penis and vagina) contain sensitive nerve tissues which, when stimulated through intercourse, create intense **pleasure**. This intercourse related sensual pleasure behaviorally conditions and reinforces Man's desire to engage in intercourse.

Although the primary object of intercourse is to produce children, no such conscious intent is required; Man's instinctual drives, his hormone-induced physiology, and his intercourse-related pleasure/response conditioning, all contribute to Man's strong and natural desire to engage in intercourse.

The initial stage of intercourse is called **foreplay**. The function of foreplay is to ready the body for **coitus**, the entry of the penis into the vagina.

Foreplay generally consists of the following actions:

- Reciprocal **kissing** of the mouths or other sexually sensitive body parts.

- The male might gently rub, stroke, kiss, or suckle the female's **breast**.

- The male may use his finger to gently rub the **clitoris**, and to enter and stroke the entrance of the female's vagina, therein stimulating the female's secretion of natural **vaginal lubrication**.

- The female may use her hand to gently hold, rub, or stroke the penis, therein stimulating its **erection**. Care should be taken not to over stimulate the male to the point of **premature ejaculation**.

- As a secondary form of stimulation, the male may kiss the vaginal area or use his tongue to lick the clitoris. The female may kiss, lick, or suck the end of the penis. These forms of mouth-to-genital stimulation, although extremely erotic, are not particularly **hygienic**, and should not become the primary means, or object of foreplay.

- **Deviant foreplay. Anal copulation**, the placement of the penis into the female's rectum, is **not** a form of foreplay; it is a form of **sexual deviancy**. Anal copulation is reproductively dysfunctional and hygienically **unsafe**.

When the penis is firmly erect and the vagina is adequately lubricated, both male and female are generally ready for coitus. There are several possible body positions which will accommodate intercourse; however, the **frontal approach** is most common. Intercourse typically proceeds in the following manner:

- The female reclines on her back and spreads her legs.

- The male then gently lays on top of the female, facing her, with his elbows off to each side of her chest (to support his upper body weight).

- While continuing to kiss the female, the male then reaches down and uses his fingers to gently open the entry to the vagina and inserts his penis.

- Both male and female then begin a gentle thrusting hip movement, causing the penis to move **in and out** of the vaginal cavity, taking care not to completely withdraw the penis from the vagina.

- The mutual hip thrusting continue until an involuntary **rhythm** is reached. This undulating rhythm typically increases in frequency until **orgasm** occurs.

- **Orgasm** is the stage of intercourse in which the male ejaculates sperm into the vagina.

The male's initial physical sense of orgasm is one of increasing titillation of the penis as the stroke rhythm increases.

Eventually, ejaculation occurs in the form of an involuntary muscular release of **semen**, followed by **involuntary** muscular contractions along the seminal tract.

The male's final orgasm sensation is typically one of great relief and pleasure.

The female's initial physical sense of orgasm is one of increasing vaginal sensitivity, stimulated by the feeling of the penis's in and out movement against the vaginal walls.

The female orgasm culminates in involuntary contractions of the vaginal muscles, sometimes accompanied by an emotional feeling of exhilaration and fulfillment.

The male and female orgasms **might not**, and need not, necessarily occur simultaneously to ensure successful cross-fertilization.

It is important that a couple **communicate** their expectations and feelings relative to intercourse, to assure that the act is physically comfortable, sensually pleasing, and psychologically fulfilling.

Individuals should always feel free to verbally express their sexual feelings and needs before, during, and after intercourse. As examples, individuals might wish to state that they:

- love their partner, or...

- have not been adequately aroused and are not yet ready for coitus, or...

- are overly aroused and are now ready for coitus, or...

- prefer that their partner do, or stop doing, some particular thing, or...

- are enjoying or dislike something, or...

- are in an uncomfortable position, or...

- would like to stop, or...

- do not wish to achieve orgasm yet, or...

- do not want their partner to have an orgasm yet, et cetera...

Again, individuals should not hesitate to inform their mate of their sexual feelings and needs!

An individual's performance of intercourse might be detrimentally affected by several factors: his general health, drugs, alcohol, age, behavioral or organic impotency, or sexual deviancy.

Should an individual experience problems engaging in normal hetero-sexual intercourse, he should seek guidance from his physician.

SUBJECT 3. Birth Control

Birth control is an intentional effort by one or both sex partners to prevent the occurrence or completion of an unintentional pregnancy. It is typically accomplished through **contraception** usage, personal **sterilization**, or **abortion**.

a. Contraception methods.

Contraceptives are **chemical** or **mechanical** means of purposely preventing pregnancy. **The following comments are general in nature and not intended to be supportive or critical of any particular brand product. The reader should consult his/her physician before employing any form of birth control discussed in this book.**

Common contraceptives include:

- **Condoms** (*rubber*). A **Condom** is a soft rubber sheath that is fitted over the penis before intercourse. It functions by containing the sperm, thereby disallowing cross-fertilization of an ovum. Condoms are relatively easy to use and effective.

Aside from preventing unwanted pregnancy, condom use is a relatively effective method of **avoiding some diseases that are venereally transmitted, particularly AIDS.**

- **Synthetic female sex hormones.** Administered orally in tablet form or through epidermal implant, such hormones chemically induce the female body to respond as though a pregnancy has occurred. The body then stops any further ovulation, therein preventing the opportunity for pregnancy.

This is currently the most popular form of female contraception in Western societies. It is convenient to use and very effective. Synthetic hormone usage for birth control does not appear to have substantial negative side effects; however, it is wise to give serious consideration before using any substance that repeatedly and substantially interrupts or alters one's natural bodily functions.

- **Spermicides.** These are chemicals that kill sperm cells. Prior to intercourse, the female may inject them into her vagina in the form of foams, suppositories, jellies, or a saturated sponge-like material.

This method is relatively convenient to use and it is effective.

- The **Intrauterine Device (IUD).** This is a mechanical device that is inserted, by a physician, into the uterus. It functions by preventing the natural attachment of a zygote to the uterine wall, thereby terminating pregnancy.

This method is relatively convenient to use and very effective. **Individuals should consult their physician regarding the potential negative side effects of this and all other means of birth control.**

- **Diaphragm**. This is a circular thin soft rubber barrier which a female can insert into her vagina prior to intercourse. It is typically used in conjunction with a spermicidal jelly, and primarily functions by preventing the sperm from entering the cervix.

Diaphragms are relatively inconvenient to use and do not enjoy the highest degree of effectiveness; however, this form of contraception appears to have few negative health side-effects.

- The **Rhythm Method** (attempting to avoid intercourse during ovulation), **Withdrawal** (attempting to withdraw the penis before ejaculation), **and Abstinence** (refraining from intercourse) are all relatively **impractical** and/or **ineffective** forms of birth control.

b. Personal Sterilization.

Surgical sterilization is a common, relatively safe, effective, and permanent form of birth control for individuals who choose to have no additional children.

- **Vasectomy** (male sterilization). This is a relatively simple operation in which a small incision is made in each side of the male's scrotum, through which the physician then surgically removes a portion of each *vas deferens*, thereby preventing them from transporting sperm to the seminal vesicles.

- **Tubal Ligation** (female sterilization). In this operation, an incision is made in the abdominal wall, through which the physician ties or surgically cuts the *Fallopian tubes*, disabling them from transporting ova.

Of these two sterilization procedures, the vasectomy is by far the easiest and safest.

c. Abortion.

Most contraceptive devices exhibit some probability of failure. Depending on the specific device being employed, the probability of failure might range from one to twenty percent; consequently, accidental pregnancy is a concern. In the event of such an unintended pregnancy, some individuals consider abortion.

Throughout Man's existence, societies have employed many methods of *culling* unwanted newborn infants. Modern medical technology has enabled Man to surgically cull such infants **prior to birth**. This medical procedure is referred to as **abortion**.

Legal abortion is the physical act of surgically removing a fetus from the womb before it is capable of extrauterine survival, therein causing its death.

Abortion is commonly used to terminate certain pregnancy occurrences:

- Those resulting from **rape**.

- Those resulting from **incest**.

- Those pregnancies which physically **threaten** the health of the woman.

- When it has been medically determined that the fetus is genetically flawed or organically damaged; to the point that it will be incapable of **normal** survival.

Abortion for **other reasons** often creates a **moral dilemma**: On one hand, it does successfully serve to abort an unwanted pregnancy, therein protecting the parents and society from the negative effects of the unwanted pregnancy. **On the other hand**, it does prevent the fetal entity from surviving, possibly undermining traditional morality systems.

In general, **morality systems** (see *What is Morality*) are man-made problem solving guidelines that consider the short- and long-term best interests of the individual.

The axiom that "**one should not kill another**" is common to most morality systems. The apparent logic of this moral imperative is to create societies in which individuals can safely live their daily lives.

The **intended** beneficiaries of this common moral axiom appear to be **existing** individuals, rather than umbilically attached fetal entities who are incapable of extrauterine survival.

Some individuals choose to employ a **marginal interpretation** of this moral axiom, extending its application to the protection of fetal entities. Such interpretations take the position that abortion is immoral.

It might help one, while judging the moral propriety of legal abortion, to comparatively **contrast** it to **spontaneous** abortions. In spontaneous abortion, also referred to as miscarriage or natural abortion, a woman's body might involuntarily abort a pregnancy for any of several reasons. The fetus might be genetically flawed, organically damaged, or ill, or there might be an anomaly in the woman's body chemistry, induced by illness, drugs, psychological trauma, or physical trauma.

Societies seldom, if ever, associate any **negative** moral significance to spontaneous abortions. In making a **causation** comparison of *legal* with *spontaneous* abortion, one might observe that:

> - In spontaneous abortion, the woman's body chemistry (or **subconscious** mind) has decided that something is **wrong** with the pregnancy (or the conditions surrounding the pregnancy) and consequently, the woman's body has taken physical actions to abort the pregnancy.

> - In legal abortion, a woman's mind has **consciously** decided that something is **wrong** with the pregnancy (or the conditions surrounding the pregnancy), and consequently, the woman has purposely taken medical actions to abort the pregnancy.

In considering the above abortion causation particulars and their relative moral significances, one might ask oneself, "**is a woman's conscious thought and decision making process equally as natural as her subconscious and involuntary systemic bodily processes?**" If the answer to this question is **yes**, then one might reason that **both** legal and spontaneous abortions are **equally moral**.

An extreme and contrary argument might assert that both legal and spontaneous abortions are equally **immoral**, and that society enjoys the right to medically monitor a pregnant mother's body to prevent it from aborting, **for any reason**.

One might further ask, "if an umbilically attached fetus of less than four months is incapable of extrauterine survival, is that fetus an **individual entity**, or is it a **part** of the mother's body?" and if it **is** a part of the mother's body, "who then enjoys the right to **control** that part of her body - **society** or the **individual?**"

Just as the act of abortion creates moral dilemmas, so might one's **failure** to have an abortion. Consider a situation in which a set of parents neither wish to bear and raise an unwanted child, nor do they wish to have an abortion. Such a predicament might raise the following morality issues:

- Should parents purposely bring an unwanted child into the world and subject it to unnatural rearing conditions, such as being raised by foster or adoptive parents or social institutions?

- Should parents force **others** in society to bear the burden of raising their unwanted child?

- Does society, by **outlawing** abortion, **force** such parents into committing the above stated morally questionable acts?

The creation and interpretation of morality systems is always **subjective**. The ultimate validity of such systems can only be tested in the **real world**. Thus, one must judge the moral propriety of abortion based upon its relative short and long term **merits**.

It is in men and women's best interest to be considerate and responsible in their approach to intercourse. If pregnancy is not desired, each partner should ask the other **"what kind of contraception are you using?"** and they should **confirm** its actual usage.

Women suffer most if an unwanted pregnancy occurs; consequently, they should be particularly **diligent** in their efforts to avoid such pregnancies.

Any society which outlaws abortion should provide its citizens with adequate **sex education** and means of **contraception**, or be prepared to deal with the moral dilemma that is posed by unwanted children.

Regardless of society's moral judgements, abortion will always be the **personal decision** of the pregnant woman. **Society might best deal with the issue of abortion by developing and practicing morality systems that minimize unwanted pregnancies.**

SUBJECT 4. Masturbation

Masturbation is the act of performing non-oral **foreplay** (see *Why and How is Intercourse Performed?*) on oneself, for the purpose of **self-inducing** orgasm.

The function of masturbation is to relieve sexual tension. Sexual tension occurs when there is lack of opportunity to engage in intercourse; consequently, masturbation is more common among juveniles and singles than among married individuals.

Masturbation should not become a preoccupation. Excessive masturbation may interfere with one's desire for, or normal performance of, intercourse.

SUBJECT 5. At What Age and How Often Should One Engage in Intercourse?

a. **Juveniles.** After puberty, an individual is generally capable of reproducing, and consequently experiences a **strong** desire to engage in intercourse.

Because juveniles lack the maturity and financial ability to maintain a healthy marriage and effectively raise children, most societies **taboo** juvenile sexual activities.

The juvenile's natural sexual desires, and society's appropriate restriction of their actualization, creates a **complex** problem situation.

Juveniles should be thoroughly educated regarding the reproductive process, masturbation, the realities of juvenile parenthood, and the use of contraceptive devices. At the same time, their participation in intercourse should be discouraged until the age of eighteen in Western societies.

Because a juvenile's sexual activities are relatively difficult to control, he should be made to understand that, if he chooses to engage in intercourse (against his parents' advice), he should try to develop **healthy** sexual habits, free of guilt or perversion, and he should **absolutely** use effective contraception.

b. **Adult Premarital Sex.** Considering Man's strong and natural desire for intercourse and the fact that one might not marry until his late twenties, premarital intercourse is **functional** and relatively **inevitable**.

Premarital intercourse, as part of a **sincere** courting process, may serve as a window to a prospective mate's emotional and sexual behavior characteristics.

Premarital intercourse does provoke **moral** issues, in that it frustrates the natural objective of intercourse, that being to have children. However, it does serve to develop a bond between the participants which might lead to marriage, and it assists the participants in judging one another's behavioral and physical characteristics, while relieving sexual tension.

For the above functional purposes, premarital intercourse might be engaged in **conservatively**. If its frequency reaches the point of **promiscuity**, a multitude of behavioral or hygienic problems might result.

c. **In Marriage.** Marital intercourse should be engaged in as often as the partners mutually desire. Frequency may vary from once a day to once a month, depending upon the partners' individual sexual motivation, age, and health (see *Marriage - Sexual Behavior*).

SECTION C. Marriage

Marriage is a **formal** cohabitation arrangement into which a man and woman enter when they are in love. A successful marriage is evidenced by the **consistent** mutual **happiness** of the partners.

The **primary** function of marriage is to provide a materially stable and complete environment for the effective nurturing of **children**; that is, it serves to provide a setting in which there is food, shelter, and the attentive presence of both parents.

The **secondary** function of marriage is to provide a mutually beneficial and efficient living arrangement for both spouses, through division of labor and the reciprocal fulfillment of companionship and sexual needs.

Most societies formalize marriage with an initial ceremony and embody the relationship with certain social/legal privileges and obligations, therein **protecting** the rights of the spouses and children.

SUBJECT 1. Communication in Marriage

A marriage will **cease** to function if it fails to meet the needs of both the wife and husband. Communication is the only means by which married individuals can express and understand one another's needs; consequently, **good communication techniques** are requisite to a successful marriage.

It is imperative that spouses communicate **every** day. Both should **express** their own **needs** and **ask questions** to uncover their spouse's needs, thereby preempting any marital problems that might result from such unfulfilled needs.

Through consistent communication such as expressing oneself and asking questions, each marital partner remains in touch with the status of the marital relationship, therein **avoiding** unpleasant surprises.

Spouses might express themselves, or ask daily questions, on the following subjects:

- How did you sleep last night?

- How do you feel this morning?

- What are your plans for the day?

- How did your day go?

- What would you like to do this evening?

- What are your plans for tomorrow?

To maintain their interpersonal relationship, spouses should regularly discuss subjects of common interest. Such subjects might include their children, vacation plans, work experiences, mutual friends, goals, finances, hobbies, et cetera.

It is particularly **difficult** for spouses to discuss adult interests or their personal needs in the presence of their **children**. Consequently, spouses need make **special** communication efforts during their child rearing years. To this end, spouses might schedule two or three **daily** opportunities for **private** adult communication. As examples, parents might:

- Converse for a few minutes each morning before their children have arisen.

- Converse on the telephone for ten to fifteen minutes, during a work break and when the children are down to naps or off to school.

- Converse in bed before going to sleep.

On occasion, the fulfillment of one spouse's needs might **conflict** with the fulfillment of the other spouse's needs. Such opportunities for marital discord can be **diminished** by practicing effective communication techniques (see *Communication Techniques*).

If a communication **impasse** is experienced, one should seek the advice of a **wise elder** or **qualified** professional **counseling**.

SUBJECT 2. Companionship

Every individual has the need for companionship. Marriage serves to reciprocally fulfill the companionship needs of the individuals. If one spouse acts in a manner that frustrates the mutual fulfillment of the couple's companionship needs, the marriage will become **jeopardized**.

The opportunity for such problems typically arises when married individuals confuse the priority of their various life activities, specifically with regard to their work or play activities in relationship to their family activities.

One should remember that family needs **precede** money or play needs. Confused logic might lead individuals to believe that **they cannot afford to be away from the office or job** because of the financial opportunity that might be lost. In reality, if individuals fail to spend adequate time with their families, they not only deprive themselves of the pleasure of the experience, but they expose themselves to the **costlier** consequences of divorce (the loss of their family and half of their assets and future income).

It is necessary and practical for the entire family to spend time together. It is equally important that spouses spend time together **away from** their children or in-laws to refresh and maintain their interpersonal relationship.

Such activities might include a weekly dinner outing, a weekly afternoon in the park, or an annual three or four day vacation (separate from the family vacation).

If grandparents or other relatives are unavailable, a couple might employ a **professional** child care service to permit themselves an evening or weekend together. The cost of such a service should simply be averaged into the family's annual entertainment budget allocation.

Family housing and food expenses certainly take priority over entertainment needs; however, entertainment should be part of every family's basic budget. Furthermore, such time together need not be expensive - one might enjoy picnics, camping, et cetera.

A couple's failure to spend such time together because of the expense or the fear of upsetting the children might result in costlier consequences. Unhappy spouses make **poor** parents, and divorce is **ultimately** expensive and upsetting to children.

Successful marriages begin with, and are sustained by, the mutually beneficial companionship of the spouses.

SUBJECT 3. Balance of Labor

A marital relationship should materially and emotionally benefit both partners **equally**. Neither spouse should enjoy a material or emotional advantage over the other.

The equality of the spouses' individual contributions should not be judged in **monetary** terms, because one partner may enjoy a greater monetary earnings potential than the other, and because it is very difficult to place a monetary value on certain tasks (like child rearing).

A spouse's material contribution to the marriage might be quantified in terms of **working hours**. If one spouse works forty hours a week, to the **mutual** benefit of both, then the other spouse should **also** work forty hours a week to the mutual benefit of both.

If both husband and wife have full-time jobs, then household duties should be shared equally (child care, cooking, cleaning, yard work, et cetera).

The marriage partners should divide work duties fairly, depending upon their preferences and the special abilities of the individuals.

Marital sexual relations (kissing, intercourse, et cetera) should **never** be considered, or used, as **barter** in balancing the equality of the spouses' marital contributions. Healthy sexual relationships, by definition, must **equally** benefit both participants.

In a healthy marriage, neither spouse need consciously maintain a **ledger account** on the equality of the other's contributions. The temporal equality of spousal contributions will vary depending upon life's circumstances. One spouse might find it temporarily necessary to contribute more than the other, in response to special educational, financial, or personal goals, or in the event of illness or extraordinary child-rearing obligations. **In a successful marriage, such temporary imbalances equalize over the long term.**

SUBJECT 4. Sexual Behavior

Because individuals have a natural need for sexual fulfillment, and because the bearing of children is a primary objective of marriage, healthy sexual behavior is **requisite** to a successful marriage.

Marital sexual relationships often **diminish** in passion and frequency as the spouses become physically and intellectually familiar with one another; consequently, a **conscious** effort is required to maintain the quality of marital sex.

a. How to maintain a healthy marital sexual relationship.

1. Married individuals should acknowledge and commit to the **reality** that their spouses are their **only** moral and functional means of sexual fulfillment.

2. Individuals should realize that their spouses were **initially** attracted to them, and sexually aroused, because of their physical **appearance**; consequently, if individuals wish to remain sexually attractive to their spouses, they should maintain their hygiene, body weight, muscle tone, stylishness of dress and grooming, et cetera.

3. Individuals should maintain their personal **modesty**; that is, they should not act in a manner that would have embarrassed themselves, or **repelled** their spouses, during their initial courtship periods. As examples:

- They should continue to practice good personal hygiene, by bathing (or showering) daily, and brushing their teeth each morning and evening.

- They should exercise privacy when using the toilet.

- They should refrain from voluntarily expelling gas in the presence of their spouse (or anyone else).

- They should wrap any potentially offensive personal hygiene materials, before placing them into an open trash basket.

By maintaining one's modesty, one projects a personal image that encourages one's spouse to focus on (and be excited by) the **sexual nature of** one's body, while minimizing attention to its mundane biological functions.

4. **Make sexual relations happen!**

a) Make time for **intimacy** and **intercourse**, and **make the first move**. It may seem difficult to get started, but one always feels **better** and closer to one's spouse after sex.

b) Both spouses should employ **sincere** foreplay techniques. A husband cannot expect his wife to be **in the mood** if he does not kiss her lips and breasts, and if he does not adequately stroke her vagina. Likewise, a wife cannot expect her husband to be attracted to her if she does not give him signals of receptiveness, like an occasional alluring glance or kiss, nor can she expect his full sexual enthusiasm, if she does not kiss his lips and stroke his penis during foreplay.

c) Occasionally, try a **different** coitus entry **position**.

d) Occasionally, have intercourse at a **different time** of day or in a different location: the living room, the shower, the car?

e) Spouses should frequently and sincerely express their feelings of love by saying **"I love you"**.

b. How to avoid extramarital relationships.

Married individuals were **initially** attracted to one another because of their personal instinctual sex drives. Regardless of the fact that individuals are happily married, and that their marriage is sexually fulfilling, individuals **continue** to possess and respond to their personal instinctual sexual drives; consequently, married individuals might experience subtle sexual attraction or receptiveness, to members of the opposite sex (other than their spouses).

Although such feelings are natural, married individuals should exercise **self-control**, lest they permit such feelings to lead them into an extramarital sexual relationship.

In particular, one might best avoid extramarital sexual relations in the following manner:

1. **Acknowledge** the fact that, regardless of the happiness of one's marriage and the strength of one's personal morality, it is normal to occasionally feel some sexual **attraction** towards individuals other than one's spouse.

2. **Avoid** personal actions that create or invite the **opportunity** for extramarital sexual encounters:

- **In social settings.** Individuals should avoid participating in **singles-oriented** social activities (such as going to **bars**, or **dancing**, or on **ski trips**), in the absence of their spouses. Such settings inherently **trigger** instinctual courtship habit pattern **responses**; men will feel a desire to compete with other males in the pursuit of available females, and women will react to a natural desire to attract and be receptive to male suitors.

- **In the workplace.** Avoid employing subordinates or associating with workmates based upon their physical **attractiveness**. Avoid going to lunch or for **after work drinks**, with attractive members of the opposite sex (especially **one-on-one**).

If a married individual is in an unavoidable work situation requiring travel or dining with an attractive member of the opposite sex, **sexually provocative** actions should be avoided, including touching one another (particularly dancing) and drinking alcohol - because it impairs one's willpower and judgement.

- **In general appearance.** All courting animals make certain physical **displays**, typified by attractive colors and mannerisms. One should avoid styles of dress, grooming, or mannerisms that signal **unintentional** sexual aggressiveness or receptiveness.

Examples of such displays in females might be excessive **make-up**, **low-cut** or **short** dresses, **furtive** glances, et cetera.

Examples of such displays in males might be the use of **strong** colognes, **excessive** body adornment (jewelry or muscle development), **flashy** cars, **suggestive** facial displays (winks), et cetera.

Individuals should most certainly act and dress in a manner that maintains their self-esteem and the sexual interest of their spouse; however, they should also be adequately discrete in their mannerisms, style of dress, and make-up, so as to avoid unintended extramarital sexual encounters.

c. The potential dangers of extramarital relationships.

Extramarital sexual relationships endanger marriages in several ways:

- **Communication**. Extramarital sexual relationships **interfere** with interspousal **communication**.

Most extramarital relationships are secretly conducted; forcing the perpetrating spouses to **mask** their feelings and to manipulate facts. Such actions necessarily **hinder** normal interspousal communication; furthermore, when the extramarital relationship is eventually disclosed or discovered, the victim spouse will **distrust** the future representations and actions of the perpetrating spouse.

Because the success of any marriage is dependent upon honest and open communication, such effects jeopardize the marriage.

- **Time and resources**. An individual spends time, and possibly money, to engage in an extramarital relationship. Necessarily then, the legal family is **deprived** of such expended monies, and the marital relationship is diluted by the loss of such expended time.

These problems are **tremendously exacerbated** if illicit children result from the extramarital relationship.

- **Health**. Extramarital sexual relationships provide opportunity for both the perpetrating spouse and victim spouse to be exposed to communicable diseases (particularly venereal diseases).

SUBJECT 5. Divorce

Marriage is not an end unto itself; it is a cooperative problem solving approach used by two individuals to fulfill their mutual reproduction and general living needs.

Divorce is the formal termination of such a cooperative problem solving relationship, and it typically occurs if the marriage becomes incapable of consistently fulfilling the needs of the involved individuals.

a. Typical reasons for divorce.

- **Wrong choice**. Before entering a marriage, one uses his best judge-ment to evaluate the physical and behavioral qualities of one's pros-pective spouse. One might later determine, due to marriage's intimate nature, that one had misjudged the spouse's qualities.

If this determination results in **considerable** unhappiness, and if there are **no** children in the marriage, divorce might be appropriate. If there are children involved, divorce should only be considered as a **last** alter-native.

- **Infidelity**. Infidelity damages marital communications, deprives the marital relationship of time and materials, and exposes both spouses to health risks; consequently, infidelity is a reasonable cause for divorce (see *The potential dangers of extramarital relationships*).

- **Empty nest**. A marriage might become unstable when established relationship routines are disrupted.

Children often become the **primary** factor in shaping a marital lifestyle. When the children eventually depart the home due to maturity, the par-ents may become **disoriented** and consequently **frustrated**.

Such disorientation and frustration might affect the manner in which the parents relate to one another. If the parents fail to identify and deal with the actual source of their discomfort, an opportunity for divorce might result.

The *empty nest syndrome*, as a potential cause for divorce, can possibly be avoided if the spouses **anticipate** and acknowledge its occurrence, and seek **qualified marriage counseling** in its resolution.

- **Retirement**. A individual's work routine often influences his sense of self-worth. When an individual's daily routine is disrupted due to retire-ment, he might experience negative psychological reactions, such as dis-orientation, depression, hostility, et cetera.

If the retiring individual has not adequately **planned** his post-retirement activities, he might find himself intruding into his spouse's established daily routine.

This combined disruption of both spouses' established life patterns might detrimentally affect their interpersonal relationship.

If the couple fails to recognize the actual source of their new relationship problems, they might **mistakenly** blame one another, introducing the opportunity for divorce.

Similar to the empty nest syndrome, this problem situation is best minimized by its **anticipation, acknowledgment,** and **qualified marriage counseling.**

- **Mid-life crisis.** As one matures, he develops a mental picture of his life **expectations,** with images of what he would like to be, have accomplished, or materially possess, in the future.

In **later** life, one might **subconsciously** sense that his actual situation is substantially **inconsistent** with his previous hopes and expectations. This subconscious realization, compounded by a heightened sense of personal mortality, might result in **depression** or **frustration.** This syndrome is commonly referred to as *mid-life crisis.*

Such depression, or frustration, might negatively impact the quality of the individual's marital relationship. Worse yet, the individual might **mistakenly** deduce that the marriage is the cause of his depression or frustration.

Individuals can best avoid mid-life crisis, or its interference with their marital relationship, by:

- Adopting **realistic** life goals and expectations.

- Practicing **effective** problem solving techniques.

- Staying in touch with their own feelings.

- **Constantly modifying** their goals and expectations in response to life's variables and practical limitations.

- Practicing effective intramarital communication.

- Seeking qualified guidance to resolve critical personal or marital problems.

b. Adjusting to divorce.

Divorce should always be approached with **civility** and **fairness**. It is in one's best interest to remain rational and considerate throughout the process, **regardless** of the actions of one's spouse. If individuals permit the divorce process to create additional agony, they are actually prolonging the negative effects of the marriage.

Both spouses should seek the advice of independent legal counsel, to assure that their individual legal rights, and those of any children, are adequately protected. If cooperation prevails, one attorney might be mutually selected to coordinate the actual dissolution paperwork, thereby **avoiding** the emotionally and financially taxing effects of a legal battle.

It should be remembered that the divorce process is a problem solving tool, **not** a **punitive** measure. Regardless of why the divorce is occurring, one should not use it as a legal *billy club*, with the intent of **beating-up** one's spouse.

All recently divorced individuals undergo a period of emotional and financial readjustment. If the marriage has left an individual emotionally scarred, or financially insecure, this period of readjustment might be **particularly** difficult.

If one must redevelop emotional security, and sense of self-worth, there are several possible approaches:

> - **Self-assessment.** If, prior to entering one's failed marriage, an individual was self-confident and self-sufficient, such **remembrance** will lend impetus to one's re-establishment of those personal qualities.

> In combination with re-awakening personal survival skills, divorced individuals should make sure that they are realistically assessing the task of **adjusting to single life.**

> To help place this readjustment task in perspective, one might consider the World War II refugees that fled Nazi Germany, or the political refugees that fled communist tyranny. Many such refugees came to the United States with no family, no job, no

money, and not knowing how to speak English; however, most of these individuals built new families, found employment, and prospered. **Recovering from a divorce is far easier.**

- **Group or individual therapy.** Many individuals **enter** marriage suffering from emotional insecurity and with limited self-sufficiency abilities. Often, such personal character flaws **contribute** to the failure of a marriage, thereby reinforcing and perpetuating the individual's personal problems.

Emotional insecurity is typically instilled in **childhood**, and the inability to be self-sufficient usually results from one's **ignorance** of effective personal problem solving skills. Divorced individuals who suffer from such difficulties, might find it very **impractical** (if not impossible) to effect their own improvement. In such instances, one might benefit from the skilled assistance of others, in group or individual therapy sessions.

Ideally, individuals should be emotionally and financially secure **before** entering a marriage. During marriage, both spouses should have **enhanced** their financial positions, thereby assuring both individuals the ability to **comfortably** return to **single life**, should divorce (or the death of one spouse) occur.

If one has failed to exercise effective financial planning while married, it may be necessary to rely on the financial assistance of family, friends, or social services, to weather divorce's initial financial readjustment period.

In such instances, the financial realities of divorce may require individuals to temporarily lower their standards of living while adjusting to single life; however, a reduced standard of living, with the possibility of **eventual** improvement, is certainly better than permanent entrapment in an emotionally painful relationship.

Although one might wish to casually date for entertainment and companionship, one should **avoid** serious romantic involvement until one has **achieved** emotional and financial security (see *Selecting a Spouse for Behavioral Traits*).

If individuals enter into a new relationship or marriage motivated by their emotional or financial insecurities, the relationship is **probably doomed** to failure - either quality-wise, or tenure-wise.

The period of time necessary for an individuals to emotionally and financially readjust their lives will vary with their particular circumstances; however, **one year** tends to be the minimal period.

Divorced individuals have successfully adjusted when they can look themselves in the mirror and **honestly** say:

- I like myself.

- I am attractive.

- I am emotionally self-secure.

- I am financially self-sufficient.

- I will only date individuals that are also emotionally healthy and financially self-sufficient.

c. Avoiding divorce.

The best divorce avoidance method is the **intelligent** selection of a prospective spouse, and personal **readiness** for marriage.

The following guidelines tend to additionally minimize the probability of divorce:

- **Spouses should communicate!** If one spouse does something that makes the other spouse unhappy, the offended individual should thoroughly communicate the nature of his unhappiness; if he fails to do so, he is equally contributing to the failure of the marriage.

Reciprocally, if one spouse senses that the other spouse is unhappy, he should initiate whatever communication is necessary to resolve the problem; if he fails to do so, he is equally contributing to the failure of the marriage.

- **Spouses should practice healthy life priorities**; that is, they should always remember that **family concerns** come **before** money or play.

- **One should not make rude statements to, or about, one's spouse;** spouses should be best of friends. One should always be quick to say "I am sorry" if an offensive statement has been unthinkingly made.

- **Spouses should frequently compliment one another and state their feelings of love.**

- **Spouses should not lie to one another, or engage in extramarital romantic relationships.** Individuals should **consciously** avoid situations that invite infidelity.

- **Both spouses should be equal partners;** neither should get the emotional or material better of the other.

- **Both spouses should remain individually strong** relative to their emotional security and financial self-sufficiency. Each should be able to negotiate from a **position of strength** to properly solve relationship problems.

If one spouse permits himself to become emotionally or financially insecure, he **sets up** the opportunity to be exploited or mistreated, therein inviting the failure of the marriage. Likewise, if one spouse knowingly permits the other to become emotionally or financially insecure, that spouse equally contributes to the potential failure of the marriage.

SECTION D. Children

SUBJECT 1. Having Children

a. Deciding to have children.

The decision to have children is primarily **instinctual**. Man has an inherent need to perpetuate his genetics and his species. His instinctual desire for intercourse **enforces** the fulfillment of this need; consequently, most individuals experience parenthood.

In primitive societies, having children also served an **immediate** survival function. All generations of a family tended to live in proximity. Children performed minor labor roles, learning as they did so, and consequently contributed to the family's **material** well being.

The primary burden of family support would shift down to the mature children as parents progressed beyond the age of strenuous physical labor. The parents would then perform the valuable **elder** functions of training the youth in skilled tasks, relationship guidance, maintaining cultural continuity, and assisting with child care.

Children played a valuable role in this **symbiotic** family relationship; consequently, an individual's instinctual desire to have children was **reinforced** by its practical survival benefits.

Modern Man's desire to have children, like primitive Man's, continues to be primarily instinctual; however, contemporary social/economic structures have **altered** the family's symbiotic interrelationship.

Unlike primitive agricultural and hunting societies, modern societies tend to be **urban** in nature. Most urban economic interstructures **do not** lend themselves to symbiotic family relationships. In primitive cultures, children could help their parents with hunting, fishing, sewing, cooking, and other survival tasks. In doing so, the child learned, while contributing to the material well being of the family. In modern urban societies, the parents typically perform specialized commercial tasks (jobs) away from the home; consequently, the children are **deprived** of the opportunity to help the parents produce, or to learn and contribute by doing so.

Because urban families are typically splintered over broad geographic areas, it has become more difficult for mature children to assist aged parents, and for parents to provide family elder functions.

These realities of modern life create special parenting **challenges**; consequently, individuals should seriously contemplate their readiness for parenthood before unthinkingly reacting to their biological urges.

b. When should one have children?

Individuals might seriously contemplate having children **after** they have married, and after the marriage has behaviorally and financially **stabilized**.

Before introducing children into a marriage, the individuals need time to test the relationship and assure themselves that they have made the **proper** spousal choices. Additionally, a marriage should be financially capable of supporting children.

The time necessary to stabilize a marriage depends upon the nature of the individuals and their living circumstances. In general, **two years** tends to be a minimal period.

c. How many children should one have?

If individuals were to simply respond to their biological urges and physical capabilities, they might have one child every two years, resulting in ten to twenty children.

Such a breeding approach was practiced by primitive Man; however, it is very **impractical** for modern Man. Consequently, one needs some criteria for determining the **proper** number of children to have.

Starting at one end of the spectrum, individuals might ask **"why they should have more than one child?"** Children enhance their problem solving and social skills by interacting with other children; consequently, it is in a child's best developmental interest to have at least **one sibling**.

One might then ask oneself, "**if children are benefited by sibling interaction, why not have many?**" Man, as a species, currently numbers in the **billions**, and has consequently driven (and is driving) other species into **extinction**, while pushing the planet to its ecological support limits.

If parents have two children, they permit the human species to maintain a **constant** population (in the billions). One should seriously question the moral appropriateness of having more than two children.

After individuals have borne their desired number of children, they should practice birth control, or consider personal **sterilization** as a convenient alternative (see *Birth Control*).

SUBJECT 2. Pregnancy and Child Birth.

Pregnancy commences upon conception, and ends with child birth. It is the natural and beautiful process by which the female body nurtures a new human entity into existence (see *How does Man Reproduce?*). **The following comments regarding pregnancy are general in nature and should not be relied upon as medical advice - pregnant women should consult and follow the advice of their physicians.**

Pregnancy need not limit a female's normal physical activities until its late stages. Some females experience **morning sickness** during the first two or three months of pregnancy. This is an early morning sense of nausea, possibly induced by a natural decrease in the level of gastric acid.

A pregnant female should maintain a normal, **healthy** diet, and anticipate a **twenty** to twenty-five pound typical weight gain. During pregnancy, a female should **absolutely** avoid the ingestion of, or exposure to, any potentially harmful substances, such as alcohol, tobacco, caffeine, heroin, marijuana, cocaine, commercial toxins, et cetera.

Fetal development is **extremely** vulnerable to the detrimental effects of toxins and abnormal body chemistry. Because delicate fetal tissues and organs are in a **rapid** state of development, their early damage (or the chemical disruption of their genetic development sequence) can result in **gross injury** to the fetus' maturing body.

Pregnancies **normally** progress in a healthy manner; however, it is wise to maintain a regular schedule of physical examinations. On occasion, the body might **spontaneously** abort a pregnancy. Such miscarriages might result from a disruption in the female's body chemistry, or the body's detection of illness or genetic imperfections in the fetus.

The term of a normal pregnancy is about two hundred and seventy days. In the final stages of pregnancy, the fetus naturally positions itself, head down, to accommodate birth.

The occurrence of birth is preceded by the onset of painful uterine contractions, referred to as **labor**. The female's **amniotic** fluid bag ruptures and drains at the inception of or during labor. The initial uterine contractions are approximately fifteen minutes in intervals, gradually increasing in frequency until birth occurs. As the female's cervix dilates, the uterine contractions force the fetus down through her lower pelvic area, and out of her womb.

The duration of labor varies, but seldom exceeds sixteen hours. A woman's period of labor tends to decrease in duration with each subsequent pregnancy.

After the physician removes the child from the womb, the **afterbirth** (placenta) is also removed and held above the child, permitting all blood to drain through the **umbilical cord** into the child's body. The umbilical cord is then severed and tied.

A woman's acute **natural** senses assist her body in physically coordinating the birth process; consequently, one might seriously **question** the wisdom of inhibiting a woman's senses by administering **anesthetics**.

Birth by **Caesarian Section** involves a surgical incision across the woman's lower abdomen, through which the fetus is removed from the womb. Some women have a Caesarian Section due to illness, improper fetal positioning, or their genetically inherent inability to give natural birth (one might question the moral appropriateness of the latter reason).

Notwithstanding physician instruction to the contrary, the infant should be initially nourished through **breast-feeding**, which is physiologically beneficial to both mother and child. By three months, the infant should be able to eat soft and pureed foods. As infants' teeth and abilities to ingest solid foods develop, they can be weaned from their mothers' breast.

SUBJECT 3. Raising Children

Successful child rearing is neither accidental nor easy. Beyond providing for a child's basic physical needs (food, clothing, shelter, medical treatment, and safety), successful parenting requires **planning, self-discipline, time,** and **commitment.**

Starting at infancy, and continuing throughout adolescence, parents should bring **emotional** and **intellectual structure** into their child's life, providing the child with a framework of **accurate facts, effective problem solving skills,** and a sense of **self-worth.** By doing so, parents help their children to develop a **reality** that will successfully guide them, throughout their entire life.

a. Infancy.

Children, in their first two years, lack the ability to fulfill any of their basic survival needs; this reality dictates the parents' primary obligations.

Because an infant is initially incapable of verbal communication, early parent/infant communication is accomplished through **voice tone** and **volume, facial gestures,** and **touch.**

Soft, comforting, or playful sounds, combined with smiles and gentle handling instill a sense of security in the infant, and encourage the infant to **trust** the parents' intentions. Such parental trust is **imperative** as a basis for the infant's responsiveness to the parents' behavioral training efforts.

Parent/child interaction encourages infants to develop and exercise their communication skills. A child's propensity for developing general problem solving skills is very dependent upon his communication abilities; consequently, **attentive** parents effectively provide their children with a **head**-start in life.

A child's walking skills will begin to develop by the end of his first year. He will clutch furniture, struggle to his feet, and take tentative steps.

Parents should encourage walking, but should not push infants beyond their physical readiness.

The parents might gently begin **behavioral training** at this time. For example, the parent might smile and use a cheerful, encouraging voice if the child swallows his food; on the other hand, if the child spits his food out, or knocks it on the floor, the parent might frown and speak in a less pleasant tone. Basic word association might also be introduced; relating *no*, *good*, *mommy*, *daddy*, et cetera, to those respective actions or objects.

Parents should teach their children how to beneficially relate to other individuals, animals, plants, and inanimate objects. Until the child is capable of intelligent verbal communication, teaching must be accomplished by **example**, the **encouragement of beneficial actions**, and the **discouragement of detrimental actions**.

The parents' encouragement of beneficial actions and the discouragement of detrimental actions are referred to as **disciplining**.

Children (and people in general) do not like to be disciplined, and will naturally resist it. Discipline, by its very nature, represents a conflict of the **wills** of the involved individuals; no one enjoys being told what to do by others.

A child's will, motivated by his immature rationale, might lead to self-injuring actions.

Parents should use their maturity to judge the propriety of their child's actions. When parents see that a child is acting in a disadvantageous manner, they should discipline the child's actions.

One parent might disagree, on occasion, with the other's approach to a particular child discipline problem. In such case, the point of disagreement should be discussed in private, between the two parents, not in front of the child, and particularly not during the subject act of discipline.

If the parents fail to demonstrate unity in their approach to discipline, the child might have divisive opportunity to play one parent against the other, weakening the effectiveness of parental discipline.

A child, when disciplined, might cry. In doing so, he is telling the parent that he does not like having his will countered, nor does he like the temporary loss of the parents' favorable attention.

Children become attuned to their parents' reactions. They sense which actions please or displease their parents. Children will naturally try to use such behavioral knowledge to manipulate their parents' actions.

As an example, a child might **pout** after being disciplined. In doing so, the child is feigning his **withholding of love** from the parents. The child does so because he knows that his parents want the child's **love**; by pouting, he is saying to the parents, "I will not love you if you discipline me!" Parents should give **special** consideration to this reality, and take care not to fall subject to its detrimental influence. A child, although immature, may be **very intelligent**; consequently, he will exercise **creative resistance** in any **discipline-associated** test of his will. Parents should realize that their children, in their efforts to influence the parents' actions, might not necessarily exercise **rational judgement**.

If the parents permit the relationship to be dominated by the child's immature manipulations, the child/parent relationship becomes frustrating and the child's social interaction abilities are affected. Children who are allowed to establish such ineffective social relationship habit patterns will find themselves in constant conflict with their parents, playmates, school teachers, spouse, employers, and general society.

Discipline, when administered in a healthy manner, does not diminish the child's love for his parents. On the contrary, the lack of proper discipline might interfere with a child's ability to love others, or himself.

Children become receptive to toilet training and the development of their language skills by the beginning of their third year.

As infancy draws to an end, the child should have a foundation of good health, basic motor skills, enthusiasm for communicating, and parental trust. So prepared, the child will be receptive to, and capable of, pre-adolescent behavioral training and character development.

b. Pre-adolescence.

After infancy, and as a child begins to develop his physical and language abilities, parents might effectively direct their efforts to teaching basic social, intellectual, mechanical problem solving skills, and character development. Formal education attempts to serve this purpose; however, there is no substitute for **one-on-one**, parental training.

Parental role modeling is a subtle, involuntary, and effective means of demonstrating proper family interaction, and of teaching general social skills and moral values. Parents should always be aware that they are **teaching by example**.

A structured life (with guidelines and discipline) certainly assists a child in building a functional **reality**; however, parents should also make a conscious effort to provide conditions that encourage their children to explore and test the limits of their environments, to exercise their problem solving skills, and to develop **creativity** and character.

This process requires discerning parental judgement; parents should encourage **individuality** in their children, while taking care not to be overly **permissive**. **As a general rule, parents should encourage their children's individual expressiveness, while making sure that their children's actions neither pose a threat to their well being, nor infringe upon the reasonable rights of other individuals.**

It is **particularly important** that pre-adolescents develop good academic **study habits**. Beyond the obvious benefits of learning the presented subject matter, this early **problem solving** environment provides the opportunity for children to establish **learning habit patterns** that will serve them for the rest of their lives.

Parents should monitor a child's studies (especially homework) in early grade school. Children might try to avoid the rigors of concentrating or studying because the child cannot intellectually appreciate the potential benefits of such efforts. This reality poses a **special** parenting task, that being to explain the benefits of such efforts, and to condition the child's learning habits.

If parents fail to accomplish this important training function, their child may become permanently disadvantaged. Parents should consider that each additional year of poor study habits will result in **missed learning**

opportunities, and the **reinforcement** of such poor habits. Eventually, their child might become unable to correct his study habits or **catch up** on missed learning.

As children endeavor to develop their motor skills, they will naturally be exposed to associated physical risks. Such learning **risks** create decision-making dilemmas for parents. On the one hand, parents do not want their child to be severely injured, and on the other hand, children should have the opportunity to test and develop their physical skills (through such activities as climbing, swimming, self-defense, et cetera).

Parents should encourage activities that develop their children's athletic and mechanical skills and at the same time attempt to minimize conditions which might lead to injury. As examples, *play sets* or climbing apparatus should be placed on **soft surfaces**, and appropriate protective gear should be worn while participating in sports.

Parents might further assist their children's social and problem solving skill development by encouraging their participation in **extracurricular school activities, and organized sports** or **youth groups**.

There is always a degree of parental ego fulfillment associated with their child's successful accomplishment of any task or activity; however, parents should take care not to allow their personal ego needs to detrimentally influence their child's healthy development.

Parents should not become **vicariously** involved in their child's academic, athletic, or hobby activities. In such instances, the child might be pushed beyond his realistic interest or performance level.

As pre-adolescence draws to an end, children should hopefully have developed their:

1. Basic athletic and manipulative motor skills.

2. Basic social and problem solving skills.

3. Creativity and character expressiveness.

c. Adolescence.

Adolescence is a **trying** period, for both child and parents. As the child makes his physical transition into adulthood, it is **imperative** that parents educationally prepare their children for the physiological changes that will occur.

> - Daughters, prior to **puberty**, should understand that they will shortly experience **pubic hair** growth, **menstruation**, and **breast development**. They should understand why their bodies are changing, exactly what function the mature body parts will serve, and what physical sensations will accompany the changes.

> - Sons, prior to puberty, should know what physical changes to expect; in particular, they should anticipate pubic hair growth, and they should understand the physical cause and functional purpose of an **erection**, and that they will begin experiencing **nocturnal emissions**.

Children should **understand** and **welcome** these natural physical changes. They should have a **complete** understanding of the sexual reproduction process (see *How Does Man Reproduce?*). They should further understand that they will **normally** desire sexual interaction with members of the opposite sex, and that they should not feel guilt relative to such sexual feelings.

A **special** responsibility rests with the parents to help their children to understand the **impracticality** of juvenile pregnancy, and to encourage the relevant self-discipline that is necessary to avoid it.

Sex education should be included in any public education curriculum; however, it best begins in the home. A parent's tactful sex education comments can be far more effective than those presented in a school film or auditorium lecture, in that they are presented **one-on-one** by a trusted love one.

While teaching children the fundamentals of reproduction, parents should also consider using illustrations from medical books. It is also helpful to ask the children testing questions and to encourage their questions.

Sex education is not a subject that should be discussed behind closed doors or in hushed tones; it should be discussed **seriously** and **openly**, with any or all family members present. It is a normal and healthy subject matter, and should be approached accordingly.

A child's sexual development should be **monitored**. This is an area that requires parental guidance, and should not be left to chance (or misguidance). Parents should question their children from time-to-time to see if they are encountering any sex-related problems, or if they have any questions.

Adolescents should also be introduced to **basic survival skills**, such as hunting, fishing, sewing, cooking, camping, wood working, construction, agriculture, et cetera.

Although many such skills will seldom be used in Western societies, their very knowledge serves two functions: first, such skills help youths to perceptually relate to their position in *nature's scheme*; second, such skills serve as an ultimate insurance policy in the event of catastrophe.

Adolescence is a period in which youths should begin to grasp their uniqueness and purpose. This is not to imply that they need determine their exact professional or family aspirations; but rather, it is a time for them to be gently introduced to the realities of **self-sufficiency**.

Regardless of a family's financial *wherewithal*, every youth should personally experience **work and material reward**, therein helping them to grasp the concept of self-sufficiency, and to perceptually value material objects. **Thirteen to sixteen** years of age tends to be an appropriate time to formalize this experience.

At one time, societies were structured in a manner that permitted their youth to gradually participate in hunting, farming, or homemaking activities, allowing the youth to learn such skills while contributing to their family's support. Because such opportunities do not exist in modern urban societies, a youth must now take an **outside** job to gain such self-sufficiency experience.

Work experience is a necessary and fundamental part of an adolescent's basic training. It is certainly as important as any individual academic course of study, sport, or social activity.

A youth need not work more than ten to fifteen hours per week to gain realistic work experience, and intermissions should be taken for family vacations, cultural experiences, and play.

As a youth engages in his work experience, the potential is created for a common shortsighted decision. Sometimes, when adolescents experience the material benefits of their labors (an automobile, nice clothing, et cetera), they become tempted to set aside long-term academic aspirations in favor of immediate financial reward.

Parents should be prepared to forewarn their adolescents against such temptations, and to explain the financial realities of such faulty logic; that is, the **earnings potential** for educated professionals is far greater than the earnings potential for an uneducated worker (see *The Problem Solving Process - Self-discipline*).

A juvenile's self-sufficiency development should include **managing** his own earned monies. Ideally, the youth should open his own commercial checking and savings account. His monies might be spent on items that fall outside of the parents' normal support responsibilities, such as the purchase and maintenance of an automobile, or special sports, clothing, or entertainment items.

An adolescent's behavior, and future interests, are strongly influenced by his **peer group** associations; consequently, parents should try to create opportunities that direct their children into beneficial peer group associations. For example, parents should endeavor to raise their children in a **pleasant** neighborhood with a **good** school system.

If a child's peers all plan to enter college and become professionals, it is highly likely that the child will be drawn in a similar direction. On the other hand, if a child's peers are all from *broken homes*, emotionally troubled, into drugs, and **down** on school, it is highly likely that the child will be drawn into similar antisocial behavior patterns.

Even under ideal circumstances, children can become aligned with detrimental peer groups; consequently, parents should monitor their children's choice of friends and be prepared to discourage such potentially damaging associations.

Formal education is important in all stages of a child's intellectual development; however, it becomes particularly important as a child begins adolescence. An adolescent's specific selection of academic curriculum largely determines his eventual vocational options.

If a child selects higher courses of study (such as mathematics, science, language, or literature), it is highly probable that the child will continue on to college. On the other hand, if the child's curriculum is primarily comprised of basic education and vocational courses, it is highly probable that the child will forego college and enter a non-professional vocation.

Adolescents should be encouraged to pursue the **most ambitious** academic study program of which they are intellectually capable. In this manner, the youth will have a broader range of vocational options.

Some adolescents **coast** through school, taking easy courses and getting average grades, planning to **find themselves, later.** Later seldom comes, and they typically find themselves slotted into some **convenient** and **mediocre** job, in which they remain for the rest of their lives, **regretting** that they did not fulfill their vocational **potential.**

By the completion of adolescence, children should be comfortably adjusted to their sexuality, they should have a basic understanding of self-sufficiency, and they should have developed academic attitudes that are supportive of broad vocational options.

d. Special child rearing considerations:

- Attention-getting.

Every individual seeks the attention of others. **Favorable attention** makes one feel good, and potentially betters one's rank or position in social groups.

Mature adults realize that favorable attention is **earned**, through their performance of **positive actions**.

Positive actions include vocational, athletic, civic, or academic accomplishments, and the individual's ability to participate in **balanced social interactions**.

Attention can also be attracted through **negative actions**, such as clamor, destruction, or shocking appearances. Such negative actions typically result in **unfavorable attention**, and tend to be self-damaging.

Parents should teach their children the benefits of favorable attention and should discourage unfavorable attention-getting tactics, such as **tantrums, screaming,** or **destruction**.

Sometimes, due to conflicting responsibilities, parents may not be able to immediately respond to their child's positive attention-getting efforts. For example, the parent might be on the telephone, or attending to another child, or in the act of grocery shopping. In such instances, a child might then experiment with a negative attention-getting tactic, such as screaming, banging toys on the wall, et cetera.

When this happens, the parents should demonstrate to the child that such tactics are **inappropriate**, thereby averting the opportunity for the child's establishment of detrimental habit patterns.

Children have no initial concept of **balanced social interaction**; consequently, children typically try to attract and maintain **all** attainable attention. Parents are faced with the task of teaching their children that there are **reasonable limits** to their attention demands, and that love is **earned** and **secured** through **socially acceptable actions**.

- Child-sitters.

Infants have no means of self-protection; consequently, they are extremely **vulnerable** to physical or psychological mistreatment. If a child is to be temporarily entrusted to another's care, that person should be a **well-balanced relative**, or a **highly-trusted** friend. In the absence of such individuals, a **professional sitter**, with references, might be considered.

Under normal circumstances, no other individuals provide a quality of child care equal to that of the parents. If practically possible, a child should have the full-time attention of his mother for the **first five years** of his development, and the joint attention of both natural parents throughout his **entire** childhood.

- Television and Movies.

The primary function of television and movies should be to **entertain** and **educate**.

One's sense of **reality** is based upon his perception of the world around him. That perception is fed by personal experiences and the information that is provided by others. Television and movies are a primary source of **information provided by others**.

As one watches commercial television and movies, the perceived information and experiences are **subconsciously integrated** into the individual's sense of reality, influencing his logic, opinions, and rationality.

Most television programs, advertisements, and movies, are fiction-based. Many such fiction-based scenarios **inaccurately** portray life's realities, and suggest or encourage ineffective problem solving approaches.

Adults, as compared to children, have had **more** time and experiences to solidify their senses of reality. In particular, adults can use their maturity to consciously **edit out** inaccuracies as they watch fiction entertainment. On the other hand, children often lack the ability to discern between inaccurate fiction and reality.

Children are particularly vulnerable to inaccurate information, because they are in the critical process of building their sense of reality. Children are at risk of developing **distorted** values and **ineffective** problem solving skills if they are frequently permitted to view **immoral or inaccurate portrayals of life**; consequently, parents should monitor the quality of television and movies being viewed by their children.

- Spanking.

Parents employ **discipline** to guide and condition their children in learning problem solving techniques and beneficial habit patterns, and in the avoidance of harmful actions. To this end, parents typically appeal to a child's reasoning ability by using verbal or gesture communication.

On occasion, a child might fail or refuse to respond to the parents' reasonable discipline efforts. In such instances, it may become necessary for the parents to **accentuate** their disciplinary approach with a **physical stimulus** (a spanking).

When children are spanked, hopefully they will associate the physical discomfort of the spanking with their failure to respond to some parental direction.

The **physical discomfort** of spanking should **not** go beyond a **mild** sensation of pain; **spanking should not inflict physical injury, nor become a frequent occurrence. Most children positively respond to the mere threat of spanking.**

If spanking is not effective within the above guidelines, parents might question their own **communication** skills, the **rationality** of their disciplinary expectations, or the health of their child's **perceptive** abilities.

All individuals exhibit some degree of personal **hostility**. Such hostility typically results from the individual's inability to adequately fulfill certain personal needs, or from previously unresolved emotional problems. When individuals suffer from excessive hostility, the opportunity exists for **displaced aggression**; that being a situation in which the hostile individual ventilates his hostility towards an object (or person) that is **not** necessarily associated with the source of the hostility.

Any time that parents are suffering from **abnormally high** levels of personal hostility, they should exercise the **utmost restraint** in their use of spanking, thereby avoiding the possibility of **inadvertently** subjecting their children to displaced aggression.

- Formal education.

A fundamental responsibility of effective parenting is to provide one's children with a formal public or private academic education. This parental obligation minimally extends through their child's sixteenth year, but more commonly through the child's **eighteenth** year.

The object of such eduction is to provide the child with adequate **knowledge**, problem solving and social interaction **skills**, and to ready them for **self-sufficiency**.

A child's academic and social performance in school is generally indicative of how he will perform in his adult life.

School grades, as indicators of academic performance, are reflective of a child's natural intellect, as expressed through the child's **reasonable** study efforts.

Although parents can do little to alter their child's innate intelligence, they can certainly affect their child's **study efforts**. To this end, parents might maintain an ongoing dialog with their child's teachers regarding their child's classroom attentiveness and homework quality.

A child's formal education through his eighteenth year is typically referred to as primary education. Upon the completion of a child's primary education, it is certainly in his best interest to consider **higher education**. Institutions of higher education include universities, colleges, professional and trade schools, and conservatories.

Such institutions prepare individuals for specific professions or trades, and provide general cultural enlightenment. The typical benefits of such higher learning are: **material rewards, broader vocational options, job satisfaction, and greater overall life success.**

Higher education, through bettering the individual, contributes to **healthier societies.**

The obligation to provide one's children with a higher education does not traditionally fall upon the parents, because the financial cost of higher education can be substantial, and because a primary education will adequately prepare a child for basic self-sufficiency.

Most Western societies provide a variety of feasible approaches to higher education, including scholarships, government loans, and government funded community colleges and state universities.

It is **practical** for students to **work** while acquiring their higher education. Granted, working students might not have the time to enjoy all of the social aspects of collegiate life; however, such individuals often experience an **enhanced perception** of the education process.

If parents are financially capable, they might permit their child to continue to live at home as the child **works his way through college**.

If parents have the financial ability and choose to support their child's entire higher education, they should also endeavor to develop and maintain their child's **work ethic**. This might be accomplished by requiring a reasonable academic effort, and by encouraging the child to take a **summer job**.

- **Divorce considerations.**

Divorce is a necessary and unfortunate problem solving tool in some marital relationships. If divorce must occur, parents should try to **minimize** its effects upon the children.

Children certainly sense the discomforts of a failing marital relationship. Because children are party to the family relationship, and because they are necessarily affected by divorce, parents should try to explain what is happening, and why. In particular, a child should understand that:

- The failing marriage is **not** representative of a **normal**, healthy marriage; in particular, children should be discouraged from emulating the problematic actions of their parents.

- The child will **continue** to be loved and emotionally and materially cared for, regardless of the divorce.

- The divorce is **not** the child's fault.

Parents should communicate such facts in a manner that is consistent with their child's ability to comprehend.

Once divorced, parents should treat each other with **civility**. In particular, parents should not demean one another for punitive purposes. Children genetically and behaviorally reflect and relate to the persona of each parent; necessarily then, if one parent is verbally or physically abusive to the other, the **child will also feel injured**. Regardless of the intensity of the parents' differences, they should absolutely refrain from any form of severe interspousal attack, particularly while in the presence of the children.

If practical, the divorced parents should share **joint** custody of any children, and try to establish a new routine that will occasion minimal disruption to the children's lives.

If one parent has legal custody and the other has visitation privileges, the parents should try to make **child visitation** a comfortable experience for both children and parents. In particular, the visiting parent should be timely when picking up and dropping off the child, and the custodial parent should have the child ready to go (and be ready to receive the child) on time. Neither parent should use the visitation opportunity to affront or intrusively interfere with the life of the other parent.

Both the custodial and non-custodial parents should meet their child support obligations in a responsible and timely manner.

- **Leaving home.**

Children should not **leave home** until they are adequately prepared to care for themselves. Most children are adequately prepared for basic self-sufficiency by the age of eighteen.

Due to habit pattern and the comfort of the family relationship, both child and parents may find it difficult to accept the child's eventual departure; however, it is in the child's best interest to eventually become domestically independent and to develop his personal sense of self-sufficiency.

It is not unreasonable for a mature child to remain with his parents as he attends college, particularly if the child is working his way through school and contributing to his support.

A mature child may need to return to his parents' home because of health or financial problems. Such occurrences should be brief and few.

- **Affluent parents.**

Effective parenting is made easier if a family enjoys adequate material wherewithal; however, **affluency** does not assure successful child rearing.

The children of some affluent parents might be sheltered from all material adversity and eventually acquire their personal wealth by gift, inheritance, or through opportunities provided by social position and nepotism.

Although affluent parents might provide such advantages with their children's best interest in mind, the ultimate effect could be **problematic**. In particular, such children might develop **distorted values** relative to material objects, and become **retarded** in their **self-sufficiency** development.

Most individuals acquire material possessions and their related benefits as the direct result of **personal labor**; consequently, the average individual values material items relative to the effort that is required to earn them.

When individuals acquire wealth without working for it, they may fail to develop an appreciation for the pragmatic relationship between **work** and **reward**. This lack of understanding might diminish the individual's respect for the earned possessions of others; consequently, when such individuals want **more** material possessions, they might be tempted to employ **immoral** means of acquisition.

Society often exhibits **respect** for individuals who have realized material wealth through hard work and creativity. When individuals acquire wealth and position through gift or nepotism, they might fail to develop an appreciation for the pragmatic relationship between **personal accomplishment** and **earned respect**.

Healthy individuals are **self-sufficient**. This personal ability affords individuals peace of mind in the knowledge that they can take care of themselves under adverse conditions.

Individuals who have acquired personal wealth or position through gift, inheritance, or nepotism might fail (through lack of necessity) to develop self-sufficiency. If such individuals permit themselves to rely upon the tenuous existence of inherited wealth or position rather than their own abilities, they might find themselves in a constant state of **emotional insecurity**.

Affluent parents might consider a variety of approaches to assist their children in developing a **functional material value system**, and a healthy sense of self-sufficiency. They might require their children to **earn** their **monetary allowance** or any other **special material gifts**, through an established work routine (**chores**) or special work projects. The eventual bestowal of substantial financial gifts, inheritance, or commercial opportunity might be delayed until their child has developed a strong personal **work ethic**.

A child's sense of **self-worth** is affected by the way that he perceive his own abilities relative to the abilities of other individuals.   Such perceptions are enhanced or reinforced by the **respected opinions** of others.   For children, **parents** tend to be a primary source of such respected opinions.

Most parents are average in their personal accomplishments; consequently, their children enjoy relative opportunity (by comparative accomplishment) to earn the parents' respect. If children believe that they have done **as well as**, or **better than** their parents, their feelings of self-worth are enhanced.

Affluent parents, on the other hand, tend to be above average in their personal accomplishments; consequently, their children might experience less opportunity to do **as well as**, or **better than** such parents. Affluent parents also tend to employ **higher** judgement standards. Under such conditions, children may fail to receive **adequate** praise and respect, or to develop a **healthy** sense of self-worth.

To assist their children in developing a healthy sense of self-worth, affluent parents should employ **practical** criteria in judging their children's accomplishments, and should avoid **forcing** their children to compete or perform in the parents' specific areas of excellence.

Affluent parents are often obsessive in their work habits, depriving themselves and their families of adequate family interaction time. Their children, although materially advantaged, may be lacking in **dedicated** parental attention.

The development of a child's problem solving skills and his sense of self-worth are both influenced by the **quantity** and **quality** of direct attention that he receives from his parents; consequently, the deprivation of adequate parental attention can **negatively impact** a child's development. Affluent parents might best avoid this possibility by practicing appropriate time allocation; in particular, **the fulfillment of one's health and family needs should precede the fulfillment of his money and play needs.**

- **Consideration for others.**

The actions of children might affect other individuals. Children, due to their **immature** judgement, may be unable to discern the consequences of their actions; consequently, parents bear a **responsibility** to protect other children or adults from unreasonable trespass or inconvenience that might be occasioned by the acts of their children.

This parental responsibility involves **work.** If individuals are not willing to commit to this responsibility, they should not have children. If parents fail to exercise the effort that is necessary to properly control and guide their children's actions, the children, the parents, and society will **all** suffer the negative consequences.

Children, by their very nature, are understandably immature in their actions, and might occasionally abuse the person or property of their playmates. Parents should take care to discourage such acts, lest they become habitual.

The normal sounds of children playing in a neighborhood are as natural as the sounds of the wind blowing or of birds singing. Children will often climb a neighbors fence or hide in a neighbors yard while playing *hide-and-go-seek.* Parents should not be overly concerned about controlling such actions and rational neighbors should be tolerant of such occurrences. At the same time, parents should discourage their children from making disturbing neighborhood noises early in the morning, or late in the evening, or damaging a neighbor's property.

Parents bear a special **child control** responsibility when in **public places.** When in restaurants, children should be discouraged from making loud noises or running around the tables. In restaurants and motion picture theaters, mothers should take crying infants to the lobby until they are calmed.

Considerate parents should refrain from bringing their young children into certain public settings in which the patrons are paying premium prices for **ambiance**. Examples of such settings are the **opera, fine dining, first class hotel, ship,** or **air accommodations,** and certain **vacation resort settings.**

Adults are typically larger, stronger, and more knowledgeable than children; consequently, adults can represent a potential threat, or source of assistance, to children. With this reality in mind, it is in a child's best interest to treat all adults with **respect.** Towards this end, parents should encourage their children to address adults by the title of **Mister** or **Misses,** and while in their presence, to refrain from actions that might inconvenience or intimidate adults (such as loud noises, or abrupt physical actions).

- **Meal time.**

Meal time can provide far more than nutritional value. It is a time for the **entire family to be together,** for information to be exchanged and for emotional security to be reinforced.

Both parents should try to be present for breakfast and dinner, and neither meal should be rushed. Parents should remind themselves that **family time** takes **precedence** over **work** or play activities. A business meeting is ultimately less important than breakfast or dinner with the family. Money cannot buy a balanced child, a loving spouse, or the inner peace that is experienced from healthy family relationships.

SUBJECT 4. Continuing Family Relationships

Ideally, parents and mature children will continue to relate in a mutually beneficial manner.

As mature children encounter challenging adult problems, their parents can provide **guidance,** based upon the parents' **previous experience** in resolving similar problems. Such guidance can be **invaluable** to their mature child, helping them to avoid unnecessary time, material, or emotional expenditures.

Parents might also assist in the rearing of their grandchildren, providing **counseling** or direct **care.**

On occasion, parents might provide financial assistance to their mature children. Such assistance should, of course, be repaid in a **timely manner**, and with market **interest**.

Reciprocally, as aging parents decline in physical ability, their mature children might assist them with certain tasks, such as special home maintenance problems.

Individuals are wise to responsibly **plan** for their retirement needs, avoiding financial reliance upon government programs or the benevolence of their children. Notwithstanding this reality, it is appropriate under **certain circumstances** for mature children to assist their aging parents with **financial support**.

Beyond material and problem solving assistance, the child/parent relationship should **continue to yield pleasure** through holiday celebrations, birthdays, mutual vacations, Sunday visits, and other festive family occasions.

PART FOUR: Money Considerations
- Contents -

SECTION D. General Business Skills (continued)

[Note - The words *Man*, *his*, *he*, *him*, and *himself* herein refer to the species in general, with **no sexist connotation intended**.]

PART FOUR: Money Considerations

This section will certainly guide the reader in **how to make money**; however, the ultimate attainment of **financial success** does not lie solely in the knowledge of how to make money. It is equally, if not more, important to **understand** money's philosophical and functional roles in life.

The financial success of individuals should **not** be judged by their earnings, or wealth **alone**. It is possible to accumulate wealth by working **long** hours, or by employing **immoral** means; however, such methods typically **frustrate** the ultimate fulfillment of one's overall needs.

Individuals are **financially successful** if they are earning **enough** money through **moral** and personally **palatable** means to **successfully** fulfill their **health, family,** and **play** needs.

SECTION A. Money

In order to effectively earn and manage money, an individual might best begin by understanding the technical concept of money.

SUBJECT 1. What is Money?

At one time, every primitive family performed the same basic survival tasks: hunting, fishing, foraging, making clothes, making shelters and making tools. As population counts increased, organized **societies** evolved. These primitive societies domesticated livestock and developed productive agricultural techniques. Tool making methods were refined and urbanization occurred.

It eventually became **impractical** for each family to perform the same set of survival tasks. As a result, different families specialized in different tasks; some tended livestock, some made tools, some worked the fields, and so on.

Individuals in these early societies exchanged their goods and services in a **barter** system economy. As villages grew in size and as **task specialization** became more diverse, formal **marketplaces** developed. These were central locations where villagers could acquire the goods and services that they needed, and could offer their particular goods and services in exchange.

The fair bartering of various goods and services required considerable negotiations, particularly when the items were not very **similar** in size, uniqueness, or quantity. For example, if one individual made *arrowheads* and another individual made *canoes*, an obvious barter problem may have resulted in determining how many arrowheads to exchange for one canoe.

The common basis for such negotiations might have been the relative comparison of the **labor** that was expended to produce the products. In the above example, more labor was necessary to produce a canoe than was required to produce an arrowhead; consequently, the canoe maker might have to accept many more arrowheads than he could personally use.

The canoe maker was probably willing to accept the **extra** arrowheads, because they could be used as barter for other desired goods and services.

Such exchange methods probably formed the basis of early **premonetary** systems. In the above example, the arrowhead actually became a form of **near-money**; that is, the arrowheads were not accepted in trade for their obvious intended use (as hunting implements), but rather for their potential **exchange value**.

The **arrowhead type of money** was relatively easy to handle, and it represented a small recognizable unit of expended labor. The **exchange value** of this near-money was secured by the ultimate usability of the arrowheads as hunting implements.

a. An implied pledge.

Societies, in time, devised other convenient and commonly accepted means of exchange, such as beads, bones, shells, coins, et cetera. These forms of **money**, unlike the arrowhead, had no **intrinsic use value**; they were simply **tokens**, secured in value by an **implied pledge** that was mutually acknowledged and agreed to by all **money exchanging** members of a particular society.

Money's sole function lies in its exchange utility for desired goods and services. All goods and services are the direct product of physical labor; consequently, money represents an implied pledge to perform labor. So, in effect, when one citizen **pays money** to another, he is giving a token pledge that he will perform a certain amount of labor **on demand**.

Money, as a **labor pledge** is in a conveniently handled and stored negotiable form. The recipient of such money may trade it to still another for other goods or service, or save it for future use.

When individuals **save** money, they are accumulating a pool of labor pledges that are backed or guaranteed by the other members of their society. Eventually, they may choose to use these saved labor pledges to fulfill (buy) their survival and luxury needs.

Individuals, as they age, might become unable to perform certain physical tasks; consequently, **saved labor pledges** (money) become very useful. This phenomena is referred to as **saving for one's old age, or retirement**.

b. Profit and Loss.

In the manufacturing and distribution of most commercial products, human and mechanical labor are used to reconfigure component **raw materials** into marketable **finished goods**. In this process, the **product** typically undergoes several progressive sales transactions: the raw material *supplier* sells to the *manufacturer*, the manufacturer sells to the *wholesaler*, the wholesaler sells to the *retailer*, and the retailer sells to the end *consumer*, with a **profit** being realized in each progressive sale.

Theoretically, such profits should **fairly** reflect the material, human labor, and other expenses that were contributed to the product in each respective marketing stage. This profit concept is commonly referred to as the **net value added** approach.

When discussing the commercial **accounting** of money, the terms **profit** and **loss** are often used. When a commercial provider (**purveyor**) of goods or services expends labor and money to bring its products to market, such expenditures are referred to as **expenses**. The purveyor will eventually receive a certain amount of money, when it sells its products to consumers; such money is referred to as **income**.

Profit is the monetary amount by which such sale's income exceeds such marketing expenses in a commercial transaction. Conversely, **loss** is the monetary amount by which expenses exceed income. The **profitability** of a commercial enterprise, is typically calculated for each monthly, quarterly, and annual period of operation (see *Understanding General Ledger Accounting*).

c. Supply and Demand.

The potential profit associated with any form of income production is directly affected by the factors of **competitive marketing** and **competitive consumption**, commonly referred to as the principle of *Supply and Demand*.

As desired commodities become scarce in supply, consumers will naturally compete to acquire them, consequently driving commodity prices up. Higher prices typically, although not necessarily, result in greater profits. Conversely, as desired commodities become abundant in supply, purveyors will naturally compete for buyers in the selling of their products, consequently driving commodity prices down. Lower prices typically result in lesser profits.

This principle of *Supply and Demand* is **universal** in nature and **unavoidable**. Being a natural marketplace phenomenon, its effects should be **anticipated** in any practical economic system.

SUBJECT 2. How Much Money is Enough?

The above question really means **"how much money should one be earning, spending, and saving?"**

If individuals fail to exercise effective financial planning, they may have insufficient money to meet their present living and retirement needs, consequently diminishing their quality of life.

Reciprocally, although less obviously, earning too much money can also diminish one's quality of life. If individuals spend time earning more money than is actually necessary to fulfill their present living and retirement needs, the time spent earning such unneeded money is literally **wasted time**. Such time is often expended to the detriment of one's health or family relationships.

The question "how much money is enough?" is best approached by considering the **basic reasons** that people need money. Individuals earn and save money for three primary reasons:

- To provide for their daily **living expenses**.

- To accumulate an **emergency reserve** to be used for their living expenses in the event that they are temporarily without income.

- To accumulate a **retirement reserve** to be used for their daily living expenses when they become to old to work.

a. Calculating *how much money is enough*:

1. Determine the monthly amount of money needed for one's reasonable **living expenses (food, shelter, clothing, utilities, health care, education, transportation, entertainment, insurance, maintenance** of assets, **capital expenditures** for cars, televisions, homes, et cetera).

2. Determine one's emergency reserve requirements. To do so, one should estimate **how long one might temporarily be without income** by asking oneself:

- How long would it take to find another job if one should become unemployed?

- What is the **worst case** time frame between sporadic incomes if one is self-employed?

One's emergency reserve needs are equal to his average monthly living expenses multiplied by the estimated number of months that one might temporarily be without income.

3. Determine one's **retirement reserve** needs. This is done by estimating:

- What will one's **annual living expenses** be during retirement?

- How many years does one anticipate living in retirement?

By multiplying the estimated **annual retirement expenses** times the estimated **number of years** that an individual expects to live in retirement, individuals can determine their estimated **total retirement cash needs**.

It is possible for individuals to **begin** their **retirement** with a lesser amount than the above mentioned total retirement cash needs, because some portion of their retirement savings should always be earning a reasonable **interest income**.

A banker or accountant, using a **loan amortization table**, can assist in estimating the actual **beginning cash reserve amount** required for retirement. Individuals should provide their banker or accountant with the following information:

> - The amount of their estimated **monthly retirement expenses**.

> - The estimated **number of years that one will be in retirement**.

> - The estimated **average rate of interest** that one anticipates receiving on their **retirement savings account**.

Normally, **a loan amortization table** is used to calculate the **monthly loan payments** when the original loan amount **interest rate** and **loan term** are all known.

Individuals should instruct their banker/accountant to use such a table in a **reverse** fashion, to deduce the **original loan amount** when the other factors are known.

Using one's estimated **retirement term (in months or years)** in place of loan term, and using one's estimated **savings interest rate** in place of loan interest rate and using one's estimated **monthly retirement expenses** in place of **monthly loan payments**, the banker/accountant can deduce the **original loan**

amount, and this figure will represent the **beginning** cash required for one's **retirement reserve**. If this computation is too complex for the reader to relate to their banker or accountant, one might simply provide them with a photocopy of this page.

By determining the **total retirement cash needed**, individuals can determine the **retirement reserve** that they should maintain at any given time in their **pre-retirement** life.

To make this determination, one should subtract his present age from his anticipated retirement age. The numeric difference equals the **number of years remaining** to earn and save one's **total retirement cash needs**.

By dividing one's **total retirement cash needs** by the **number of years remaining**, one can determine how much he should be saving **each year/month** for a **retirement reserve**.

4. After performing the above calculations, one can reasonably approximate **how much money is enough** as follows:

   - The amount of money that an individual needs to earn on a monthly basis is equal to his monthly **living expenses, plus** his necessary **monthly savings for retirement reserves**. This assumes that the individual has previously earned and saved an amount equal to his estimated **emergency reserves** requirement; if the individual has not saved his emergency reserves, he should do so, prior to estimating and starting his retirement reserves savings.

   - The amount of money that an individual should have saved, at any given time, is equal to his **emergency reserves** requirements plus his **retirement reserves** requirements.

As a numeric **example** of the above method of calculating *how much money is enough*, consider an individual with the following financial profile:

   - present monthly living expenses = **$2,500** (Note: this particular amount has been arbitrarily used for demonstrative purposes only and may not necessarily reflect typical living expenses)

- estimate of the time required to find another job or the worst-case time frame between sporadic self-employed incomes = **6** months

- emergency reserve = **$2,500** times **6** months = **$15,000**

- estimated monthly retirement expense = **$2,000**

- estimated number of years to be in retirement = 35 **(420 months)**

- total retirement cash needs = **420** months x **$2,000** per month = **$840,000**

- **$840,000 reverse amortized** over 420 months, using an 8% savings rate = **$281,300** = beginning cash required for retirement savings

- individual's present age = **25** years old

- anticipated retirement age = **65** years old

- number of years remaining, to save retirement reserve = retirement age (**65**) - present age (**25**) = **40** years

- annual/monthly savings required for retirement reserve = **$281,300** divided by **40** years = **$7,000** per year or, divided by twelve = **$586** per month

- monthly earnings necessary for the individual to pay his living expenses and to save for his retirement = **$2,500** + **$586** = **$3,086**

- **total reserve savings** necessary at any given time = emergency reserves of $15,000 plus retirement reserves (starting at $586, increasing by $586 each month, thereafter, until $281,300 is saved)

The individual in the above example would have **enough** money at twenty-five years of age if he earned **$3,086** per month, and if he had a total of **$15,586** in his combined emergency and retirement savings accounts. Again, this assumes that the individual has previously earned and saved $15,000 for his emergency reserves prior to beginning the above suggested $586 per month retirement saving.

If one's emergency reserves become depleted, he might shift funds from his retirement reserves to his emergency reserves. To compensate for this reduction in his retirement reserves savings, it becomes necessary to re-estimate (increase) the monthly amount that one should be saving for his retirement reserves.

b. Retirement income planning.

It is in an individual's best interest **not** to anticipate or rely upon **government** or **private industry retirement programs**, because they are not subject to the individual's control.

Individuals should attempt, through **their own** earnings, savings and investments, to provide for their retirement. It is a **risky misjudgment** to expect one's children or society to financially provide for one's retirement needs.

Retirement may seem very distant to most people; consequently, **vision** and **self-discipline** are necessary to plan for one's retirement. One must remember that a poorly planned retirement can be **mentally and physically torturous**.

In marriage, **both** spouses (particularly full-time **homemakers**) should take special care to **understand** and **monitor** the financial soundness and implementation of their family **retirement reserves** plans. In the event of divorce, both spouses should **equally** enjoy the eventual financial benefits of their mutual retirement planning efforts.

c. Healthy financial motivations.

The amount of money that one earns and spends is determined by his basic living needs, and his **attitudes** towards money.

An individual's chosen **monetary habits** and **standard of living** should be reflective of **good emotional health**.

Some individuals, due to **misinformation** or **harmful experiences**, develop emotional problems that affect their financial motivations. Such individuals **might mistakenly seek** or **avoid** money to palliate their emotional discomforts. As examples:

- An **emotionally insecure** individual might amass **excessive** wealth to compensate for inadequate feelings of self-worth, or to protect himself from misperceived threats. If an individual has suffered extreme financial deprivation, he might develop an insatiable desire for money.

- Some individuals might pursue and use the **power** afforded by wealth to ventilate personal **hostility**.

- Some individuals, depending upon how they acquired their wealth (through inheritance, for example), might experience **guilt** in its possession; consequently, they might **decry** wealth, and its means of acquisition.

- Some individuals, if they have been subject to an **abusive** economic system, might develop **contempt** for wealth and its means of acquisition.

- Some individuals, due to **misguided** religious beliefs, might **discourage** financial accomplishment.

Individuals should periodically assess their **priorities** and **motivations** regarding their earning, spending, and saving habits, particularly if their **money-related habits** are **interfering** with the successful fulfillment of their **health, family,** or **play** needs.

Assuming that one is participant in a **fair** economic system, he should neither envy, nor deny, the financial success of others. It is far better to live in a society in which **all** individuals enjoy the **opportunity** to achieve financial success, rather than being subject to an economic system in which all individuals are **limited** to financial **mediocrity**.

SECTION B. How to Earn Money

Individuals can earn money by one of two moral means: through their **personal labors**, or through **investment**.

SUBJECT 1. Earning Money Through Personal Labor

Individuals can earn money through personal labor by providing goods or services to others. The specific manner in which an individual chooses to provide such goods or services is referred to as his **vocation**.

a. The selection of a vocation.

Laboring for money (working) is **not** a particularly pleasant experience. Vocations vary in potential and palatability; consequently, it is very important for individuals to give **intelligent** consideration to their vocational options. When selecting a vocation, individuals should be guided by **three** considerations:

1. Personal skills.

As individuals mature, they develop a set of **personal (problem solving) skills**. Such skills might render a person particularly talented in the **arts**, **athletics**, **manual dexterity**, **linguistics**, **finance**, **mathematics**, et cetera. Because individuals vary in their personal experiences and genetic predispositions, they develop **unique** skill **strengths**.

Most vocations have formal training or apprenticeship programs; however, it is certainly to one's advantage (efficiency wise) to select a vocation that effectively utilizes one's natural inclinations.

2. Financial needs.

As individuals mature, they envision a desirable **lifestyle**. In that different lifestyles necessarily **vary** in their financial support requirements, it is important that individuals select a vocation that will **accommodate** their lifestyle expectations. One's failure to do so predestines him to **mid-life crisis**.

3. Self-image needs.

As individuals mature, they develop opinions, attitudes, and prejudices about the types of individuals who typically engage in various vocations. Such feelings result from personal experiences. For example, an individual might have had an uncle who was a **plumber**; in such instance, the individual might forever associate his uncle's image with the plumbing profession. Public media representations or the comments of respected individuals also influence such perceptions; one's father might have said "never trust a salesman," therein prejudicing one's image of salespeople.

An individual's vocation-related **self-image needs** are strongly influenced by such perceptions, **regardless** of their accuracy; consequently, an individual should engage in a vocation that is **personally palatable**. An individual might mistakenly engage in a vocation that adequately fulfills his **financial needs**; however, he might (consciously, or subconsciously) disrespect the type of individuals who characterize his chosen vocation. Consequently, he might continuously suffer **self-image-related discomfort**.

Individuals should exercise considerable forethought in selecting a vocation which realistically **balances** their **self-image** and **financial needs**, while capitalizing on their **personal skills**.

b. Earning potential.

The **earning potential** associated with any chosen vocation is largely determined by **three** primary factors:

1. The **uniqueness** of the vocation.

An individual's labor will be of **greater** market **value** if few other individuals possess equal ability to perform the same labor (assuming, of course, that such labor is in demand).

2. The **economic environment** in which one's labor is performed.

An individual's potential for enjoying substantial earnings is increased if he performs his labor in an **economic environment** which is conducive to **individual and national prosperity**.

Such environments have **two** common characteristics:

> - **Fair economic systems**. Such systems support an equit-
> able distribution of wealth, permit social/economic mobility,
> and encourage individual financial accomplishment. Capit-
> alistic/free enterprise economies, operating under the admin-
> istration of a democratic government, are representative of
> **fair economic systems**.
>
> If individuals are working within such an economic system,
> they might give further consideration to their nation's
> **geographic** distribution of commercial prosperity. It is
> certainly in one's best interest to perform his labors in a
> region of the country, or specific city, which is enjoying
> general prosperity.
>
> - **Affluent industries**. Individuals enjoy a higher proba-
> bility of financial accomplishment if they associate them-
> selves with an industry that is characterized by profitable
> **high dollar volume transactions**. For example, an indi-
> vidual who prefers a **commission** remuneration might real-
> ize a higher earning potential in **real estate sales** as
> compared to **shoe sales**. Although a shoe salesperson
> might be paid a higher commission **percentage**, the real
> estate salesperson might enjoy a better **overall earning
> potential** because of **comparative** annual monetary trans-
> action volumes of the two vocations.

Additionally, one might consider the **spectrum** of **affluency**
within one's chosen vocation. For example, the **real estate**
industry can be subdivided into areas of product specialization:
commercial, **residential**, **agricultural**, and **special use**. If one
has chosen commissioned real estate sales as a prospective
vocation, he might further compare the relative affluence of
different **sub-industry** product specializations. In doing so, he
might determine that the average commercial real estate sales
agent enjoys a greater earning potential than the average
residential sales agent.

3. The **method of remuneration**.

The manner in which employees are remunerated for their labors varies with vocation. Different **remuneration methods** have respectively associated benefits:

- **Salaries** and **hourly wages** tend to assure an employee of a relatively **consistent** periodic income.

- **Profit participation, commission,** and **piece rate** remuneration tend to encourage and reward individual **initiative**; such approaches typically favor the employee's financial betterment.

c. Earning money as an employee.

Individuals might choose to perform their chosen vocations in one of **two** capacities: in the **employment of another**, or **self-employed**. Working for an employer is characterized by the following benefits:

- The employer typically provides the direction, facilities, equipment, training, and capital, that are necessary to accommodate the employee's work objectives.

- Employees have an immediate market for their labor.

- Such employment provides the individual with the opportunity to test the earning potential and palatability of various vocations, without having to invest considerable time or personal capital.

- Individuals might use such employment earnings to fund their future **self-employment** or **investment** ventures.

There are three primary **disadvantages** to being an employee:

- Employees do not typically realize the **optimum** economic benefits of their labors, in that their employers share in a portion of their produced income.

- The employee is subject to the employer's business judgement; if the employer makes unprofitable business decisions, the employee may be negatively impacted.

- The employee is subject to the control of the employer; if the employer practices ineffective management techniques, the employee might experience very uncomfortable working conditions.

1. **Types of employers.** There are four general types of employers:

a) **Sole proprietorships.**

Sole proprietorships are owned and operated by one individual. Because the proprietor's income is directly affected by his employee's **morale**, and because such firms are typically small in size, sole proprietors are often sensitive and responsive to employee needs.

b) **Partnerships.**

Partnership firms are owned and operated by two or more individuals. Smaller partnerships, like **sole proprietorships**, are often sensitive to **employee needs**. As partnerships grow in company size and/or number of employees, this benefit tends to diminish.

c) **Corporations.**

Larger corporations generally provide excellent training opportunities for inexperienced workers. Such corporations often provide good **indirect benefits**, including paid vacations and holidays, medical and dental care, stock options and pension plans, et cetera.

On the negative side, the corporate **management mentality** is typically (if not necessarily) **insensitive**. Corporations are owned by **stockholders**. The stockholders of most corporations are not actively involved in the management of the company; they elect a **board of directors** who employ professional managers (**executives**) to run the company.

Many such **executives** advance their careers by *job-hopping* from one corporation to another; this practice is encouraged by corporate proselytizing. When executives have relatively **short** company tenure, they may not personally know the employees who are subject to their management decisions; consequently, corporate employees who have performed many years of **dedicated** service may fall **victim** to insensitive **cost cutting** or **reorganization** programs.

d) Governments.

Governments, as employers, provide very **stable** work environments; that is, very few employees are ever **laidoff, forcedout,** or **fired**. Government employees often enjoy generous **indirect benefits**, such as paid holidays and vacations, medical insurance, and pension programs.

On the negative side, government workplaces (by their very nature) lack profit motivation; consequently, an employee's economic opportunities tend to be **limited**.

With the exception of the highly motivated or altruistic few, most government employees lack a sense of **vested interest** in the overall success of their particular operational entity. Additionally, government work environments are often austere, bureaucratic, and inflexible.

- Labor Unions

Although not employers *per se*, labor unions are employee organizations that endeavor, through collective bargaining, to protect employees from economic and physical abuses. Unfortunately, unions occasionally become the object of criminal manipulation. In such instances, the quality of union representation and union finances become at risk.

2. How to get a job (and prosper as an employee).

The specific approach to becoming employed necessarily varies with each vocation; consequently, the following suggestions are general in nature and should be adapted to the particular employment position being pursued. Regardless of the vocation being pursued, one should first secure the appropriate education or apprenticeship experience that is necessary to minimally qualify for employment.

a) Creating an Employment Opportunity.

One should **first** make a **list** of prospective employers. In doing so, one might consider the following sources:

- The newspaper classified advertisements.

- Leads from friends, relatives, or business associates.

- A membership list from the local chamber of commerce.

- Academic, professional, or government job placement agencies.

- Personal canvassing.

Next, one should prepare a **single** page (typed, if possible) **resume**, including one's name, address, telephone number, educational background, apprenticeship training, related work experience, and any outstanding academic, professional, or civic accomplishments. Also prepare a **one-half** page resume **cover letter** of introduction, requesting an **employment interview**.

If feasible, use a **word processing system** to set up the prospective employer mailing list, therein permitting the personalized preparation of each resume cover letter and envelope.

Prepare and mail one-third of the **position inquiry** letters, and then evaluate the responses. Depending upon the responses, the individual might wish to modify his resume or cover letter approach.

Depending upon the nature of the desired employment position, one might experience very few positive responses; consequently, one should attempt to send out as many **position inquiries** as possible.

If the individual cannot prepare a resume and does not have access to a **word processing system**, he should **personally** call on each prospective employer and ask to speak with the **person in charge**.

The key to eventual employment is **persistence**. Granted, one might feel quite insecure and uncomfortable, while looking for a job, but continued effort is the only course of action. When one is **looking for a job**, it is literally like being *on the outside looking in*. One must simply continue to **actively canvass** for employment. It only takes **one good opportunity**, and then one is comfortably on the *inside* - potentially, for years!

b) Controlling the job interview.

It is wise to have some general information about a prospective employer before the **job interview**. An **annual stockholders' report** or **marketing brochure** are good sources of such general information; the company receptionist will often have such literature available. Such pre-knowledge will help one to intelligently converse with the interviewer, and to better judge the employment opportunity.

First impressions can be made only once; consequently, one should dress in a clean and business-like manner. One should avoid the use of heavy colognes or perfumes and keep hairstyles conservative. One's style of clothing and grooming should not distract from the business object of the interview; that is, one's appearance should not overly accentuate one's sexuality, or prompt the prospective employer to make unintended **value judgements.**

One should refrain from smoking or chewing gum in employment interviews, even if the interviewer is doing so. One should be cordial, but not **overly friendly**, lest such behavior be perceived as casual **disrespect.**

One should appear to be **prepared**; bring a briefcase (if appropriate), and **always** bring a pen and pad of paper. It is wise to write down the names of the individuals that one meets during the interview. In this manner, one avoids misstating names, and readies oneself for the preparation of an **interview follow-up letter.**

Upon meeting the interviewer, an individual should offer his hand and make a **firm** (but not over powering) handshake, regardless of the sexes of the individuals. A **limp** handshake is typically perceived as being indicative of **weak resolve, deceptiveness,** or **illness**. If one's hand is perspiring, one should try (discreetly) to wipe it before shaking hands; a wet handshake exposes one's sense of anxiety.

The prospective employee should endeavor to **subtly control** the interview. To this end, one might **initially** thank the interviewer for granting the meeting, and **then** ask him to expand upon the details of the **job opening**. One should **listen** to the interviewer rather than attempting to dominate the conversation; a **challenge** of egos will surely result in **no job**.

If there is no present job opening, one might ask the interviewer to comment on the history of the company. In this manner, one can then use the interview opportunity to build a rapport with the interviewer, and to inform him of one's job related skills and enthusiasm. On occasion, an employer will actually **create** an employment position to accommodate an impressive (apparently valuable) individual.

Towards the end of the interview, politely ask **who else** will be involved in the **hiring decision**; such knowledge permits one to react appropriately, should he be introduced to that individual, and it helps to **qualify** the interviewer's decision-making capacity.

After the interview, one should write a letter to the interviewer, thanking him for the interview and expressing one's pleasure in meeting the involved individuals. Individuals should also reiterate how their professional background will enable them to proficiently perform the duties of the subject employment position. They might also restate their enthusiasm about the subject employment opportunity and ask what the **next** step is in the employer's decision-making process.

If an employment position is very attractive, and if there are many others competing for the position, an individual might offer to work **without pay** for a two-week **trial basis**. By doing so:

> - One **demonstrates confidence** in his abilities and enthusiasm for the employment position.

- The employer's **risk** is **minimized**, encouraging him to give the prospective employee an opportunity.

- The individual creates an opportunity to get his **foot in the door**, and once **in**, it is probable that the employer will retain him.

c) Negotiating employment terms.

1) Remuneration.

Employees, **at the time of hiring**, should try to negotiate an advantageous remuneration package (see *Negotiating*).

An employee's opportunity to **negotiate** his remuneration will be dependent upon the nature of the job position and the employment market. If people are **lined up out the door** for the same job position, negotiating becomes impractical. On the other hand, if there are few other qualified applicants, the employee should be **aggressive** in his remuneration negotiations.

Remuneration negotiations generally involve four considerations:

- **Direct Pay**

Direct pay is the monetary consideration paid to employees for their labor.

Profit sharing, piece rate, or **commission oriented** pay arrangements particularly benefit ambitious employees, because they are paid in direct relationship to their efforts.

Hourly and **salaried** pay schedules tend towards consistent income; however, they might inhibit an individual's productivity and limit his earning potential.

Salaried employees should, at the time of hiring, negotiate how they will be compensated for **overtime** work. Salaried employees should not be expected to work overtime **free of pay**. Salaried individuals should be paid for overtime on a **pre-agreed to** hourly rate, or they should be compensated with an equal amount of **time off**.

- **Indirect benefits.**

There are many forms of **indirect benefits**; for example, employer provided **medical and dental insurance coverage, paid vacations and holidays, reimbursement of educational expenses, pension plan coverage, stock options**, et cetera. Additionally, some such indirect benefits are free of government taxation.

2) Work duties.

The appropriateness of any remuneration arrangement is dependent upon the employee's work duties and schedule. In particular, before completing one's remuneration negotiations, he should understand the specific work tasks that he will be expected to perform, and what his working hours will be.

3) Labor amenities.

Labor **amenities** influence one's comfort and effectiveness in accomplishing his work responsibilities. Amongst those that should be considered, are:

- **Facilities**, such as a **private office, desk assignment, bench assignment, locker assignment**, et cetera.

- **Tools** provided by the employer.

- **Vehicle usage**, such as a **company car or truck**.

- **Expense allowance**, for the reimbursement of the employee's business-related (transportation, entertainment, uniforms, et cetera) expenses.

4) Severance terms.

All employment relationships eventually end. Upon termination, an employee is of no further value to an employer; consequently, an employee enjoys **minimal** negotiating leverage **at the time of his termination**. With this reality in mind, it is in one's best interest to negotiate his severance terms **at the time of hiring**. In particular, one should negotiate and define the **time frames** required for **notice of termination** and the **monetary amounts** of **severance pay**, relative to the nature of any termination.

All terms of employment, once negotiated, should be **in writing**. Employees should not hesitate to have their attorneys review or modify the employer's **printed form contract**, as such forms are typically worded in the **employer's** best interest.

An employee's negotiating leverage will fluctuate with circumstance throughout his term of employment; consequently, an employee might periodically consider renegotiating his remuneration package if **later** circumstances afford him a **stronger** negotiating position.

d) Good employee attitudes.

- Employees should be **honest, timely, hard-working**, and should **not waste** their employer's **assets**. By helping a **good** employer to prosper, employees are actually helping themselves. A prosperous employer is better able to **fairly** remunerate its employees, particularly those that are directly responsible for the employer's success. This **assumes** that the employer is rational and practicing good business judgement.

If an employer **substantially** profits, due to the employee's conscientious and special work efforts, the employer should formally **recognize** and materially **reward** such efforts. If the employer fails to do so, the employee should formally voice his expectations; if the employer still fails to properly respond, the employee should seek **other** employment.

- An employee should practice **effective problem solving techniques** (see *Problem Solving Skills*). Being a **problem solver** rather than a **problem identifier** is in the employee's **best interest**, because it helps the employer associate **positive** thoughts with the employee's image.

When employees do or say something to improve their employer's financial position, it makes the employer **feel good**, and the employer will associate that good feeling with the image of the employee who helped to induce it. The following are examples of employee actions or comments that might make an employer *feel good*: "we will have that job ready on time", or "I just negotiated a very profitable sale", or "our company is great to work for."

All individuals desire personal respect and attention. Normally, respect and attention are earned through the accomplishment of **good deeds**. Such accomplishments typically require **work** and **self-discipline**. Some employees try to get their employer's attention by **identifying problems**. Such an approach, although much easier than **solving problems**, is ultimately **detrimental** to the employee.

If individuals must **identify** a problem, they should also be ready to suggest a solution; better yet, they should try to solve problems **before** their employer becomes aware of them. Naturally, there will be some problems that employees cannot solve or avoid; in such instances, the employer should certainly be involved.

Employers make many decisions regarding their employees. Such decisions include *pay raises, promotions, lay-offs*, et cetera. When making such decisions, the employer might mentally picture the **faces** of the subject employees, and subconsciously recall any associated incidents or feelings. If employers recall **good** associated feelings relative to an employee, they will probably make decisions that are favorable to that employee; consequently, employees can **best** assure their employment well-being by creating and maintaining **positive image associations** in their employer's minds.

e) Controlling the workplace environment.

Employees should try to create and control a workplace environment that is conducive to their personal well-being without distracting from their employer's profit objectives.

Employees can enhance the beneficial nature of their workplace and diminish the detrimental nature through their assertive actions. Generally speaking, it is in the employee's best interest to **assume** the authority to act, unless such permission has been **specifically** denied. As an example, some employees might be inconvenienced because other employees are pilfering their company-issued tools. Although the victim employee has not been specifically directed to do so, he might mark or identify his tools with a particular paint color, thereby discouraging others from pilfering them.

In the above example, the individual has **assumed the authority** to solve his work environment problem, rather than seeking the authority or accepting the solution of another.

Another method of controlling one's employment environment is through **suggestion**. There are many employment situations in which an employee is subject to the control of the employer. An employee can affect the way that its employer exercises control by making subtle or direct **suggestions**. When making such suggestions, employees should take care **not to affront** the authority of their employers or supervisors.

An effective technique when making suggestions is to offer **three possible approaches** for the employer's consideration and decision. One of the suggested approaches should be the employee's **desired** approach, and the other two should be relatively **impractical**. The employer will most likely select the employee's desired approach. In this manner, the employee achieves his desired result, while at the same time **allowing** the employer to exercise its decision making **prerogative**.

d. Earning money through self-employment.

When individuals are employees, their employer typically funds and directs their work tasks. Employers either consume their employees' labor efforts (to produce a product), or market their employees' services to the general public.

Self-employed individuals typically **fund** and **direct** their own business operations, and provide their goods or services **directly** to the general public.

In contrast to being an employee, the primary advantages to self-employment are **superior earning opportunities**, and **self-determination**.

1. Selecting a vocational field of self-employment.

Selecting a vocation for self-employment involves the same methodology as that stated in *The selection of a vocation*, above. One should test various prospective vocations by first working as an employee. There are several advantages to doing so:

- An individual can judge the prospective vocation, before investing substantial time and capital into his own business.

- An individual can enjoy the material benefits of being trained in a vocation, on his employer's time and money.

- An individual can develop the client, vendor, supplier, and general business base, that will be necessary to form and support his own business; unless he is restricted from doing so in his employment contract (some employment contracts have a **covenant not to compete, non-use** or **non-disclosure of company proprietary information clauses**).

- An individual can save part of such employment earnings to use as capital in the formation of his own business.

Individuals greatly increase the probability of their self-employment success by first working as an employee in the same field (and preferably in the same geographic area). Conversely, if individuals start a new business in a geographic area, or vocation with which they are unfamiliar, they often assure its failure.

2. Starting one's own business.

There are **three** prerequisites to forming one's own business:

- **First**, individuals should have the **expertise** that is necessary to provide the goods or services that are expected of their particular self-employment vocation. Such expertise is typically acquired through one's previous work experiences, or through formal education.

- **Second**, individuals should be well developed in their personal problem solving skills (see *Problem Solving Skills*) and their general business skills (see *General Business Skills*). Such business skills are typically acquired through previous work experiences, or through formal education.

- **Finally**, individuals should have adequate funds to set up (or purchase) their new business, to support its initial operating costs, and to support themselves, until the new business is sufficiently profitable.

Business expenditures are generally categorized as **capital** or **operational**. Capital expense items tend to be relatively permanent in nature, and used for the general production of goods and services. Such items would be part of one's **set-up** costs. Examples of capital expenditure items include **office equipment, production equipment, vehicles, furniture, patents**, or **facilities**.

Some business expenditures are for **operational** costs. Operational expenses are typically for items that are directly consumed in the production and marketing of goods and services. Examples of such expenses might be **payroll, raw materials, utilities, rents**, or **transportation**.

Before starting a new business, individuals should **realistically** estimate their **set-up** costs, a monthly **operating budget**, and their **personal living expenses**. These figures should then be used to plan their capital needs. In particular, individuals should have adequate resources to:

- Fund the initial set-up costs.

- Provide for the operational expenses until the business is consistently generating planned profits, typically a **minimum of one year**.

- Provide for one's personal (family) living expenses until the planned profits are consistently doing so, typically a **minimum of one year**.

When starting a new business, it is advisable to be **conservative** in one's capital expenditures; that is, one should avoid acquiring more facilities or equipment than is **absolutely** necessary. If one has acquired larger facilities, more equipment, or more employees than are initially needed, the associated expenses might prove **fatal** to a marginally profitable business venture.

It is financially prudent to start conservatively and then increase one's capital expenditures as the business **grows** in volume and profitability. If there is a surge in one's business volumes, one can temporarily operate under cramped facility conditions, or with two shifts working on limited equipment. One should not expand facilities, or buy additional equipment until it is justified by **consistent** business volume and **profits**.

Individuals should **minimize** the borrowing of funds for initial capitalization, expansion, or to cover operating expenses. Interest payments for borrowed money add a heavy burden to operating expenses. Most operating expenses can be reduced if business volumes drop. On the other hand, **loan interest payments** often remain **constant** until the loan is paid off; in a troubled economy, this reality can doom a marginally profitable business.

There are some justifiable reasons for business-related borrowing:

> - If one is purchasing an **existing business** which has a reliable **profit history**, some financing might be appropriate.

> - As one's business grows and consistently prospers, commercial credit lines might be employed to stabilize **cash flow** demands.

> - One might use a **real estate loan** for the purchase of operating facilities, because such expenditures are typically impractical to self-capitalize.

Like borrowing, the renting or leasing of business furniture, equipment, or facilities, should also be **minimized**. Like loan interest payments, lease or rental payments remain constant when business volume falls. Similarly, such fixed expenses might prove fatal to a marginally profitable business.

There are, of course, some reasonable justifications for the leasing of business facilities (offices, retail outlets, manufacturing buildings, warehouses, et cetera):

- Initially, a business may lack the capital or credit rating that is necessary to finance the purchase of its operating facility.

- It is unwise to purchase a business facility until one is confident that the new business venture is viable.

- It is unwise to purchase a business facility until one can accurately determine the business' long-range facility needs.

- **Retail store** locations and **branch office** locations must typically be leased, because they are often part of a larger investor-owned commercial property.

3. Operating one's own business.

To successfully operate one's own business, he should practice **integrity** and **be willing to spend money**.

a) Practice integrity.

The **first rule** of good business is to be **fair** with one's clients, employees, business associates, society in general, and the environment. If individuals conduct their businesses both **intelligently** and **morally**, profits **typically** follow, notwithstanding economic or market conditions that are beyond one's direct control.

To this end, individuals should provide their clients with value for their money, pay fair wages to their employees, maintain healthy employee working conditions, pay business obligations on time, honor commitments, maintain a pollution free environment, conserve natural resources, be considerate of ecological balances, and exercise common courtesy.

The above comments are not based in mysticism or altruism, but rather in the practical realities of **effective problem solving** (see *What is Morality?*).

b) Be willing to spend money.

To make money, one must be willing to spend money! Many self-employed businesspeople find it difficult to grasp this **simple** concept. In particular, many entrepreneurs bleed their companies to death by personally drawing out their **cash flow** monies as though they were **profits.**

To better understand this detrimental phenomenon, one should understand the relative definitions of **cash flow** and **profits.**

Businesses realize **cash flow monies** by selling their goods or services to consumers. These cash flow monies are then used to pay for the expenses of operating and expanding the business.

After the business operating expenses have been paid and some reasonable amount has been set aside for maintenance and expansion reserves, the remaining cash flow monies may be paid out to the business owner in the form of **profits. Only then** should such business-generated monies become the personal monies of the business owner.

When business owners mistakenly consider their business cash flow monies to be their **personal monies**, they find it very difficult to spend those monies on necessary and legitimate business expenses. Worse yet, such owners often withdraw cash flow monies from the business, **before** they have become profits; leaving insufficient funds for the payment of the business operating expenses.

SUBJECT 2. Earning Money Through Investment

Investment income is money received from others in compensation for their use of the investor's possessions (usually money or property).

There are three typical means by which one might earn investment income:

- **Financial** investment. In this manner, investors charge a fee for allowing other individuals to use their money.

- **Income property** investment. In this manner, investors charge a fee for allowing other individuals to use their property.

- **Capital gains** investment. In this manner, the investor purchases an object, and then resells it at a higher price. The monetary difference between the original purchase price and the resale price is referred to as the **capital gain.**

a. Financial investment.

The following are common forms of financial investment:

- **Savings Accounts.** Most individuals deposit their savings into commercial financial institutions (such as **commercial banks, savings and loan associations,** or **credit unions**). This is the simplest form of financial investment. Such institutions **pay** their **depositors,** for the use of their funds. Such payments are typically based upon a *pre-agreed to* annual percentage rate of return, commonly referred to as the **interest rate.** The interest rate varies, depending upon the **amount** of the deposit, the **term** of deposit, and **market** conditions.

- **Government Notes and Bonds.** An individual may loan money directly to municipal, state, or federal governments by purchasing government obligations (**notes** or **bonds**). Similar to commercial savings accounts, such investments produce annual investment income that is based upon a pre-agreed to percentage rate.

- **Private Loans.** An individual (**lender**) might invest his funds, by making **loans** to others (**borrowers**). The terms of such investments are spelled out in the **loan note**, and are typically **secured** by a written agreement (such as a **trust deed**) that permits the lender to legally **seize** designated real or personal property in the event that the borrower **defaults** on the loan. Similar to other forms of investment, the lender will receive annual investment income, typically based upon a pre-agreed to annual percentage rate. Such loan interest rates are determined by the amount of the loan, the duration (**term**) of the loan, the nature of the security agreement, and market conditions.

- **Corporate Stocks.** Corporations raise capital (money) by issuing and selling incremental shares of company ownership, referred to as **stocks.** Such stocks are publicly traded in **stock markets.** As stock-issuing companies realize and accumulate profits, a portion of their profits are typically designated for distribution to the **stockholders,** and each stockholder is paid a share of such profits, proportionate to his stock holdings. Such payments are commonly referred to as **dividends**, and are paid quarterly or annually.

Dividend earnings are primarily dependent upon the **profit performance** of the subject company, stock market **trends**, and **fluctuations** in the national economy. Because the typical stockholder has relatively little control over such variables, corporate stock investments are **relatively risky**.

- **Debentures.** Corporations also raise capital by selling **debenture bonds** to investors. By purchasing such a bond, the investor is loaning money to the corporation and earning investment income. The bond specifies the term for repayment of the principal, and the annual **interest rate** upon which the investor's income payments will be calculated. Like savings accounts and private loans, the interest rate varies with the size and term of the bond. The interest rate will also be influenced by the financial stability of the bond issuing company; weaker companies typically pay higher interest rates.

Such investments are typically compared by their relative **yield** percentages. A financial investment's yield is calculated by dividing its annual net income by its acquisition cost. For example, if an investor placed $100 into a savings account and received $8 in annual interest income, the yield would be 8% ($8 of annual income, divided by the $100 initial investment capital = an 8% yield). Likewise, if an investor purchased a corporate bond for $1,000 and received $90 a year in interest payments, the resulting yield would be 9% ($90 of net annual income, divided by the $1,000 bond purchase price = a 9% yield).

b. Income Property Investments.

- **Real Property.**

Real property is **land**, and that which is **permanently attached** to the land. If an individual owns real property, and if others wish to use that property, the owner might then charge a fee for such usage, thereby producing investment income. Such **income properties** typically include agricultural land, residential dwellings, mobile home parks, and industrial, office, or retail facilities.

Income properties are **leased** to tenants (**lessees**) for a specific duration (the lease term). The **lease** is the written document that delineates the particulars of agreement; it typically specifies the rents to be paid, the time frames involved, and the respective obligations/rights of the lessee and the property owner (**lessor**).

Most investment property leases are **net** or **gross** in format:

- The term **net** is in reference to the expenses that are typically associated with property ownership and use, those being **taxes, insurance**, and **maintenance**. Net leases require the lessee to pay a fixed monthly rental fee to the lessor, and to **also** pay all other property-related expenses (taxes, insurances, and maintenance).

- **Gross** leases, on the other hand, require the tenant to pay a fixed monthly rental fee **only**, with the lessor paying all other property related expenses (with the typical exception of **utilities**).

The net annual income (**net income**), produced by an income property is the monetary difference between the rents that the lessor receives and the expenses that the lessor must pay. For example, a lessor receives $40,000 of annual rental income, pays $3,000 for property taxes, $1,500 for property insurance, and $1,000 for property maintenance; consequently, the **net income** would be $34,500 ($40,000 of income, minus $3000 for taxes, minus $1,500 for insurance, minus $1,000 for maintenance = $34,500 net income).

The net income, under a net lease, is usually **equal** to the rental income, because the owner does not pay any property-related expenses (with the possible exception of a **property management fee**).

The **relative yields** of various investment income properties are **compared** by their **capitalization rates**, commonly referred to as their **cap rate**. A property's cap rate is calculated by dividing its **net annual income** by its **purchase price**, and then expressing the fraction as a percentage. For example, if a property's annual net income is $90,000 and if its purchase price was $1,000,000, then the resulting cap rate is 9% ($90,000 of annual net income divided by a $1,000,000 purchase price = 9% cap rate).

Cap rates also permit investors to compare income property yields to those of other investment forms.

- Personal Property.

Personal property is that which is **not** permanently **attached** to the land. If an individual owns personal property, and if others wish to use such property, the owner might charge a fee for such usage, therein producing investment income. Such income properties include vehicles, ships, aircraft, machines, tools, patents, copyrights, et cetera.

c. Capital Gain Investments.

When an investment holding increases in value, it is referred to as **appreciation**. If one chooses to sell his investment holding after it has appreciated, the resulting profit is referred to as the **capital gain**.

Some investment holdings are purchased with the **specific intent** of producing capital gains profits; collectors' items (classic autos, art objects, coins, guns, precious stones, jewelry, antiques, et cetera) are representative of such objects. As an example, an individual might purchase an **oil painting** for $100, and resell it in five years for $150, realizing a fifty (50%) percent profit on his investment. Such investments often appreciate at a **faster** rate than the prevailing economic annual rate of monetary inflation. Additionally, such investments might also provide the holder with **entertainment** or **aesthetic** utility.

Publicly traded agricultural, mineral, and precious metal commodities may also be acquired for capital gain resale.

Many investment vehicles enjoy capital gains profits as a **secondary** benefit. For example, an investor might purchase one share of corporate stock for $15, with the primary intent of enjoying a annual dividend income of $1.50 (a 10% annual yield). If the investor sells the stock for $18 after one year, he will realize a $3 capital gain profit. The investor's combined (dividend and capital gain) rate of return would then be 30%

($1.5 dividend + $3 capital gain = $4.5 annual yield, divided by the original stock purchase price of $15 = 30%). In this example, the secondary capital gain benefit substantially improved the investor's **overall** investment yield.

Real property is limited in supply; that is, there is a finite amount of desirable land available. As populations grow, the demand for real property directly increases. The combined effects of **limited availability** and relatively **unlimited demand**, necessarily cause **appreciation** in the value of real property; consequently, real property is a common investment vehicle for enjoying capital gains profits.

Additionally, the rate of appreciation enjoyed by real property often exceeds the prevalent rate of an economy's **monetary inflation**; consequently, appreciation tends to protect an investor's capital from the **erosion** effects of monetary inflation. As an example, if a $100,000 property appreciates at an annual rate of 6%, and if the annual rate of economic monetary inflation is 5%, then the property's effective value (after one year) becomes $101,000 ($100,000 initial value, plus $6,000 of annual appreciation, less $5,000 for annual economic monetary inflation, equals $101,000). If such a property did not enjoy appreciation, its effective value (after one year) would be reduced to $95,000, due to the diminutive effects of monetary inflation.

Some investments, such as **savings accounts**, produce **no** capital gains profits. To better understand the potential benefits of **appreciating** investments, one might compare the two following investment scenarios:

> - **An appreciating investment.** An investor pays $100,000 for a income property that has a 7% cap rate, meaning that the property produces $7,000 of annual **net income**. One year later, the investor re-sells the property, for an appreciated value of $106,000. The investor realized $7,000 of rental income, and $6,000 in capital gains profits, providing the investor with a total of $113,000.

> - **A non-appreciating investment.** An investor places $100,000 into a commercial savings account that yields a 9% annual interest payment. At the end of one year, the investor will have received $9,000, providing a total of $109,000.

Both investments required an initial $100,000 capital outlay. In comparing the two investments, the savings account paid a higher annual earning amount ($9,000, as compared to the income property's $7,000); however, the income property enjoyed a higher **overall** investment return ($13,000, as compared to the savings account's $9,000), **because of** the income property's appreciation-related capital gains profits.

The above examples were offered simply to illustrate the **potential** benefit of capital appreciation. Investments that enjoy appreciation potential may also be subject to additional associated **risk factors**; for example, such investments may actually **depreciate** in value, **diminishing** the investor's capital.

d. General factors influencing investments.

1. Expertise.

Individuals increase their probability of successfully investing, if they invest in something that they **understand**.

In order to invest, most individuals earn and save the necessary funds by laboring in their chosen vocation. The fact that they were able to make an adequate living and save extra money for investment purposes is indicative of their relative vocational expertise.

With this simple reality in mind, an individual should first consider his own area of vocational expertise for the investment of his excess capital. To this end, an individual might use part of his investment savings to do the following:

- Purchase an ownership position (possibly **stock**) in his employer's company.

- Purchase an ownership position (possibly stock) in a company that competes with, supplies, or buys from his employer's company.

- Start a new business in his field of vocational expertise.

- Expand one's existing company, if self-employed.

Unfortunately, many individuals place their hard earned savings into investment vehicles that are **unrelated** to their area of vocational expertise. Typical of such investments are **commodity futures, precious metals, collector objects, drilling or mining ventures, alternative energy sources**, et cetera.

Exotic investments often offer the lure of **exceptional income tax shelter**; typically, such investments are characterized by **equally** exceptional **risk** factors.

If one is compelled to invest in a field in which he possesses little vocational expertise, it is **highly advisable** to employ **expert guidance**. One should also understand that there will always be a **cost** for such expert guidance (usually in the form of a **fee** or **commission**), and that such costs will necessarily diminish the investment's net yield.

2. Risk.

Investment scenarios typically require investors to hand their money (or property) over to other individuals in anticipation of investment income, and with the expectation of eventually recapturing their capital.

All forms of investment have some associated risk; in particular, the investor's capital might not be returned in full, or the anticipated earnings might not be realized.

Factors influencing investment risk include:

- **The means by which an investment is secured.**

The risk factor on some investments, such as **private loans**, is reduced by the use of **security devices**. The written form of security device employed (promissory note, trust deed, mortgage, et cetera), its specific wording, and the nature of the property that is offered as collateral, all affect the ease with which a lender might legally recover on a defaulted loan.

Loans secured by valuable properties, and through legal instruments that are easily enforced, are necessarily of **lower** investment risk.

A borrower, tenant, or company (when selling its stocks or bonds) might provide an investor with **financial statements**, or **credit history** information. Credit histories indicating bankruptcies, loan defaults, breached contracts, or late payments are indicative of the provider's **likelihood** for future defaults, **increasing** investment risk. Financial statements that indicate **consistent profits** and a **substantial net worth** are reflective of **good business habits**; additionally, they **reveal** assets that an investor might legally **pursue**, should the tenant/borrower **default** on his loan or lease obligation.

Such documentation provides a *security* **comment** about its provider, helping the investor to **judge** the relative risk factors.

- The geographic location of an investment.

An investment's risk is directly influenced by many location-related factors, such as:

> - The prevailing **economic/political** environment.

> - Proximity to **hazardous conditions**, such as flood zones, earthquake faults, pollution, et cetera.

> - Proximity to beneficial **natural amenities**, such as lakes, oceans, mountains, et cetera.

> - Proximity to beneficial **commercial amenities**, such as airports, farm land, industrial centers, et cetera.

> - Proximity to beneficial **cultural amenities**, such as schools, museums, theaters, et cetera.

Depending upon the nature of the investment, such factors will increase or decrease its risk element; consequently, the investor should consider such factors when evaluating the **appropriateness** of a particular investment.

- The physical condition of an investment property.

If a property is very old or damaged, it may have considerable **deferred maintenance**. Deferred maintenance occurs when a previous owner (or tenant) fails to properly repair or replace a property's fatigued capital components. The following property components are often objects of deferred maintenance: roofs, paint, asphalt parking or yard areas, floor coverings, air conditioners, et cetera. Such conditions increase the risk of **unplanned** expenses, or **interruptions** in planned income streams; consequently, an investor should thoroughly evaluate the maintenance condition of various property components prior to purchasing any **income property** investment.

- The nature of a tenant's property use.

An income property owner's investment risk might be substantially increased due to the nature of the tenant's business operations (its usage of the property). Certain tenant **uses** are particularly conducive to property **damage** or **waste**. Examples of such uses might include: foundries or chemical plating operations, or any operation that involves the processing of toxic materials or the by-production of hazardous waste.

Under a worst case scenario, a tenant might substantially **damage** a property or environmentally **pollute** it, and then **go bankrupt**. In such instance, the investor (lessor) is left with the expense of **repair** or **clean-up**, and **lost rental income**; consequently, an income property owner should evaluate the associated risks of any prospective tenant's business operations. To this end, an owner might inspect the prospective tenant's previous operating facilities for any damage that has been occasioned by their tenancy.

3. Financing investment purchases.

In general, one should **avoid** borrowing money; however, under **appropriate** conditions, there are two potential benefits to **financing** the purchase of an investment:

a) Financing permits individuals to make investment acquisitions **beyond** the limits of their personal monies (capital). As an example, an individual might finance his purchase of an income property, then lease the income property to a tenant, and then use the resulting rental income to make his payments on the purchase loan. In this manner, one uses the **lender's** money to purchase the income property, and uses the **tenant's** money to pay back the lender; **ideally**, the investor will eventually **own** the income property, **without having to invest any of his personal capital.**

b)   An investment's yield might be **substantially** increased by financing the investment purchase. As an example, an individual might use $100,000 of his own money and borrow $300,000 more, to buy a $400,000 income property investment.

For purposes of this example, assume that:

- The income property has a cap rate of 9%, thereby producing an net annual income of $36,000 (9% cap rate times a $400,000 acquisition cost = $36,000 net annual income).

- By the end of one year, the investment property will have appreciated 10% in value, permitting the investor to resell it at a $40,000 profit (10% annual appreciation times $400,000 acquisition cost = a $40,000 increase in value).

- The investor borrowed the extra $300,000 of acquisition funds, under the conditions that he would make annual interest payments equal to 11% ($33,000) of the principal borrowed ($300,000 loan, times 11% interest   = $33,000 annual loan payments).

Under the above set of circumstances, at the end of one year, the investor will have earned $36,000 in rental income and $40,000 in **capital gains** profits (from the resale of the property), producing a total investment income of $76,000.

Subtracting the investor's $33,000 loan payments from his $76,000 net investment income, the investor will enjoy a net investment profit of $43,000.

In the above example, the investor has earned a 43% overall yield, commonly referred to as the **cash on cash** investment return. His cash on cash return is calculated by dividing the investment's $43,000 net profit by the investor's initial $100,000 capital investment (the cash that the investor has in the investment). An investment's cash on cash return indicates the annual profit that an investor will receive, expressed as a percentage of the cash that they have invested.

For comparative purposes, assume the same set of investment parameters described above; however, **now assume** that the investor uses **his own** $400,000 cash to purchase the property (rather than financing the purchase). Again, the investor's cash on cash return is calculated by dividing his net annual income (which will be the same $76,000), by his $400,000 cash investment, yielding a 19% **cash on cash** return.

In comparing the two investment scenarios, one will observe that the purchase prices, rental incomes, and resale profits were respectively equal; however, the **financed purchase** yielded a **43%** cash on cash return, as **compared** to **19%** for the **all cash** purchase!

The above examples were specifically designed to demonstrate the **potential** benefits of **financed** investment purchases; however, the reader **should not** assume that such comparative benefits can be realized under all investment circumstances.

4. Government income tax consequences.

An individual's annual income, for **income tax** purposes, is typically segregated into **earned income** (that which results from his labors), and **passive income** (that which results from his investments).

Investments vary in their associated income tax consequences, as determined by the prevailing government tax laws. Certain types of investments might reduce an investor's overall income tax exposure. Income property is generally representative of such investments.

The **tax savings** potential of income property investments stem from their **structural nature**. Most income properties consist of land and **improvements** (such as buildings, roads, sewer systems, et cetera). Such improvements tend to wear out or dissipate in time, and as they do, the property naturally **depreciates** in value.

For business accounting purposes, investors annually estimate and record the monetary amount of their property's **depreciation**. As an example, if an income property consists of land and a building, and if the building cost $310,000 to construct, and if the estimated usage life of the building is thirty-one years, then an investor might reasonably determine that his property is **depreciating** in value by $10,000 a year ($310,000 building cost, divided by a 31 year life = $10,000/yr).

Although there is no actual **cash outlay** associated with **depreciation expenses**, they are traditionally treated as legitimate **operating expenses**. Such expenses are often referred to as **book expenses** only; that is, the investor has recorded them into their accounting records, however, there has been no relative **cash outlay**.

Most government taxation laws permit investors to **claim** and subtract (**deduct**) their depreciation expenses from their **taxable income**. The resulting amount by which their taxable income is reduced will be **deferred** from any immediate taxation; however, should the investor ever sell the property, **all** previously claimed depreciation expenses will become immediately taxable. The resulting benefits of such deferred taxation can be **substantial**; in particular, the investor retains the use of his capital for **further** investment purposes.

It is a prudent business practice for an investor to establish a **reserve account**, equal in amount to the depreciation expenses that are being claimed. In this manner, the investor will be financially prepared to replace such improvements when they actually wear out.

On occasion, an investment's depreciation expense deductions might actually exceed the investment's gross income. In such instance, the investment will show a **net operating loss**. **Depending** upon the prevailing government income tax laws, investors might be permitted to deduct this investment loss from their **other** investment profits, **and** from their **earned** income. This is referred to as **tax sheltering**; that is, the investment's book depreciation expenses have completely sheltered the investment's income from **any** immediate taxation (and may have partially sheltered the investor's **other** passive and earned income as well).

To further exemplify tax sheltering, consider an income taxation scenario with the following parameters:

- An individual owns two income property investments: properties A and **B**.

- Income property A has an annual rental income of $3,500, annual operating expenses (loan payments, maintenance, et cetera) of $2,500, and an annual depreciation expense of $6,000, resulting in an annual taxable income **loss** of $5,000 ($3,500 income, less $2,500 operating expenses, less $6,000 depreciation = a <$5,000> income loss).

- Income property B has an annual rental income of $8,300, annual operating expenses of $2,300, and annual depreciation expenses of $4,000, producing an annual **taxable income** of $2,000 ($8,300 income, less $2,300 in operating expenses, less $4,000 of depreciation, = $2,000 of taxable income).

- The investor also works as a *schoolteacher*, receiving an annual taxable **earned income** of $25,000.

- For purposes of this example, assume that the prevailing government income tax laws permit the investor to:

    a. Estimate and deduct his investment's depreciation expenses from its taxable income.

    b. Use one investment's loss to off set the taxable income of another.

    c. Use his investment losses to off set his taxable earned income.

Under the above circumstances, the investor can use $2,000 of property A's $5,000 income loss to shelter property B's taxable income. Additionally, the investor can use the remaining $3,000 of property A's income loss, to shelter $3,000 of his $25,000 taxable teaching income.

Under such conditions, property A's depreciation expenses permitted the investor to defer paying income taxes on $5,000 of (otherwise taxable) income. If the investor was in a 20% income tax bracket, the $5,000 of **tax shelter** would result in a $1,000 income tax **deferral** ($5,000 of tax sheltered income, times 20% taxes = $1,000 tax deferral).

[**Note - Government taxation laws are in constant revision. The financial examples and suggestions offered herein are conceptual in nature. The reader should consult with his CPA and attorney before employing any financial approaches discussed herein.**]

5. Marketplace demand.

Most investment vehicles (such as *bonds, stocks, income properties,* or *loans*) are **traded** in investor marketplaces; consequently, they are subject to classical **supply and demand** price influences. The **price** of an investment is the amount that an investor must pay to acquire it. If an investment is particularly **desirable** (having a **high yield and low risk**), investor competition will drive its price up. Conversely, if an investment is less desirable, the lack of investor demand will drive its price down.

An investment's income production, as determined by a **lease agreement**, or **loan note**, or **bond terms**, et cetera, remains **relatively constant**, regardless of the investment's market induced price fluctuations.

An investment's **yield** is calculated by dividing its annual net income by its acquisition price; consequently, an investment's yield **declines** if its annual net income remains **constant** while its price **rises**. Conversely, an investment's yield **increases** if its annual net income remains constant while its price **falls**. For example, an individual purchases a income property for $400,000. The property is leased to a tenant for ten years, producing a net annual lease income of $36,000. The resulting cap rate is 9% (a $36,000 net annual income, divided by a $400,000 acquisition price = 9% cap rate). The first investor then sells the property to another investor for $450,000. Because the investment's net annual income is fixed by the Lease, the second investor will experience an 8% cap rate (a $36,000 net annual income, divided by a $450,000 acquisition price = 8% cap rate). In effect, the investment's price increase has caused the property's cap rate (yield) to drop from 9% to 8%.

As investments are **traded, market demand** will drive down the yields of **desirable** investments; **until** they **fail** to compete with alternative investments. **Likewise,** market demand will drive up the yields of unattractive investments until they become **competitive** with alternative investments.

SECTION C. How to Manage Money

Effective **money management optimizes** one's use of money; permitting individuals to either acquire **more** goods or services, or to **reduce** the number of hours that they must labor to fulfill their monetary needs. In either instance, effective money management can **increase** an individual's **quality of life.**

The effective management of one's money involves two disciplines: **financial conservatism** and **tax planning.**

SUBJECT 1. Financial Conservatism

Financial conservatism is a mental attitude that favors conservation of capital and the optimal utilization of money. It is most commonly reflected in an individual's **lifestyle, spending priorities,** and **payment methods.**

a. Lifestyle.

An individual's **lifestyle** is primarily expressed by the manner in which they consume goods and services. One's choice of lifestyle is dictated by his **personal tastes,** and **limited** by his **financial means.**

Certain characteristic lifestyles are associated with respective **income groups.** For example, individuals with $30,000 of annual income might typically own automobiles which cost $17,000 and wear watches which cost $80. Comparatively, individuals earning $100,000 per year might typically own automobiles which cost $30,000 and wear watches which cost $200.

The material possessions associated with **different** income groups are generally reflective of their comparative lifestyles.

It is financially conservative to maintain a **material** lifestyle that is **consistent** with or **below** that typically associated with one's income group. It is both financially **imprudent** and **pretentious** to feign or maintain a material lifestyle that is typically associated with a **higher** income group.

As a general rule of financial conservatism, an individual's material lifestyle should be like **the tip of an iceberg**; that is, one's **obvious** possessions should reflect only a **minor** portion of his overall net worth.

b. Spending priorities.

Individuals use their money to fulfill their material needs. The fulfillment of one's material needs results in an associated **pleasure,** or **avoidance of discomfort.** The fulfillment of certain material needs necessarily take precedence over the fulfillment of others, according to their **comparative** pleasure/discomfort avoidance consequences.

The **priority** of one's **spending** should be **consistent** with the relative **importance** of the needs that are being fulfilled; that is, individuals should spend **first** on their most **basic** needs, and spend **last** on the fulfillment of their **least important** needs.

The following list of **general needs** have been numerically prioritized relative to their typical comparative importance, with the first being the most important, and the last being the least important. Individuals might consider **similar** priorities, in **guiding** their personal spending:

1. **Basic survival needs**: food, shelter, clothing, medical care, transportation, education, entertainment, et cetera.

2. **Emergency reserve savings**: enough money for six months of survival.

3. **Retirement reserve savings** (see *How Much Money is Enough?*).

4. **Replacement of capital items**: such as automobiles, appliances, furniture, homes, et cetera.

5. **Extravagances.**

Breaching the above suggested spending order typically results in a **diminished** overall quality of life.

c. Payment methods.

When acquiring goods or services, there are four primary methods of payment: **cash**, **financing**, **barter**, or **direct labor**. Considering their comparative incident, this presentation will address **cash** and **financing** only.

Generally speaking, financed purchases should be **avoided**, because debt costs money to maintain (in **interest payments**) and creates property **liens** and personal **obligations**. Additionally, debt expenses tend to remain **fixed**, regardless of one's income fluctuations; consequently, debt exposes individuals to **insolvency** in lean economic times. A financed purchase might be **justified** under the following circumstances:

> 1. If an individual wishes to purchase an object and has adequate cash to do so, he might consider financing the purchase if he can safely invest an equal amount of his own cash elsewhere, at a rate of return that exceeds the cost of borrowing equal funds to purchase the subject item.

> 2. If an individual does not have sufficient funds to pay for the purchase of a **high priority** personal or business **necessity** (such as a home, or transportation vehicle), and if the individual has the **realistic** ability to repay debts that might be incurred in the financed purchase of such items, then the individual might prudently consider making such financed purchases.

SUBJECT 2. Tax Planning

Most income is subject to government taxation. If individuals can reduce the amount of taxes that they must pay, they will retain more money for their personal use; consequently, the object of tax planning is to **minimize** (or **defer**) the amount of taxes that an individual must eventually pay.

a. Understanding tax laws.

The **first step** in minimizing one's taxation exposure is to **understand** the prevailing government tax laws. It is neither practical, nor necessary to read and understand all tax laws; however, individuals should endeavor to understand those specific laws that primarily affect their taxation. At a minimum, individuals should thoroughly review the instruction package that accompanies their annual federal and state tax forms.

Ideally, each individual should maintain a reference library, including such publications as:

- Federal Income Tax Regulations (typically in five volumes)

- Internal Revenue Code (typically in two volumes)

- Annual Federal Tax Code Update (usually a single volume)

- Pension Plan Regulations (typically in one summary volume)

Such reference materials are available through commercial publishers and public libraries. These books are priced well within the means of the general public, and are conveniently available by telephone order.

Most government taxing authorities publish a variety of **tax guides**; such publications are typically free, and available by telephone request.

Some commercial publishers market a **tax handbook** that provides a broad selection of summarized taxation information; such a publication might serve as a **minimal** tax reference library for most individuals.

Government tax laws are continually changing; one should stay abreast of such changes to minimize their detrimental effects, and to take advantage of their beneficial effects.

Should one lack the resolve to become informed about government tax laws, he should employ the services of a qualified **tax specialist**, preferably a *C.P.A.* Even if one has developed a functional working knowledge of government tax laws, he should not hesitate to employ the services of a tax specialist to review his **tax planning approaches** and **income tax filings**, or to render an opinion on matters of extreme technical complexity.

b. Income reporting, or *tax filings*.

Most governments require their citizens to file an annual statement of income, commonly referred to as an **income tax filing**. The government then uses this information to compute one's taxes. Typically, the amount of one's taxable income may be reduced by certain permitted expenses, referred to as **deductions**. It is in one's best interest to maintain detailed accounting records regarding such incurred **deductible** expenses.

If possible, individuals should prepare their own **income tax filing** forms. The form preparation task is not unreasonably difficult, the process is educational, and it is helpful in developing tax planning approaches.

Should it become impractical for an individual to prepare his own income tax filings, he should employ a competent income tax specialist. When allowing another individual to prepare one's income tax filing, the taxpayer should thoroughly review and understand every line item of the prepared tax forms before permitting them to be submitted to the government. In particular, one should make sure that **all income** has been reported, that all claimed **deductions** are **valid**, and that the preparer has **creatively** and **aggressively** endeavored to **minimize** the amount of taxes payable.

c. Taxation deferral and reduction approaches.

Tax planning should begin **early** in one's tax year, before income is earned and expenses are incurred. In this manner one has time to design and implement approaches to minimize detrimental taxation consequences.

Individuals should be **creative** and **aggressive** in their interpretation of government tax laws, and in their tax planning approaches. **Because tax laws are constantly changing, it is impractical for this book to suggest specific tax planning approaches; consequently, the following examples might not conform to prevailing government tax laws, and are offered for conceptual consideration only.**

- Example one.

For purposes of reporting his annual taxable income, a self-employed individual uses a **calendar** accounting year (one that begins January 1 and ends on December 31). He **withhold**s estimated taxes from his income, and forwards the withholdings to the government on a monthly basis, with his final taxation adjustments due in April of the following calendar year, when he submits his **income tax filing**.

The individual wishes to defer making his **estimated tax** payments so that he might continue to use his cash for operating capital. To this end, the individual has **incorporated** his business activities, and designated himself as the only employee of the corporation. As the individual sells his goods or performs his income producing services, all received income is now channeled through his corporation.

He establishes a corporate accounting year that begins February 1 and ends on January 31. As his corporation receives revenues, it **loans** the money back to him. Money that is received **as a loan** is not normally classified as *income*, and consequentially **is not** generally subject to estimated income tax withholdings.

The individual continues to borrow such monies throughout his personal accounting year; by December 31, he has still received no income (only loaned monies), and has made no estimated tax payments. At the end of his corporate accounting year (during late January, following the end of his personal accounting year), his corporation declares and pays him a **year-end bonus**. The amount of the bonus is calculated to equal the sum of the previous loans, permitting the individual to make a corporate accounting entry in which the individual's **accounts receivable** (for the loans) is offset by a **bonus expense** entry (involving no actual cash transaction).

Through the use of this **incorporating approach**, the individual has had the use of all corporate revenues throughout his calendar year, and he has deferred making estimated tax payments until the last month of his corporation's accounting year. In this manner, although he will eventually pay the same total taxes, the individual has gained the opportunity to profit on the use of funds that **previously** were not available to him.

The process of incorporating is relatively easy to accomplish, by using *do it yourself* guides; such books are typically available through retail book stores, and contain the necessary filing forms.

To enhance the above example with numbers, assume that the individual would earn $100,000 during his 1990 calendar year, and forms a corporation to receive such revenues.

His corporation then loans him $100,000 throughout 1990, as it receives the revenue. The individual has not declared income throughout 1990, because he received the monies as a loan.

His corporation's 1990 accounting year ends on January 31 of the individual's 1991 accounting year. During the final month of his corporation's 1990 accounting year (January of 1991), his corporation declares and pays him a salary bonus of $100,000. The individual **now** estimates his tax withholdings for the $100,000, and sends the payment to the government.

With regard to corporate accounting, the year end salary bonus is used to offset the $100,000 that the corporate owner/employee had previously received in loans; there is no cash transaction, and the corporation is left with no 1990 taxable income (that is, the corporation's $100,000 revenue was offset by the $100,000 **bonus expense**).

In effect, the individual has used his corporation's $100,000 of revenues, throughout 1990; however, he did not claim such income until making his **tax filing** in 1992.

In this scenario the individual might also have chosen to distribute his income over two accounting years. For instance, he might have received $40,000 of the $100,000 corporate revenues in 1990 salary, and $60,000 in 1990 loans, with the loans being offset by a January 1991 corporate year-end bonus. In such case, the individual has distributed the $100,000 1990 income over two years ($40,000 in 1990, and $60,000 in 1991). This process creates an **income averaging** effect, possibly bettering the individual's tax bracket placement.

As individuals anticipate their current and future deductible expenses, **this form of income averaging** might become a valuable money management tool.

The above example, again, is demonstrative of a **conceptual approach** only, and does not consider any of the negative taxation or expense effects that might be associated with the creation and maintenance of a corporation. **Again, the reader should consult the relative government taxing authority or his expert counsel regarding the legality of any such tax planning approach, prior to considering its use.**

- Example two.

Assume a similar scenario to that described in *Example One*. Additionally, assume that the individual establishes a **pension and profit-sharing plan** for his corporate employees (he being the only emlployee), and designates himself as the **trustee** of his profit-sharing and pension plan **trust account**.

All pension plan formats must be approved by the appropriate regulating government agency. For purposes of this example, assume that the subject pension plan allows the corporate employer to contribute an annual amount, equal to 25% of the employee's annual salary.

Further assume that the individual, by selling goods or providing services, generates $125,000 of revenue, which is channeled through his corporation. His corporation then pays $100,000 of the revenue to the individual (in salary) and places the remaining $25,000 (25% of the individual's salary) into the individual's profit-sharing and pension plan **trust account**.

The corporation, when it makes its annual **tax filing**, claims the entire $125,000 as an operating expense deduction, offsetting its $125,000 of revenue, consequently leaving no taxable corporate profit.

The individual is taxed on the $100,000 of salary only; the $25,000 that was placed into the profit-sharing and pension plan trust account is not subject to income taxes as long as it remains in the trust account. If the individual would normally have paid 40% taxes on his income, he has effectively deferred having to pay $10,000 of taxes (40% times $25,000 income).

The individual, as the designated **trustee** of his profit-sharing and pension plan trust account, can now invest those trust monies (within certain government regulation limitations). As those invested monies accumulate investment profits, the profits are also deferred from taxation.

Under certain conditions, the individual can also borrow monies from the trust account.

When the individual is of retirement age, he can then take (**distribute**) all or part of the trust account monies. At that time, all monies received will become taxable; however, the individual will possibly be in a lower income tax bracket than when he earned the monies.

If the individual needs some portion of the trust account monies prior to his designated retirement age, he can take a **premature distribution** from the trust account, and pay any relative penalty and taxes.

This hypothetical tax planning approach permits the individual to **defer taxes** on substantial portions of his income, to personally **control** and **invest** those monies, and to create additional tax deferred **profits**.

- **Example three.**

Assume that a self-employed individual is disallowed the complete income deduction of certain personal expenses, such as medical and dental care; consequently, he establishes a personal corporation, and deducts such expenses through his corporate books.

To illustrate, assume that an individual has $5,000 of annual medical expenses that are not permitted (under the prevailing government tax laws) to be deducted from his personal taxable income.

Further assume that he earn $100,000 of gross annual income, and that his permitted annual expense deductions are $40,000, yielding a net taxable income of $60,000 ($100,000 income, less $40,000 of deductions, = $60,000). Also assume that he is in a 40% (combined state and federal) income tax bracket, resulting in $24,000 of taxes ($60,000 net income, times 40% = $24,000 taxes).

Now, in comparison, assume that the individual has established a personal corporation. The $100,000 produced by the individual's labor is now channeled through his corporation.

To encourage corporations to provide their employees with certain benefits (such as medical and dental expense coverage), governments often permit corporations to deduct such expense items from taxable corporate profits. For purposes of this example, assume that such an incentive permits the individual's corporation to use $5,000 (of its $100,000 corporate revenues) to pay employee medical and dental expenses (remembering that the individual is the only employee of his own corporation).

The corporation then pays the remaining $95,000 to the individual, in the form of salary; this leaves the corporation with no taxable income ($100,000 revenue, less $5,000 employee benefit expenses, less $95,000 employee salary expense = no taxable profits).

The individual's medical and dental bills have been paid, he has $95,000 of gross income and the same $40,000 of deductible personal expenses, leaving him a net taxable income of $55,000 ($95,000 salary, less $40,000 expenses = $55,000).

The individual, being in a 40% tax bracket, pays $22,000 in taxes ($55,000 taxable income times 40% = $22,000 taxes), as compared to the $24,000 that he previously paid, before incorporating.

By processing his medical and dental expenses through his corporation, the individual reduced his income taxes by $2,000.

Although the above scenarios cites relatively affluent individuals, there are tax planning benefits that can be enjoyed at **all** income levels.

Each of the above examples were hypothetical in nature, and were specifically designed to illustrate potential tax planning concepts. It is not the intention of this book to suggest or encourage, by comment or example, any reader actions that might violate or conflict with prevailing government taxation laws. The reader should consult with the appropriate government agency or a tax expert prior to employing any tax deferral, avoidance, or filing approach discussed in this book.

Governments provide their citizens with valuable social services. Such services must be supported through the taxation of the recipient citizens; consequently, each individual has a moral obligation to pay government taxes, in consideration of the services that they have received. Notwithstanding this moral obligation, individuals should avoid unnecessary taxation. To this end, individuals should understand and aggressively interpret their government's tax laws and employ effective tax planning.

d. Government income tax filing audits.

On occasion, the taxing government authority will find cause to question the accuracy of one's income tax filing. In such instances, the government typically sends a **notice of audit** to the individual (**taxpayer**), either requesting additional information, or his presence at an **audit** meeting.

Individuals should not fear tax audits, as they tend to be **inevitable**, particularly if one has exercised creativity and aggressiveness in his tax planning approaches.

In preparation for a tax audit meeting, individuals should thoroughly re-familiarize themselves with the subject tax filing documents. When one attends such an audit meeting, he should bring writing materials, and copies of the pertinent documents.

Tax auditors perform a necessary and valuable civic function; it is morally proper, and in one's best interest, to treat the tax auditor with respect and courtesy. There are many individuals that literally **cheat** on their tax filings, in effect taking government services without paying for them. Such dishonesty results in higher tax payments for honest citizens; consequently, tax auditors (theoretically) are working in society's best interest.

During audit meetings, answer questions honestly but do not offer more information than is **specifically** requested, unless an additional response is necessary to adequately explain a point.

Individuals might be audited for a variety of causes:

- The taxpayer, or his tax filing preparer, may have made an information error in the completion of the income tax filing. In such instance, the taxpayer should **willingly** provide the correct information; if an additional tax obligation results, the taxpayer should **apologize** for the error, and promptly pay the appropriate amount (including any **interest chargers** or **penalties**). In some instances, if the oversight was obviously innocent, the auditor might **waive** any punitive interest charges or penalties.

- The government might question or **disallow** a taxpayer's filing approach, because they disagree with the taxpayer's **interpretation** of a particular tax law. In such instances, one should be prepared to **politely argue** and defend his interpretation of the relative tax law. To that end, one should bring copies of the applicable tax codes/regulations and copies of any precedent tax court rulings supporting the subject interpretation.

In the process of resolving such interpretations, **always** be prepared to appeal any unfavorable ruling to the next authority level.

- An individual might be selected for **random** audit. In such instance, individuals should be polite, honest, and brief in their responses.

If the auditing tax authority insists on deepening the audit, with the **obvious** intention of increasing one's tax liability, one should request a **continuance**; that is, the meeting should be terminated and re-scheduled for a future date.

Prior to the continued audit meeting, one should **thoroughly** review the subject filing documentation, with the specific intent of **minimizing** previously calculated tax obligations. In particular, one should creatively rethink his previous tax filing approach, using aggressive tax law interpretations to uncover **additional** tax savings. If appropriate, one might employ **expert assistance** in this effort.

When the audit meeting continues, the taxpayer should be prepared to submit an **amended** tax filing, requesting a **tax refund** (if appropriate). If the government insists upon continuing the audit, the taxpayer might begin creatively reviewing his previous years' tax filings, in search of additional tax refunds. **If one's time is going to be taken for a random audit, he should attempt to profit from the encounter.**

In summary, taxpayers might consider the following guidelines when being audited:

- **Prepare** for the audit meeting.

- Be **polite.**

- Be **honest.**

- **Appeal** unfavorable rulings.

- Use creativity to **reduce** tax obligations.

SECTION D. General Business Skills

An individual's ability to earn and manage money is directly dependent upon his/her **financial problem solving techniques**, typically referred to as business skills. The most common of such skills are:

(1) **Negotiating**	(6) **Civil Law Application**
(2) **Salesmanship**	(7) **Commercial Development**
(3) **Management**	(8) **Escrow Coordination**
(4) **Accounting**	(9) **Exercising Discretion**
(5) **Computer Usage**	(10) **Skill Diversification**

SUBJECT 1. Negotiating

The fulfillment of one individual's needs often **conflicts** with the fulfillment of another individual's needs; **negotiating** is a dialog process for resolving such conflicts.

a. Negotiating positions.

To successfully negotiate, one should understand the respective **needs** and **limitations** of the involved parties as they relate to the object of negotiation. Such needs and limitations establish the parties' **negotiating positions.**

An individual should start by defining his own **negotiating position.** To this end, the first step is to determine the **exact nature** of the object to be acquired or marketed. The objects of most negotiations are typically *material goods, services,* or *privileges.* If one is acquiring or marketing a **material good**, he should begin by knowing the exact **quantity** and **quality** to be transacted. If one is acquiring or marketing a service or privilege, he should begin by understanding the specific **actions** that will be performed, or **rights** that will be enjoyed.

An individual, next, should realistically assess the **importance** of acquiring or marketing the subject item; that is, how important is the success of the negotiations, relative to his overall life needs? This determination will help to shape the individual's negotiating **strategy**; if the subject need is relatively unimportant, the individual can afford to be **very** aggressive in his negotiating approach. To the other extreme, if the success of the negotiations is pivotal in one's life, he should exercise the utmost **finesse**.

Finally, one should realistically assess the **limitations** affecting his negotiations. Such considerations might include: **monetary budgets, time frames , skills, product availability**, et cetera.

As an example of determining one's own **negotiating position**, consider the following scenario, in which an individual wishes to purchase an automobile:

1. In defining the quantity and quality of his needs, he has determined that he wants a new, four-door car.

2. The individual presently has an older car that is in satisfactory operating condition; consequently, acquiring the new car is not of extreme importance.

3. In assessing his negotiating limitations, he has determined that:

- He has $15,000 cash, to purchase a new car.

- The model that he desires typically sells for $14,000.

- There is an abundant supply of the subject model.

Once an individual understands his own negotiating position, he should next try to understand that of his business adversary (the *auto dealer*). By doing so, he becomes better able to form an effective negotiating strategy. In demonstration of this step, consider the following continuation of the above example. The automobile buyer has conducted research, and determined that:

1. The auto dealer's (the seller) cost for the desired model is approximately $12,000.

2. The particular auto dealer with whom he has chosen to negotiate has a surplus inventory of the subject model.

As the buyer comparatively considers his own negotiating position relative to that of the seller, it becomes obvious that the buyer enjoys a negotiating **advantage**; that is, he does not critically need the new car, he has adequate cash to make the purchase, there is an abundant market supply of the desired model, and the seller is holding an excessive inventory of the desired model. With this knowledge, the buyer can plot his negotiating strategy accordingly.

b. Fundamentals of negotiating.

Beyond understanding **one another's negotiating positions**, the negotiating parties should employ the following mechanics:

1. Be courteous. Courtesy, aside from being virtuous, encourages cooperation. When an adversary senses consideration, he becomes receptive to **fair** bargaining.

2. Be ethical. The objective of negotiating should be a **fair** and **equitable** resolution for all involved parties. If an individual tries to take unfair advantage of another, such actions will **ultimately** frustrate the fulfillment of that individual's overall needs (see *What is Morality?*).

3. Employ effective communication techniques (see *Communication Techniques*).

4. Be objective. Remain unemotional during negotiations; do not permit personal ego needs to interfere with business objectives. An adversary might be insensitive or offensive; however, one should avoid taking it personally, lest it frustrate the attainment of one's business goals. This generalization, of course, has practical limits; if one's adversary becomes obviously **rude**, it is advisable to **terminate** the negotiations and pursue other opportunities.

5. Exercise self-discipline. The negotiation process will vary in complexity and tenure, depending upon the object of negotiations. Some negotiations are concluded in minutes, while others take years.

If the negotiations are particularly **complex** and **protracted**, one must make a special effort to keep them moving forward. Such efforts might require the coordination of associated events, such as **appraisals, inspections, surveys, financing, title searches, testing, transporting pertinent documents or materials,** et cetera.

Complex (or lengthy) negotiations **invite failure**, not because of the parties' unwillingness to reach an agreement, but rather because of the parties' inability to **maintain** the negotiating process. Consequently, such negotiations demand **exceptional** self-discipline. Each negotiating party should **energize** and lend momentum to the negotiating process, at the same time taking care not to be perceived as overly eager or rudely aggressive.

6. Develop a negotiating strategy. Negotiating typically consists of a series of oral or written **offers** and **counter-offers,**

through which business adversaries state their desires or expectation. Each party will, of course, suggest (or demand) terms that are in his own best interest; for instance, buyers typically demand low prices, high product quality, and quick delivery. Reciprocally, sellers typically seek high retail prices, minimal product costs, and loose delivery schedules.

In order to maneuver an adversary towards one's desired negotiation objectives, it is advisable to begin with a set of **pre-planned negotiation sacrifices**. Such items include **marginal amounts** or negotiation **points** upon which one is willing to **acquiesce**.

If the object of the negotiations is multifaceted, one might itemize the various negotiating points (both quantitative and qualitative) into **two** lists: one list of those points that are **essential** (a **hard list**), and one list of those points that are **marginal** in consequence (a **soft list**). The material difference between the two lists, in effect, becomes one's planned **negotiating cushion**. As the negotiations progress, one should first acquiesce on his **soft list** items; by doing so, he will (hopefully) induce his adversary to reciprocally concede upon, or grant those items embodied in the individual's **hard list**.

To demonstrate this process, again consider the above exemplified automobile buyer. In review:

> a) The buyer wanted a new, four-door sedan with basic amenities, of which there is a readily available supply.
>
> b) He would use the automobile for general transportation purposes; however, he could also continue to use his presently owned car, if necessary.
>
> c) He had $15,000 to purchase a new automobile.
>
> d) The particular model of automobile that he desired, typically sells for $14,000.
>
> e) The approximate dealer cost for this model is $12,000.

In considering the above facts, the buyer might develop the following **hard** and **soft** negotiating lists.

Hard list (essential requirements):

- Purchase price of $14,000 or less
- standard radio
- chrome hub caps
- fabric seats
- manual transmission
- white paint

Soft list (negotiable points):

- Purchase price or $12,000 or less
- sunroof
- AM/FM/CD stereo player
- leather seats
- alloy wheels
- automatic transmission
- metallic silver paint

Next, the buyer might initiate the following negotiating sequence:

- First, he might offer the dealer $11,500 for a new car which possesses the amenities stated on his soft list.

- If the dealer counter-offers at $15,000, the buyer might offer to give-up one of his soft list amenity items and counter-offer at $12,000.

- If the dealer counters at $14,000, the buyer might offer to give-up another soft list item and counter at $12,500.

- If the dealer declines to lower his price any further, the buyer might express his appreciation for the dealer's negotiating efforts and state that he now wishes to **think about it** or to **shop around** a little more. Just before walking out of the dealership, he might casually mention that he would be willing to buy the auto, right now, for $13,000 cash. It is highly probable that the dealer will accept that final offer.

In the above scenario, the buyer exercised his **pre-planned** price and feature sacrifices to negotiate his desired end result.

7. One should prompt his adversary to make the *first offer*. Doing so, establishes a beginning **reference point** for negotiating, and exposes the **practicality** of the adversary's position.

The need for aggressive negotiating is diminished if the adversary's first offer is relatively close to one's ultimate negotiating goal. Conversely, if the adversary's first offer is ridiculously unrealistic, one might choose to **forego** negotiating, thereby avoiding frustration and wasted time.

This technique is particularly functional if the negotiations are being **arbitrated** by a third party. By encouraging one's adversary to make the first offer (or argument), one stages the opportunity for his adversary to create a **contradictory** or **hostile** relationship with the arbitrator. For example, consider a situation in which two salespeople are engaged in a commission dispute and they appeal to their manager to resolve the dispute. The manager asks each salesperson to state his respective position; when the first salesperson does so, he speaks with such hostility and aggressiveness that he offends the manager. As a result, the manager decides in favor of the other salesperson. As exemplified, the second salesperson prevailed over his adversary without speaking a word.

8. Generally speaking, one should always *counter-offer*. When negotiating, one should try to **better his position**, by counter-offering. Although a negotiating adversary might not necessarily accept the terms of one's counter-offer, there is always a **possibility** that he might; consequently, the simple act of **passing air across one's vocal cords** (asking) might better one's material position by hundreds, thousands, or millions of dollars.

Again referring to the above presented *automobile purchase* example, the auto dealer (after concluding the sale) might offer the buyer a **maintenance insurance** package, to extend the coverage of the new automobile's standard maintenance warranty.

If the dealer offers the insurance package for $600, the buyer might counter at $300. The dealer might eventually agree to $450.

The point is, that for thirty seconds of verbal effort, the buyer might save himself $150.

One should, of course, know (or sense) **when to stop** countering for a better deal. Generally speaking, it is unwise to continue to negotiate once an individual has reached his pre-planned objective **(lest greed ruin the opportunity)**.

The most **important** point for the reader to grasp, regarding this subject, is that one can potentially realize substantial material (or intangible) benefits, simply by **asking for them**. Again, the act of **asking** requires no more than **passing some air across one's vocal cords**, yet it can yield valuable benefits!

9. One should always be prepared to *walk away from a bad deal.* Certain **psychological mind-sets** are conducive to effective negotiating. For example, if an individual has relatively little need to acquire or market the object of negotiation, he tends to negotiate more effectively; because he has little to lose, he tends to remain calm, and drive an advantageous bargain. **On the other hand**, if an individual is desperate to acquire or market the object of negotiations, he might be less effective in his negotiating efforts; that is, he might exhibit extreme anxiousness, or unnecessarily acquiesce to adversarial demands.

Before entering negotiations, one should endeavor to assume a psychological state in which he feels and acts as though he **does not** necessarily need the object of negotiations. In this manner, the individual increases the probability that he will negotiate objectively and be able to **walk away from a bad deal**.

10. Do not permit minor negotiating points to spoil the overall negotiations (or, as the old proverb goes, "one should not allow the tail to wag the dog"). As an example, a buyer might be negotiating the acquisition of an object, commonly valued at $1,000,000. For purposes of this example, assume two occurrences: first, that the buyer has negotiated a very favorable acquisition price of $900,000, and second; that the seller, rather than accepting a mailed cashier's check, has oddly insisted that the buyer personally deliver an **all cash** payment to the seller's office (which is several hundred miles from the buyer's office).

Granted, the seller's odd request will cause the buyer to suffer the inconveniences of having to withdraw cash from his bank, of having to spend money on an airline ticket, and of having to lose a half day of travel time. **On the other hand**, the buyer is obtaining the **object** of negotiations at $100,000 below market price. The monetary value of the buyer's inconvenience might be $300 for airfare, and $500 for lost office time. **Comparing** this $800 inconvenience cost to the $100,000 bargain savings, the buyer would be ill-advised to complain about the requested method of payment (**at the risk of queering the entire agreement**).

11. Be patient. One should not permit himself to be rushed by his adversary, nor should one rush himself, nor should he **appear** to rush his adversary in the negotiating process.

Hurried negotiations typically induce **judgement errors**. If the parties to a negotiation feel unsure of their decisions, it increases the probability of **eventual** problems. This is not to suggest that they should unnecessarily delay their decisions; they should simply grant them **appropriate** consideration.

12. Time is of the essence. If the negotiating parties have reached a point of **mutual agreement**, they should **promptly** conclude the transaction.

To this end, individuals should anticipate and remove as many negotiation obstacles (delays) as possible. For instance:

- Documents might be prepared in advance, requiring only amounts and signatures to be added.

- If products are to be demonstrated in support of a decision, the appropriate materials should be staged and ready.

Unnecessary delays in concluding a transaction, **invite reconsiderations** or the introduction of new and **disruptive** variables.

13. One should honor (perform on) his commitments. Once an agreement has been negotiated, do not **renege** or **complain**; such actions **injure** others, demean one's **reputation**, and establish detrimental **precedences**.

The above suggested negotiating approaches are generally applicable to **business** and **personal** *conflict resolution* situations.

SUBJECT 2. Salesmanship

Salesmanship is a communication technique whereby one person (the **salesperson**) convinces another person (the prospective **buyer**) to purchase certain *goods* or *services*. In a more general sense, salesmanship is used to convince others to act in some **desired** manner.

Typical applications of salesmanship beckon images of *automobile salespersons*, or *door-to-door salespersons*; however, salesmanship techniques are effectively utilized in many **non-marketing** or **non-commercial** situations: a physician may wish to convince his bank to finance the expansion of a new clinic, or a cleric may wish to convince his congregation to fund a special church project, or one individual may wish to romantically pursue another. These, and many other such situations, require some use of **salesmanship**.

All individuals can employ and benefit from salesmanship. They need simply understand and practice certain salesmanship fundamentals, such as:

- **rapport building**   - **completing the sale**

- **qualifying**   - **saying "thank you"**

- **imparting information**

a. Building a rapport with the prospective buyer.

It is far easier for a salesperson to convince a prospective buyer to act in some desired manner if the buyer **trusts** and feels **comfortable** with the salesperson. A prospective buyer's initial feelings of trust and comfort will be dependent upon his perception of the salesperson's **image**. A salesperson's image is created by the salesperson's **physical appearance** and **mannerisms**.

- **Physical appearance.**

Individuals often associate particular physical appearances with certain **behavioral tendencies** or **value systems**; for example, **unkempt appearances** might be perceived as being indicative of **disorganization**; a university **class ring** might be associated with **expertise**; a fine **leather briefcase** might be considered as reflective of **professionalism**; **obesity** might be associated with **lack of self-discipline**, et cetera.

A salesperson's image is partially created by his grooming and his possessions, such as his clothing, briefcase, automobile, jewelry, wrist watch, residence, et cetera.

The personal values **shared** by a salesperson and a prospective buyer create **common** reference points and form a framework for **communicating**; consequently, a prospective buyer will be more responsive to a salesperson that **appears** to have **similar** or desirable personal values. Conversely, a prospective buyer will tend to reject the influence of a salesperson whose apparent personal values are undesirable, intimidating, or simply **different** from those of the prospective buyer. Consequently, the first step in rapport building is for the salesperson to present an **image** that projects familiar or admirable **personal values** (as perceived by the prospective buyer).

Salespeople should be sensitive to the **range** of values exhibited and adhered to by their typical prospective buyers. With such a spectrum in mind, salespeople should attempt to purposely project an image that is conservatively **in the middle** of that spectrum. By doing so, salespeople increase the probability that they will appeal to a broad range of prospective buyers.

- **Mannerisms.**

After observing the apparent values displayed by their prospective buyers, salespeople should **adjust** their own mannerisms to reflect and complement such values. In this **chameleon-like** manner, salespeople further project a comfortable and trusted image, as perceived by their prospective buyers.

- **Common interest.**

Beyond physical appearances and mannerisms, effective salespeople might **reinforce** a favorable image by discussing subjects of common interest, such as the weather, sports, fashion, family, current events, et cetera. Such simple conversation provides the salesperson an opportunity to identify values that are commonly held by both the salesperson and the prospective buyer, thereby further strengthening their rapport.

Also, in this manner, salespeople and prospective buyers can better develop a common framework for **verbal communication**, that being the salesperson's single **most influential** persuasion tool. Successful verbal communication is dependent upon the parties' mutual understanding of the **language** used and the underlying **values** implied. By bantering about simple subjects of common interest, a salesperson is also preparing the prospective buyer's communicative **receptiveness**.

b. Qualifying a prospective buyer.

It is far easier to persuade someone to purchase certain goods or services if he actually has a **need** for the subject goods or services, and if he has the **financial means** to acquire the subject goods or services. Logically then, the salesperson's next step should be to discover the prospective buyer's needs and financial capabilities (as they relate to acquiring the subject goods or services). This step is referred to as **qualifying** the prospect.

This step benefits both the salesperson and the buyer. It helps the prospective buyer to understand his own needs, and to make sure that he is purchasing a product that will actually fulfill his needs. At the same time, it permits the salesperson to minimize wasted time and effort.

To demonstrate the **qualifying process**, consider the following example, in which a prospective buyer has walked into an automobile dealership showroom. The salesperson, after **building rapport**, might ask the following **qualifying questions**:

- What type of automobile would you like to purchase?

- When do you plan to buy a new auto?

- For which specific purpose do you plan to use the new auto: to commute to work, for household errands, for off-road recreation, for hauling materials, et cetera?

- What kind of auto do you presently own?

- Do you wish to trade in your present auto?

- Do you require financing to purchase a new auto?

- Are you presently employed?

- How much do you earn?

- What are your monthly living expenses?

Such questions permit the salesperson to determine if the prospective buyer has the **need**, **desire**, and **ability** to purchase an auto at that time.

When asking such qualifying questions, a salesperson must take special care not to appear **unnecessarily intrusive**; such questioning should be **obviously pertinent** and **tactfully subtle**.

c. Imparting information to the prospective buyer about how the subject goods or services will fulfill his needs.

After the salesperson has *developed a rapport* with and *qualified* the prospective buyer, he must next inform the prospective buyer of how the subject goods or services will fulfill his relevant needs. This step might be accomplished through physical demonstration, written text, diagram, or oratory.

A new automobile **test ride** is an example of **demonstrating** how a product might fulfill a prospective buyer's needs. During this step of the sales process, it is helpful if the salesperson uses terminology that **presumes the sale to have already been made**; for instance, the salesperson might state that "you will feel very proud next week, when you drive this new automobile to the office." By doing so, the salesperson helps the buyer to **visualize** the benefits of acquiring the subject goods or services. Furthermore, this subtle technique helps to psychologically **obligate** a prospective buyer to completing the transaction; that is, after the salesperson implies that the **sale has been made,** and the buyer fails to argue the point, it becomes a bit more difficult for the buyer to renege on his **implied** (although not intended) concurrence.

It is imperative at this stage in the sales process, that the salesperson confirm the prospective buyer's **understanding** of and **concurrence** with the salesperson's **representations.** This is commonly referred to as uncovering the buyer's **objections,** and is accomplished through subtle or direct questioning, such as "don't you agree?", or "doesn't that sound great to you?", et cetera. If the prospective buyer refuses to "buy" and at the same time has no stated objections to doing so, the salesperson should restate the benefits of purchasing the subject goods or service and re-inquire as to the prospect's understanding. The salesperson should actually **welcome** the opportunity to address the prospective buyer's objections, because once done, there should be no further obstacles to completing the sales transaction.

d. Completing (closing) the sale.

After the salesperson has developed a rapport with and qualified the prospective buyer, and informed him how the subject goods or services will fulfill his needs, the final step is to **complete (or close) the sale.**

Most often, the **closing of the sale,** typically involves the **final exchange** of possessions; that being the salesperson's goods or services for the buyer's cash (or barter). Depending upon the nature of the product, this step might also involve the **signing of a contract,** specifying some specific future performances by the buyer and the seller, such as a product delivery date, or the date that services are to be performed, or a buyer payment schedule.

Ideally, the *close* should be **subtle** and **perfunctory,** taking care not to invite any buyer objections. A salesperson should choose his words carefully when closing the sale; in particular, he should avoid **open-ended** questions that might prompt the buyer to rethink his purchase decision. As an example of an **ill-worded** closing question, a salesperson **should not** ask "can you think of any reason not to buy?", or "are you sure that this is what you want?"

Effective closing questions **assume that the sale is already made,** and **prompt** a buyer response that is **affirmative.** Examples of such questions include "would you like this delivered on Monday or Tuesday", "would you like one more, just to be safe?", "will that be cash or credit card?" Such questions beckon an affirmative response **only**. As an **alternative** to asking any closing questions, a salesperson might simply state, "you have made a wise decision, I will write it up."

Care should also be taken in the consummation of sale's documentation. Although a buyer may have orally agreed to the purchase, he might change his mind if he becomes apprehensive about **signing** documents; consequently, questions such as "will you sign this contract?" should be avoided. Signing sounds very **official** and **encumbering**; it is far more effective to **casually** direct a buyer to "**please endorse here.**"

If a sales document requires the signatures of **both** the salesperson and the buyer, the salesperson should casually sign the document **first**, and then hand it to the buyer (along with an ink pen). By signing first, the salesperson **induces** the prospect to follow in a likewise manner; furthermore, it creates the **illusion** that the transaction has now been formalized, making it difficult for the prospect to balk. It is also effective to make casual conversation during such **signing mechanics**, to **defuse** any associated decision-making significance.

While closing a sale, the salesperson should be particularly (although not obviously) sensitive to a prospective buyer's final **moment of decision**. As the prospective buyer reaches into his pocket to withdraw his money, or as he picks-up the ink pen to sign the sales agreement, the salesperson should **do nothing to distract or delay that pivotal act**. Any such delay or distraction might create an opportunity for additional buyer objections and the **potential** failure of the transaction. As an example of an **insensitive closing comment** (*what not to do*), one might envision a sales situation in which a senior and junior salesperson are sitting across the desk from a prospective automobile buyer:

> - The senior salesperson has been negotiating for hours and has now brought the prospective buyer to his final **moment of decision**.

> - The senior salesperson has laid the sales agreement in front of the buyer, the buyer has reviewed it, and has picked up the ink pen to sign.

- A **pregnant** moment has passed, as the buyer pensively stares at the signature line. Tension pervades the room, as the ink pen slowly drops towards the document. The junior salesperson, becoming uncomfortable with the tension of the moment, blurts out, "so what do you think about this weather that we have been having?"

Obviously, a very ill-timed and insensitive question, as it presents the buyer an opportunity to *get off of the hook*!

In the event that a prospective buyer **does object** to the closing of the sale, the salesperson should tactfully ask the buyer to explain the nature of his reservation or objection. It may be necessary for the salesperson to again review the buyer's needs, and how the subject goods or services will fulfill such needs. This routine should simply be **repeated** until the buyer's objections have been appropriately addressed.

The following continuation of the above example demonstrates one approach to addressing a buyer's final objections:

The prospective buyer, after the ill-timed *"weather question"*, has decided not to sign the purchase agreement. In a final objection, the buyer states to the senior salesperson, "I just can't afford it." The salesperson then addresses this objection in the following manner:

> **Salesperson:** "I can appreciate your concern; purchasing a needed automobile is a major decision. Let's take a moment to review the facts. Your family auto is ten years old, and on the verge of mechanical breakdown - correct?"

> **Buyer:** "Yes."

> **Salesperson:** "You need a reliable auto, to take your children to school and to do the household errands - correct?"

> **Buyer:** "Yes."

> **Salesperson:** "The new auto will permit you to confidently meet your needs for many years, and it is competitively priced - correct?"

> **Buyer:** "Yes."

Salesperson: "We have arranged financing for your purchase of the new auto, and we have agreed to take your old auto in trade, eliminating any need for you to make a cash down payment - correct?"

Buyer: "Yes."

Salesperson: "You earn $2,500 per month, and your living expenses are $1,700, leaving $800 of discretionary spendable income - correct?"

Buyer: "Yes."

Salesperson: "The monthly payments for your new car will be $450. This amount is well within your budget, and still leaves you $350 of extra discretionary spendable income - correct?"

Buyer: "Yes."

Salesperson: "So, in review, it appears that your **need** for a new auto is **justified**, that the subject auto will **fulfill** your needs, and that the purchase is financially **prudent** - correct?"

Buyer: "Yes."

Salesperson: "There appears to be no reason for concern, so I must assume that you are now ready to proceed."

Buyer: "Yes."

If a salesperson cannot successfully redress the buyer's objections, the sale might not be justified.

e. Saying *thank you.*

Once a sale has been completed, the salesperson increases his probability of repeat business by saying **thank you** to the buyer, and to any **other** individuals that may have been involved in helping to complete the transaction. Depending upon the nature of the product marketed, the salesperson might express his thanks by giving a gift to the buyer. Such gifts should be appropriate for the situation, and not in the form of cash. As a general rule, the value of such gifts should equal about **five percent** of the salesperson's net remuneration. **The giving of such gifts is not based in civility; it is an effective approach to securing future profits.**

SUBJECT 3. Management

Management is the process of **motivating** and **directing** the actions of others, in a joint problem solving effort.

Management techniques are equally useful in commercial and non-profit environments. For purposes of this presentation, a commercial application shall be presumed; however, the same principles are effective in social, family, church, school, or other problem solving settings.

A successful manager should exercise good **problem solving skills** (see *Problem Solving Skills*), but most importantly, a manager must attain the **respect** of the individuals to be managed.

a. Attaining respect.

Individuals consistently (and enthusiastically) respond to a manager's direction only if they **respect** the manager.

In order for a manager to attain his staff's respect, the manager must demonstrate that:

- He is considerate of his staff's **well-being.**

- He possesses the professional **expertise** that is necessary to guide his staff in the accomplishment of their mutual goals.

In demonstrating concern for his staff's well-being, a manager should:

- Employ common **courtesy** when addressing his staff; he should say please, thank you, and refrain from condescension, or rudeness. If a manager wishes to be addressed as *Mister* or *Misses*, he should address his staff in the same manner.

- Encourage the **self-betterment** and career advancement of his staff.

- Protect his staff from harmful working conditions, such as mechanical, chemical, radiation, organic, or psychological hazards.

- Make sure that work schedules do not unreasonably interfere with the fulfillment of his staff's **health**, **family**, and **play** needs.

It is equally important that those to be managed are confident in their manager's **professional expertise**. To this end, a manager might tactfully inform his staff of the **educational** and **vocational** accomplishments that qualified him for the management position. A manager will also earn such respect by **properly** explaining and demonstrating the work tasks to be accomplished.

b. Motivating individuals.

Individuals are best motivated through **positive inducements/rewards**, rather than through **intimidation/punishment**.

Positive inducement/reward motivation is exemplified by the following task performance process:

1. The manager **politely asks** a staff member to perform a specific task.

2. The manager **intelligently explains** (or demonstrates) the task to be performed.

3. The manager informs the worker of the **benefits** that will result from the successful accomplishment of the subject task.

4. Upon successful accomplishment of the subject task, the worker is **rewarded** with a **thank you**, **praise**, and/or **pay**.

The above motivation approach tends to induce staff **loyalty** and **consistent** quality of workmanship.

Managers should refrain from attempting to motivate their workers through **intimidation or punishment**. Such ineffective approaches include:

- Yelling or snapping at staff members.

- Scolding staff members in the presence of others.

- Scolding of all staff members for the mistakes of the few.

- Threats of **wage** or **personnel cuts** to motivate the achievement of arbitrary goals.

Such management techniques typically yield **low** productivity, **high** employee turnover, and **inferior** quality workmanship.

c. Directing individuals.

A manager should make himself available to his staff, to assist them in problem solving and in guiding their work activities. To this end, a manager should constantly (but subtly) monitor the activities of his staff, and maintain an **open door** policy.

Because a manager's primary function is to **motivate** and **guide** his staff, he should avoid becoming embroiled in excessive paperwork. If paperwork begins to conflict with a manager's prime duties, he should delegate a portion of the paperwork to one of his staff members.

-    **Meetings.** Meetings, with other than subordinates, remove a manager from direct supervision, and often waste time by providing a podium and captive audience to egotistic or talkative peers.

Certainly, managers should participate in productive meetings with their superiors, other managers, staff, vendors, customers, or others; however, one's participation in such meetings should be **minimized** or **avoided**, unless the meeting **directly contributes** to the accomplishment of the manager's work responsibilities.

-    **Giving instructions.** Individuals should be instructed in a **clear**, **polite**, and **patient** manner. The manager should ask the individual to repeat the instructions, to make sure that they were understood. A manager should instruct his workers by using **specific language** and **a degree of detail** that is **commensurate** with the worker's education and vocational experience. When in doubt, the manager should assume that the worker's skills are minimal, and instruct at that level. By doing so, a manager ensures that all individuals will understand his **initial** instructions. As workers respond, the manager can then assess their abilities, and appropriately modify his guidance approach.

- **Reprimanding others.** Individuals occasionally make judgement, technical, or policy errors, such as breaking a tool, damaging stock, offending a client, being tardy, being insubordinate, et cetera. In such cases, the individual should be reprimanded in a **constructive** manner; that is, the manager should attempt to correct the specific shortcoming and refrain from general character attacks.

Reprimands are intended to **correct** an individual's erroneous work habits, **not** to publicly **embarrass** the individual; consequently, reprimands should be administered in **private**. In the event that the workplace does not afford a private area for such purpose, the subject worker should be tactfully reprimanded in a calm manner.

Reprimands should be **personal**; that is, managers should avoid reprimanding a **large group** of individuals for the infractions of the unidentified **few**. For example, it is very ineffective when a manager stands before a large group of individuals and states in a **scolding tone** that "many of you arrive late in the morning." The offending individuals are typically unresponsive to such approaches, while the timely (innocent) individuals are unfairly subjected to a general reprimand, thereby provoking their alienation. If a manager must administer such a general reprimand, he should **first** state the non-applicability of his following statements to the **non-offending** majority.

- **Delegation of work.** A manager, by definition, **must** delegate work. When work is delegated to an individual, he becomes **responsible** for its accomplishment; it is imperative that a worker also be delegated adequate **authority** to accomplish the work for which he has become responsible. Once an individual has been delegated the responsibility and authority to accomplish a task, his manager should not interfere with the worker's efforts, unless the individual is obviously experiencing problems. Unwarranted management interference **wastes** both the manager's and worker's time. Additionally, it **discourages** the development of a worker's individual problem solving abilities.

SUBJECT 4. Understanding General Ledger Accounting

An understanding of accounting **enhances** one's earning abilities and enables one to **better** manage his financial affairs.

a. The concept.

Accounting is a formal **record-keeping system**, intended to assist any entity in the **monitoring** and **controlling** of its finances.

The *Dual Entry* General Ledger Accounting System was developed in Fifteenth-century Italy, with its primary attribute being increased accuracy. This particular method is the most common accounting system in Western societies. Though equally useful for personal or business purposes, the following presentation presumes commercial application.

b. Terminology.

- **Assets.**

Businesses, in the course of their operations, acquire legal rights to use certain **properties**. Examples of such properties are: cash, raw materials, finished goods inventory, pre-paid expenses, patents, equipment, real estate, et cetera. For accounting purposes, such properties are commonly referred to as **assets**, and are expressed in **monetary** values.

- **Liabilities.**

During their course of operation, businesses become encumbered to perform certain actions. Examples of such **legal obligations** are: credit purchases payable, loans payable, incurred taxes payable, et cetera. For accounting purposes, such obligations are commonly referred to as **liabilities**, and are also expressed in monetary values.

- **Capital.**

The monetary value of a business can be determined by subtracting the sum total of its liabilities from the sum total of its assets. The resulting amount is commonly referred to as the business' **net worth, capital,** or

equity. For purposes of this presentation, the term **capital** shall be used.

The basic accounting formula for determining **capital** is:

$$\text{Assets - Liabilities = Capital}$$

- Income.

When a business provides its goods or services to a buyer, it typically receives money in payment. As such payments are received, they are recorded into the business' accounting records as **income**, assuming that the business conducts its accounting on a **cash basis**.

- Expenses.

Most businesses expend money on items that are consumed in the **direct** production of **income**; such expenditures might include rent, utilities, taxes, payroll, advertising, raw materials, et cetera. As such expenditures are recorded into the business' accounting records, they are referred to as **operating expenses**.

Operating expenses should not be confused with **capital expenditures**, the latter being for the purchase of general purpose **assets** that are not consumed in the direct production of income.

- Profit or Loss.

The inherent purpose of any business is to **increase** its owner's **material holdings**. A business' monetary **effectiveness** for any given operating period is measured by subtracting the **sum total of that period's expenses** from the **sum total of that period's income**. If the resulting monetary difference is positive, it is commonly referred to as **profit**; if it is negative, it is commonly referred to as a **loss** (see *What is Money?*).

The basic accounting formula for determining a business' profit or loss is:

$$\text{Income - Expenses = Profit or Loss}$$

- Accounts.

All business transactions and accounting entries fall into one of the above described general groupings: Assets, Liabilities, Capital, Income, or Expenses. Within such general groupings, an accounting **record** is established for each of the specific types of transactions. These records are then referred to as **accounts**.

- General Ledger.

All **accounts**, once designated, are contained in a record-keeping file, commonly referred to as the **general ledger**. The general ledger might be in **book** or **ledger card** format, and maintained through manual entries. More often, a company's general ledger is stored on magnetic or optical scan media and maintained through computer entry.

Organizationally, the general ledger typically lists all asset accounts first, then liability accounts, then capital accounts, then income accounts, and finally expense accounts.

The **Assets** grouping might be comprised of the following accounts:

- Cash
- Receivables
- Stock
- Office Equipment
- Production Facilities (real estate)
- Pre-paid expenses

The **Liabilities** grouping might be comprised of the following accounts:

- Payables due
- Loan obligations
- Employee Income Tax Withholdings

The **Capital** grouping might be comprised of the following accounts:

- Stockholders Equity (in corporations)
- Capital Contributions
- Retained Earnings
- Current Earnings

The **Income** grouping might be comprised of the following accounts:

- Sales Income
- Interest Income

The **Expense** grouping might be comprised of the following accounts:

- Payroll
- Rent
- Telephone
- Advertising
- Postage
- Supplies
- Materials
- Taxes

Each such account grouping is typically assigned a major **control number**, with individual accounts being assigned a **sub**-number of its general account grouping. As examples:

- The Asset group might be #100, and the Cash account assigned a sub-number of #101.

- The Liability group might be #200, and the Payables Due account assigned a sub-number of #201.

- The Capital group might be #300, and Capital Contributions account assigned a sub-number of #301.

- The Income group might be #400, and the Sales Income account assigned a sub-number of #401.

- The Expense group might be #500, and the Payroll account assigned a sub-number of #501.

All accounts are then listed in the **general ledger** in **numeric order.**

- Chart of Accounts.

The **chart of accounts** is the general ledger's **table of contents**, indexing the **name** and **number** of each listed account. This is for quick reference purposes only and displays no account balance information.

- General Journal.

As a business conducts its daily operations, its monetary transactions are first noted in the **general journal.** Each such entry is made in a **line item** fashion, reflecting the **date, monetary amount,** and **description** of the transaction. The general journal often consists of sub-journals, such as the **cash receipts journal, cash disbursements journal, payroll journal,** et cetera.

In smaller businesses, the **check register** often serves as a general journal, becoming the **source document** for general ledger entries.

- Debits and Credits.

On a periodic basis, each general journal **line item** entry should be transcribed (**posted**) into the specific general ledger account that has been designated to record that **type** of business transaction.

When the account postings are made, they are referred to as **Debit** or **Credit** entries. These terms have been carried forward from antiquity. Debit comes from the Latin word *Debere*, which means "to owe", and Credit coming from the Latin word *Credere*, which means "to trust".

As entries are made in each account, debits are placed on the **left** side of a column and credits are placed on the **right** side. An account's balance is equal to the mathematical difference between the sum of its debit and credit entries. The balance is expressed in terms of the excess debit or credit quantity; that is, an account has a **debit balance**, or **credit balance.** As an example:

- Assume that an account has a zero beginning balance.

- Next, assume that a $10 debit entry is made.

- Finally, assume that a $3 credit entry is made.

This combination of account postings would result in a $7 debit balance.

Asset and expense accounts are increased by debit postings, **decreased** by credit postings, and normally maintain a **debit balance**. Liability, capital, and income accounts are **increased** by credit postings, decreased by debit postings, and normally maintain a **credit balance**.

In computerized accounting systems, credit entries are usually preceded by a **negative sign** to mathematically differentiate them from debit entries. In both manual and computerized accounting systems, debits are typically abbreviated as **Dr** and credits are typically abbreviated as **Cr**.

- Trial Balance.

In a **dual entry** accounting system, as implied by its name, the sum total of all debit entries must always be offset by an equal total of credit entries. The object of this **dual entry offsetting** approach is to provide a mathematic tool for checking **accuracy**. To this end, a periodic **cross-check** is performed, in which the total of all debit balance accounts is compared to the total of all credit balance accounts. This process is referred to as taking a **trial balance**.

In a **trial balance**, the total of all Asset and Expense accounts should equal the total of all Liability, Income, and Capital accounts. If there is an **imbalance**, it indicates that a posting error has been made subsequent to the last trial balance.

- Financial Statements.

In order to assess and control the financial condition of a business, one must be able to determine its **profitability** and **net worth**. This task can be accomplished by reviewing the business' general ledger accounts. Such reviews have evolved into two written formats: the **income state-**

ment, and the **balance sheet**. These reports are commonly referred to as a business' **financial statements**.

- The Income Statement.

The profit for a given period of operation is determined by totalling the income for the subject period and then deducting the period's total operating expenses. This accounting information is formally provided through the **income statement**. It is presented in a columnar fashion, with total income listed first, then total period expenses, and finally the mathematical profit or loss difference, which are also referred to as the **current earnings**.

At the end of a business' accounting year, the current earnings account is **closed out** (returned to zero) by transferring the account balance into the **capital** account. In this manner, the current earnings account is readied for the accumulation of the next accounting period's entries, and the business' capital accounts become reflective of the increase resulting from the period's profits.

- The Balance Sheet.

The balance sheet reflects the **net worth** of the business. It is prepared by separately listing and totalling all asset, liability, and capital accounts in three respective columns, with the total assets listed first, then the total liabilities, and finally the total capital.

The total of the asset accounts column less the total of the liability accounts column should equal the total of the capital accounts column. As an alternative format, some balance sheets are prepared with the total assets equalling the combined totals of the liability and capital accounts.

- Interpreting financial statements.

The following guidelines are general in nature and should not be relied upon in the judgement of any particular financial situation. The reader should seek the advice of expert counsel, prior to making any financial decision that depends upon the interpretation of financial statements.

The first consideration, when reviewing a business' financial statements, is its **source** of preparation; that is, **who prepared the documents, and what method was employed**? Ideally, the preparer should be a **reputable** independent accounting firm which has **audited** the accounts and **confirmed** the assets through appraisal and visual inspection.

Certain types of businesses exhibit characteristic operating norms, such as **profit margins**, or **expense to income ratios**. For example, a particular industry might experience an average profit margin of 20%, meaning that their profits equal 20% of its gross receipts. Another industry might typically experience a 35% expense to income ratio, meaning that its operating expenses typically equal 35% of its operating income.

When reviewing a business' income statement, it is helpful to be familiar with the profit margins, expense to income ratios, or other standard measures that typify that business' general industry. By doing so, one can better judge the business' efficiency of operation.

When reading the **balance sheet**, one should first look at the assets; large receivables, and minimal cash balances might be indicative of **ineffective** cash management. It is ideal if a business' assets are easily convertible to cash (**liquid**), with little or no discount in value. Such assets include cash, certificates of deposit, prime real estate, and general purpose business equipment. Less desirable assets include accounts receivables, specialized trade equipment, raw materials, and finished goods inventory; the latter assets should be discounted in determining their disposable value. **Intangible assets**, such as **good will** or **engineering cost** are very difficult to evaluate, and should be **cautiously** considered.

Assets and liabilities are generally classified as **current**, or **fixed**, in nature. **Current assets** are those that can be converted to cash within one year, and current liabilities are those that will come due within **one year**. For example, a ninety day certificate of deposit would be a current asset, and an invoice for payment of material purchases due in sixty days would be considered as a **current liability**. As a general rule, a company's current assets should be equal to **twice the amount** of its current liabilities (the *current ratio*).

SUBJECT 5. Understanding Computers

People fulfill their needs through problem solving. Often, **tools** are employed in the problem solving process. As examples, one might use a hammer to drive or remove a nail, one might use an oven to cook a meal, or one might use an automobile to drive to their place of employment. In these examples the hammer, the oven, and the automobile are all problem solving **tools**.

The **effectiveness** of one's problem solving approach may be dependent upon his **choice** of tools. For example, an individual might select a bicycle, an automobile, or an airplane, for the purpose of commuting from one city to another. Depending upon **which** such tool he selects, his commute might take **days, hours,** or **minutes** to complete.

The computer is a tool, designed to **process, store,** and **display** information, and to **control** electronic or electro-mechanical devices. Computers, as problem solving tools, offer **substantial time and energy savings**, particularly when compared to their manual or mechanical predecessors.

Often, people fail to employ tools simply because they do not **understand** the tool; consequently, they become **deprived** of the tool's potential **benefits**. The object of this subject presentation is to **familiarize** the reader with **computers**, thereby making it **easier** for the reader to **select, use,** and **benefit** from the computer as a problem solving tool.

The following terminology should be minimally sufficient to acquaint the reader with computer concepts and usage:

- **User.**

A user is an individual who is using a computer.

- **CPU.**

A CPU is the computer's **brain**, an abbreviation for **central processing unit**. The CPU is constructed from electronic circuitry.

- I/O Devices.

I/O Devices are the computer's **eyes, ears, voice,** and **limbs.** I/O abbreviates **input/output.** The most common **input** device is the **keyboard console,** and the most common **output** devices are the **video console** and **printer. Magnetic tape and disc units** and **optical disc units,** can function as input or output devices.

- Computer Languages.

Computer languages are special **instruction formats** using alphabetic, numeric, and other symbols to direct a computer's processing. Most computer languages are designed to accommodate certain user application needs. Such languages tend to be **user friendly;** that is, they employ recognizable **near-English** command words (*mnemonics*).

- Computer Programming.

A **program** is an intelligent sequence of computer language instructions, intended to direct the computer in the performance of some desired task. Most programs fall into one of two categories, **operating system** or **application** programs.

    a. Operating system programs instruct the computer in the performance of **the fundamental** operational routines that are necessary to support the processing of most **application** programs. Such fundamental routines might include:

        1. How to interpret the application language being used.

        2. How to coordinate the I/O devices being employed.

        3. How to assist the user with common needs, such as **copying information,** or **setting up files,** et cetera.

    b. Application programs instruct the computer in the performance of the user's **specific** processing (problem solving) needs.

- **Software Packages.**

Software packages are **application** programs, designed with sufficient format **flexibility** to **accommodate** the **common** processing needs of many users. Examples of such programs include:

Word Processing

Database Management

General Ledger Accounting

Order Entry/Inventory Control

Material Requirements Planning

Production Scheduling

Scientific Applications

- **Custom Software.**

Custom software, is a specific application program, initially written to accommodate the processing needs of **one** user only.

SUBJECT 6. Understanding (business-related) Civil Law

An understanding of Civil Law affords individuals the ability to **protect** their **property**, to **enforce** their contractual **rights**, and to **avoid** unnecessary **litigation**.

Creating and retaining wealth involves the use of certain business tools and objects, such as **contracts, real and personal properties, concepts**, et cetera. The rights and privileges enjoyed by individuals and business entities, relative to such business tools, are defined and enforced by societal **civil law systems**. Most such legal systems in Western societies have evolved from **English Common Law, or Roman Laws.**

It is certainly advantageous, when playing any game, to understand the **rules of play**. In business, the prevailing **civil laws and procedures** are the *rules of play*, consequently, it is in one's best interest to have a basic understanding of such laws and procedures.

It is impractical to advise the reader on the whole of this subject, as such legal systems are voluminous and vary in text and case law from one jurisdiction to another.

The object of this section is to **familiarize** the reader with **legal terms** and **civil procedures** that are often associated with business litigation. **The following presentation is general in nature, and should not be relied upon as a definitive source; individuals should seek professional legal counsel when engaging in any personal or business actions that might affect their legal rights.**

a. Contracts.

Most business transactions involve the use of a written document, referred to as a **contract**. The function of a contract is to delineate the expectations and obligations of the parties, therein creating legal **rights and duties**.

Legal systems sometimes assume the authority to dictate the textual format of contracts, because they might be called upon to protect or enforce the rights and duties that are created by such contracts. For a contract to be **enforceable**, it should generally embody the following characteristics:

- It should be for a **legal purpose**.

- It should **clearly** represent the **agreement** of the parties and show their **genuine assent**.

- It should clearly delineate the nature of the **acts to be performed** and state a **finite time frame** for their performance.

- There should be **adequate consideration** specified to justify the actions of the parties.

Additionally, the parties to a contract should be of **sufficient mental capacity** to enter into a contract; that is, they should be of adequate age and maturity, mentally sound, not intoxicated, and free from the influence of duress.

If a contract is lacking in any of the above elements, a court might render the contract **unenforceable** or **voidable**, or choose to selectively enforce various parts of the contract.

b. Common Torts.

A **tort** is a **wrong-doing**. Relative to contracts, the most common torts are:

- **Breach of contract.** This condition exists, when one of the parties, without just cause, refuses to honor its contractual obligations, therein injuring another party to the contract.

- **Misrepresentation.** This condition exists when one party to a contract fails to disclose or misstates certain material facts, therein **damaging** another contract party.

- **Fraud.** This condition exists when one party to a contract willfully misrepresents material facts with the intention of gaining an unfair material advantage over or causing inconvenience to another party.

- **Interference with Contract.** This condition exists when an entity, for the purpose of gain, intentionally interferes with one party's contractual performance, thereby materially injuring another party to the contract. This section's use of the term **entity** refers to both animate objects (such as individuals) and inanimate objects (such as corporations).

Other business related torts include:

- **Defamation.** This condition exists when one entity makes malicious public accusations about another, therein actually or potentially injuring the esteem or reputation of the defamed entity. Such defamations might be oral in nature (referred to as **slander**), or written in nature (referred to as **libel**).

- **Intentional Interference with Prospective Economic Advantage.** This condition exists when one entity uses unlawful means to gain an economic advantage, to the detriment of a competing business entity.

c. Civil Procedures.

Civil procedures are the specific **methods** and **processes** of civil litigation. When one entity is materially **damaged** by the wrongful acts of another, the injured party may seek **remedy** through the civil court system. A legal remedy is the procedural means by which a right is enforced or the violation of a right is prevented, redressed, or compensated.

The most common civil procedure, seeking remedy, is referred to as a **lawsuit** and is initiated with the filing of a **complaint**. A complaint includes a formal **pleading** of the circumstances that resulted in the subject damages, and a delineation of such damages.

The specific nature of the litigation will determine if **jurisdiction** lies with a Municipal, State, or Federal court, and the **venue** (court location) for filing the complaint. Once a complaint has been filed with the appropriate court, the defendant must be formally (and personally) **served** with (handed) a copy of the complaint.

The damaged party is referred to as the **plaintiff** and the accused party is referred to as the **defendant**. Once served, the defendant typically has thirty days to file an **answer** with the court. The defendant's answer will generally take one of three tacks:

- Deny the plaintiff's **allegations** and request a **dismissal**.

- Deny the plaintiff's allegations and initiate a **cross-complaint**, wherein the defendant claims that it is actually the damaged party.

- Acknowledge the plaintiff's allegations, but offer justification for the defendant's actions, therein attempting to prevent the plaintiff's recovery of damages or enforcement of rights.

The court, after considering the pleadings of both plaintiff and defendant, may dismiss the action or remedy the plaintiff's damages by rendering a **judgement**. Judgements are **court orders** obligating the subject parties to **respond**. Failure to respond to such court orders can result in additional fines, the seizure of properties, or imprisonment. Examples of judgements relative to the above discussed torts might be:

1. **Specific Performance.** In the occurrence of *breach of contract*, the court might force the breaching party to perform a specific contractual act, such as the delivery of certain goods.

2. **Recovery of Damages.** In the occurrence of *breach of contract, defamation, interference with contract, interference with prospective economic advantage, misrepresentation*, or *fraud*, the court might force the defendant to remunerate the plaintiff for damages incurred by the defendant's actions (or inactions). The award of such damages might be **compensatory** and/or **punitive** in nature.

> - **Compensatory** awards compensate a litigant for **actual** damages incurred, as a direct result of the defendant's wrongful acts. Such damages might include **lost income, legal fees, court costs**, et cetera.

> - **Punitive** damages might be awarded the plaintiff, if the wrongful actions of the defendants were particularly outrageous and if they resulted in considerable compensatory damages. Such damages tend to be awarded in instances of fraud, particularly when multiple defendants have acted in **collusion**.

3. **Injunctive Relief.** In the occurrence of certain torts, a court might initially grant a **temporary restraining order**, prohibiting the defendant from performing some specific *act*, and subsequently grant a **preliminary injunction**, assuming that the plaintiff can convince the court that the subject *act* poses an imminent physical or economic threat to the plaintiff. If the court so judges, the preliminary injunction may be replaced with a **permanent injunction** (permanently forbidding the defendant from performing the subject act).

d. Litigation avoidance.

Being involved in a lawsuit, either as a plaintiff or a defendant, can be **time consuming, emotionally taxing**, and **very expensive**; consequently, it is in one's best interest to **avoid** litigation. To this end, one should:

- Employ **ethical** business practices and avoid personal or commercial interaction with individuals of questionable moral character.

- Practice **attention to detail** in business transactions.

- Structure contracts **succinctly**.

- Agreements should always be in writing, regardless of the trustworthiness of the individuals involved.

- **Document** pertinent communications relative to a business transaction, and draft *memos to file*, summarizing any legally sensitive telephone conversations.

- Maintain **organized** computer and document files, with copies of all correspondence, notes, telephone messages, et cetera.

- Use **registered** or **certified** mail for all correspondence of particular legal consequence (such as **demands** or **notices**).

- Be **tactful** and avoid making enemies.

There are certain instances in which civil litigation is appropriate; however, **it should be used only as a final resort. Unfortunately**, some legal systems invite or permit frivolous/greed motivated lawsuits. **Plaintiffs and their attorneys should seriously consider the moral propriety of their actions, prior to initiating lawsuits** (see *Greed*).

If an individual (or corporation) believes that he has been the victim of contrived and meritless litigation, most civil law systems permit him to file a counter-suit, alleging that his adversary had employed the **malicious institution of a civil proceeding**. In order to prevail in such a pleading, one must first have **successfully** defended against the questionable lawsuit, and furthermore prove that the other party lacked **probable cause** for initiating the questionable lawsuit.

Considering the additional time, emotions, and legal fees that are expended in such defenses and remedies, one should make special efforts to avoid litigation.

SUBJECT 7. Commercial Development

Commercial development affords individuals the **opportunity** to make **vast** amounts of income. Unlike many vocations, commercial development **does not** require any particular academic nor licensing credentials; consequently, it is an excellent vehicle for economic mobility.

Commercial development is the **implementation of a concept for the purpose of creating a profit.** Such concepts might include inventions, musical scores, songs, motion picture productions, literary works, real property uses, et cetera.

The commercial development **process** is relatively similar, **regardless** of the commercial concept being exploited. For purposes of example, one might consider the development of **commercial real estate.** When most individuals see an office building, industrial building, government building, motion picture theater, shopping center, or other such structures, they seldom consider (nor understand) the provenance of such structures; in actuality, most are privately owned investment properties that originated as **commercial developments.**

In the developing of commercial real estate, the **developer** might **build-to-suit**; that is, he might develop a **project** to meet the facility needs of a specific **user** (the intended buyer or tenant of the developed property). As an alternative, the developer might engage in a **speculative** development; that is, the project might be developed and **marketed** with the intention of **eventually** securing a **user** to purchase or lease the property. In either approach, the **first step** in the commercial real estate development process is to determine a **profitable use concept** for the property to be developed.

Although a developer might have a lucrative concept and the skills to develop it, many developers **lack** the personal finances that are necessary to capitalize their development projects; consequently, the **next step** in the development process is to seek **financing**. Such financing might take the form of a commercial bank loan, or the securing of private investor funds. Most typically, a combination of such approaches are used. Often, a **joint venture** partner (a money partner) will provide the necessary capital to begin the development project. The joint venture partner might be an individual investor, a group of investors (a **syndicate**), or a commercial institution, such as a bank or insurance company.

Once the joint venture partner has been secured, the remainder of the development capital is secured through commercial loans, typically from banks, saving and loan associations, or insurance companies. Such loans usually consist of a **construction loan** and eventual **permanent financing**, also referred to as a **take-out loan**.

With the development *concept* and *financing* in place, the project mechanics may **then** be commenced; that is, an **architect** can complete the plans and a **general contractor** can complete the property improvements. If the development is **speculative** in nature, its **marketing** might also commence at this time.

Finally, with the project complete and the **user** in place, the developer and joint venture partner can divide the development profits as dictated by their partnership agreement. It should also be understood that many developers draw a **periodic** and **continuing fee** from the construction loan proceeds; such fees remunerate the developer for his project coordination efforts, and financially sustain him until the development is producing profits.

In review of the above, the development process consists of:

- Creating a development concept.

- Securing development financing.

- Maturing the concept into a physical reality.

- Marketing the matured concept.

- Realizing the development profits.

The **development process** is functional across many fields of endeavor: **book publishing, motion picture production, consumer product development**, et cetera. Many development vehicles, though **less obvious**, are **equally** lucrative. As an example, some development exploits are guised as **religious projects**. In such instances, an individual (possibly a **religious leader**) might propose the construction of a religious **edifice** (such as a statue of some **favorite deity**), or an extravagant religious **theatrical production**. The **religious developer** then coordinates the project in much the same manner that a commercial developer might, funding such a project through direct parishioner **contributions** and through commercial loans.

Such religious developers, like commercial developers, often earn hundreds of thousands or millions of dollars, as often evidenced by their lavish personal lifestyles. **Unlike commercial development, the moral propriety of such personal profit making is questionable.**

SUBJECT 8. Escrow

Most individuals first experience an escrow when purchasing a home; escrows are also used to accommodate a broad variety of business transactions. The object of this subject presentation is to acquaint the reader with common escrow terminology, and to remove any mystique surrounding the subject. Such familiarity will better enable individuals to manage their financial affairs.

Most business transactions require the involved parties to perform reciprocal acts of consideration. For example, one party to a transaction (the Seller) might be obligated to sign a document that conveys the ownership of his property over to another; while the other party (the Buyer) might be obligated to hand the Seller a specific amount of cash, in consideration of receiving title to the Seller's property.

The Buyer and Seller might **not trust** one another to perform their respective acts; consequently, the Buyer and Seller might mutually select and employ a **trusted third party** to temporarily hold the Seller's legal documents and Buyer's cash, until all elements of the transaction have been completed. Thus, the term **escrow holder**.

Such escrow holders are typically licensed and controlled by government authorities, to assure their **trustworthiness**. The **fee** charged by an escrow holder is usually proportionate, on a **percentage basis**, to the monetary value of the subject business transaction. The specific individual who coordinates the escrow is referred to as the **escrow officer**.

If individuals wish to **open** an escrow, they must select an escrow company and instruct the escrow officer as to the particulars of the subject transaction. This might be accomplished via telephone, FAX, or in person. The principals (such as the Buyer or Seller) can personally initiate the escrow, or their agents/employees can initiate escrow on their behalf.

Based upon the Buyer's and Seller's oral or written directions, the escrow officer will prepare written **escrow instructions**, delineating the specific performance obligations of the parties. The Buyer and Seller will then review the escrow instructions and endorse them, assuming that the instructions accurately reflect the particulars of the business transaction. Once endorsed, the escrow instructions become a **legally binding** agreement, obligating the parties to perform accordingly.

If the sale of real property is the object of the business transaction, the escrow officer (on behalf of the principal parties) usually employs a **title insurance company** to **research** and **insure** the condition (deliverability) of title; the written result of such research is referred to as a **preliminary title report**.

A property's **title** is a body of information specifying the legal usage rights that are enjoyed by various entities, relative to that property. Such title information is usually located in the property records of the jurisdictional government offices.

The individual who coordinates the title research is commonly referred to as a **title officer**. The preliminary title report assures the Buyer that the Seller has the legal authority to transfer title. Furthermore, it discloses the existence of any **liens** or **encumbrances**, such as trust deeds, unpaid taxes, pending lawsuits, rights of access or possession by other parties, et cetera.

After the Buyer accepts the disclosed condition of title, the title insurance company issues a **commitment of title insurance**, in which it promises to guarantee the stated condition of title, until the property title is transferred to the Buyer. Prior to issuing such a commitment, the title officer might **except** coverage on certain title items, or request specific title clearing actions. Such items are commonly referred to as **exceptions**. As examples, there might be a **mechanic's lien**, or a recorded **leasehold interest**. Such items are commonly referred to as **clouds on title**.

To clean the title, the title officer might require the escrow officer to prepare a **quit claim deed**, for endorsement by any parties with a questionable title interest. A quit claim deed, when endorsed by such parties, relinquishes any legal rights that they might have had in the subject property.

When the title to real property is to be conveyed from Seller to Buyer, the escrow officer typically prepares a **grant deed**. The grant deed is then signed by the Seller, and eventually entered into the official government records.

Often, Buyers find it necessary to borrow money to purchase a piece of real property. The **Lender** of such funds might be a commercial entity, a private investor, or the Seller. The Lender will typically send its **loan documents** to the escrow officer for coordination. The loan documents generally consist of the **loan note** and the **trust deed**.

The note states the Buyer's promise to repay the loan, and delineates the method of repayment. In the note, the Buyer is referred to as the **Payor** or **Maker**, and the Lender is referred to as the **Payee**.

The trust deed is a document which secures the note; that is, it gives the Lender certain legal rights to the subject property, in the event that the Buyer **defaults** (fails to repay) on the note. Such rights typically include the right to take possession of, and to sell, the subject property through a legal **foreclosure** procedure. The proceeds of a foreclosure sale are then used to **pay off** the defaulted loan balance.

The trust deed designates an impartial third party (a **trust deed company**), referred to as the **Trustee**, whose function is to coordinate the transfer of title, in the event of a foreclosure. In the trust deed, the Buyer is referred to as the **Trustor**, and the Lender is referred to as the **Beneficiary**.

Because most properties are purchased with real estate loans, preliminary title reports often disclose the existence of a trust deed (securing an existing loan). Another of the escrow officer's responsibilities is to coordinate the payoff of such existing property loans, and to remove any related trust deed encumbrances from the property's title. To this end, the escrow officer submits a **payoff demand** to the Lender of any existing loans, wherein such Lender is requested to provide the escrow officer with the outstanding loan balance.

After a Lender has been paid in full, it releases its interest in the property by **reconveying** the trust deed. A copy of the reconveyed trust deed is eventually entered into the appropriate government records, and the original document is sent to the loan **Payor**, along with their cancelled note.

At the appropriate time, the escrow officer **records** the grant deed, trust deed, and any quit claim deeds or trust deed reconveyances. To **record** such documents, the escrow officer sends them, via messenger, to the jurisdictional government office that houses such **property records**. A government clerk then formally enters such documents into the government records.

Next, the escrow officer determines any **prorations** and **charges**. Prorated items include Seller prepayments or arrears of rents, tenant security deposits, taxes, insurances, et cetera. Charges might include escrow fees, title insurance fees, commissions, et cetera. After the prorations and charges have been determined and posted against the appropriate Buyer or Seller escrow accounts, the escrow officer will **disburse funds** (if any) to the Seller, and prepare a **closing statement** that delineates the accounting of the escrow transaction. This final step constitutes the **closing** of escrow.

SUBJECT 9. Exercising Discretion

When individuals **guard** their business expertise, they **protect** both their **earning ability** and their **material possessions**.

Each member of Earth's growing population constantly **competes in the consumption of** Earth's **limited** (and dwindling) resources. This reality is exemplified when two or more individuals vie for one **job position**, or for one **sales opportunity**, or compete to purchase one **rare object**, et cetera. In more primitive terms, **all individuals are hunters in a common field possessing limited game.**

When competing against others, an individual's ability to earn and retain material wealth is **directly dependent** upon their **business expertise**. Such expertise might be classified in two general categories: knowing *how to do something* (**technique expertise**), and knowing the *condition* of something (**condition expertise**).

Examples of **technique expertise** might include knowing:

- How to grow food crops.

- How to lay bricks.

- How to cut precious stones.

- How to perform surgery.

- How to analyze an investment.

- How to use a weapon.

- How to skin and dress out a carcass.

Examples of **condition expertise** might include the knowledge of:

- Where water is located.

- Where a mineral vein is located.

- Who will sell or purchase certain objects.

- Which investment will yield the highest return.

- Which plants are edible.

- Where abundant quantities of fish or game are located.

Typically, individuals spend **years** acquiring technique expertise, through academic studies, apprenticeships, by trial and error, et cetera. Likewise, it may take an individual years to acquire certain condition expertise, through study or experimentation. For example, after many years of labor, a fisherman might have developed a bait preparation **technique** and tidal **condition** knowledge, both of which enable him to enjoy **extraordinary** fishing success.

If the fisherman **indiscreetly** shares his technique and condition expertise with other fishermen, he will soon discover that there are **less** fish available for him, simply because the other fishermen will use the subject expertise to catch the fish. Likewise, if a businessperson indiscreetly discloses his productive business techniques or his sources of business opportunity, he **increases** the probability that competing businesspeople will use such expertise to **their** business advantage, therein **diminishing** the earning potential of the indiscreet businessperson.

There are, of course, some justifiable circumstances under which valuable business expertise might be disclosed to others:

> - If one is **commensurately remunerated** for the disclosure of such expertise, as in the case of an employee, a consultant, or an author, et cetera.

> - If such expertise is divulged for the purpose of helping a **friend** or member of one's **family**. In such instances, the individual is actually strengthening a common material support base, upon which they might draw in time of personal need.

In reiteration, the **discreet** use of one's business expertise **is not selfishness**; on the contrary, such discretion is **dictated** by the **competitive nature** of Man's existence.

SUBJECT 10. Skill Diversification

There are a multitude of **ancillary** business and personal tasks which support one's earning and money management efforts. Such tasks include:

> - Maintaining accounting books.

> - Preparing income tax filings.

> - Becoming incorporated.

> - Registering trademarks and fictitious business names.

> - Copyrighting material.

> - Filing patents.

> - Drafting a personal will.

- Setting up a pension plan.

- Marketing one's real or personal property.

- Coordinating an escrow.

- Drafting a contract (such as a loan note, partnership agreement, a lease, a sales agreement, et cetera).

- Coordinating probates.

- Filing civil litigation.

- Publishing materials.

- Coordinating travel bookings.

Society often perceives such tasks as being shrouded in professional **mystique** and beyond the ability of the layman to perform; consequently, most individuals employ professionals to assist them with such needs. In reality, many such tasks are **reasonably** performed by the **average** individual, often requiring nothing more than **minimal** research and performance effort.

There are a multitude of **reference** and **do-it-yourself** books available, with easy instructions and tear-out forms for tasks such as incorporating, income tax filings, divorce filings, et cetera. Many **government agencies** provide published or telephone **instructions** and **forms** relative to civil procedures. On occasion, one might **avoid** sizeable professional fees through such an inquiry and the completion of a simple form.

One might also approach many such tasks by reviewing **copies** of professionally prepared documents. Such documents are often available through **law libraries**, **friends**, **business associates**, et cetera. Using such source materials, one might simply copy the general format, and then **edit** the information that is unique to one's particular situation.

The obvious benefit to performing such tasks oneself is the **cost savings**; however, there are other **potential** benefits. By researching a task's procedure and then doing it oneself, an individual is **better** assured that it has been done **correctly**. Furthermore, by coordinating such tasks oneself, they are more likely accomplished in a **timely manner**. Finally, by **personally** doing such ancillary tasks, individuals **enhance** their general business skills and **reduce** their **dependency** upon others.

There are, of course, appropriate times to seek **professional assistance** with regard to the performance of such ancillary business and personal tasks:

- An individual must **necessarily** take time away from his primary income production efforts (his vocation), to research methodology and personally accomplish such ancillary tasks. One might employ another to do such tasks, if the **cost** of such employment **is less** than the income lost due to one's personal performance of such tasks.

- An **error** in the performance of some such tasks might potentially result in **substantial** material damages; in such instances, one might be wise to employ the services of a professional. As an alternative, one might at least employ a professional to **review** one's plans, or to **monitor** one's efforts (as in the instance of *in pro per* court representation).

- If the method of task accomplishment is so **esoteric** or professionally **guarded**, as to be **indiscernible** to the layman, one has no choice other than to employ a **professional.**

- If individuals **choose not** to practice effective personal problem solving habits (such as organization, self-discipline, planning, attention to detail, et cetera), they **must** rely upon the skilled efforts of others in the performance of such ancillary tasks.

PART FIVE: Other Considerations

- Contents -

[Note - The words *Man*, *him*, *his*, *he*, and *himself* herein refer to the species in general, with **no sexist connotation intended**.]

PART FIVE: Other Considerations

SUBJECT A. Play

An individual's *need to play* is **equal** in importance to his health, family, and money needs. Relatively, however, play assumes a **lower** need fulfillment priority.

1. Understanding Play.

In many instances, play serves the function of developing, refining, and maintaining one's intellectual and mechanical problem solving skills. Play might also serve the function of diversion or inducement.

An individual's chosen forms of play will be determined by his age, physical and intellectual abilities, unique needs, and cultural orientations.

Some play is in the form of **athletic** (sport) or **intellectual games** that **indirectly imitate** primary survival skills. Such play forms are often characterized by **territorial protection, pecking order challenges**, or **physical sparring**. Examples of such athletic play include boxing, Karate, fencing, Judo, football, basketball, polo, et cetera. Examples of such intellectual play might include parlor games, chess, or card games (such as bridge). Other play forms might involve the **direct imitation** of survival skills, such as **playing house**, or **playing army**.

Individuals, through such **low-risk** scenarios, are provided the opportunity to **safely** develop their social and survival skills.

Some individuals create **art** as a form of intellectual play. The fine arts typically permit individuals to exercise and develop their creative intellectual and mechanical skills. Such play might include **dance, sculpture, song, painting, acting**, et cetera.

The liberal arts permit creative play expression through the use of language. Such play might include the writing of poetry, fiction novels, screen plays, et cetera.

The participants in artistic play might be classified in two categories: the **creators** of the art (the artist, poet, actor, et cetera), and the **end users** of the artistic products (the audience, viewer, reader, collector, et cetera).

Artistic play can provide the creator, or end user, with a **diversion** from stress, boredom, or fear. Equally so, artistic play can be used to **induce** a desired **physiological** state in the creator or end user. The induction of a desired physiological state by artistic play can assist an individual in the fulfillment of a basic life need. As examples, an individual might sing or whistle to subdue the fear of the moment, or an individual might read a novel to induce sleep, or an individual might dance with another to induce sexual arousal, or an individual might paint a pleasant scene or look at such a painting as a diversion from an unpleasant reality.

In addition to play's **educational, diversionary**, and **inducement** functions, it might also serve as a vehicle for **ego fulfillment**. Normal individuals seek a positive self-image, with their feelings of self-worth being shaped by their life accomplishments. If one's job, marriage, or friendships fail to provide them an adequate sense of self-worth, the individual might use play to enhance his self-image. For example, an individual might serve in a subordinate employment position, performing mundane tasks; consequently, to enhance his sense of self-worth, such an individual might strive to be the champion of his company sponsored bowling or baseball team. Likewise, an individual might feel neglected by his spouse; consequently, he might participate in social play activities (cards, athletics, et cetera), using the associated peer attention to help fulfill his ego needs.

2. Scheduling Play.

It is both **proper** and **necessary** for individuals to take rest or play **breaks** from their work; failure to do so may impact the **effectiveness** of one's work and the overall **quality** of one's life.

When taking such breaks, individuals should be **consciously** aware of their intentions and actions; that is, the individual should purposely discern and separate **work time** from **play** or **rest time**. One's failure to do so can result in a potentially **problematic confusion** of the two activities. For example, an individual's work might require him to use a computer, possibly to look up information or to perform calculations, with such tasks being in support of his **primary** work duties. Under normal circumstances, the individual's computer usage might consume ten percent of his work day. A problem situation might develop in which the individual's computer usage starts to consume fifteen to twenty percent of his work day, while his overall work output is declining. Upon analysis, the individual might determine that he **particularly** enjoys using his computer, and consequently, he is doing so as a form of play and to the detriment of his overall work performance.

When individuals permit their work to become a form of play, they risk the **misprioritizing** of their life activities. The **primary** objective of work is to earn enough money to fulfill one's living needs. To this end, work time (although of lesser relative priority) **occasionally** conflicts with one's health time (for meals, exercise, or rest), or with one's family time (for interacting with one's spouse or nurturing one's children).

If one permits his work and play time to become indiscriminately **intermingled**, the opportunity is created for such play activity to **precede** or **displace** not only his work objectives, but also the fulfillment of his health, family, and **legitimate** play needs. Representative of this problem syndrome is the individual that works **excessively** long hours, with **no** financial **necessity** to do so. Such individuals often permit play (disguised as work) to interfere with the fulfillment of their health, family, or legitimate play needs, as typically evidenced by their substantial wealth, ill health, alienated families, and general unhappiness.

More often than confusing play with work, most individuals simply fail to take **adequate** time for rest or play breaks, thereby becoming **fatigued** and **bored**. Fatigue and boredom diminish both productivity and quality of life; consequently, all individuals should take rest or play breaks that are **commensurate** in **frequency**, **intensity**, and **duration** with the nature of the work that they perform.

As individuals age, they often settle into life routines that are relatively **devoid** of play; consequently, one should **plan** play in his daily activities.

Such planned play might include:

- vacations

- athletic hobby activities, such as golf, sailing, biking, et cetera

- dining out

- theater attendance

- reading

- sewing

- gardening

- crossword puzzles

- chatting with friends

- daydreaming

- enjoying a cup of tea or coffee

- smelling the roses

As a general guideline, one might consider the following schedule for planned rest/play:

- **five minutes** of rest/play for every half hour of work

- **two days** of rest/play for every work week

- **three weeks** of rest/play for every work year

- a **six month** rest/play sabbatical for every ten working years

In accommodation of healthy rest and play habits, individuals should remember that work is a **means** of need fulfillment, rather than an end in itself. Likewise, employers should remember that unhealthy employees produce **inconsistent** profits, and that such profits are **ultimately devalued** by an unhealthy society.

SUBJECT B. Violence

The object of any **problem solving action is** to fulfill some rational need. Problem solving approaches, by their nature, vary in **efficiency.** Violence as a problem solving approach is **necessarily inefficient.**

Violent problem solving approaches (such as war, rape, harassment, armed robbery, slavery, murder, et cetera) might successfully fulfill the immediate needs of the perpetrating individual or group; however, such approaches necessarily alienate, disable, or kill animate victims, or destroy inanimate objects, rendering them either hostile, uncooperative, or unusable in the fulfillment of the perpetrator's future needs.

Any problem solving approach that fails to consider the individual's **immediate** and **long-term needs** is **ineffective** and therefore **immoral,** by definition (see *What is morality?).*

Violence may be morally **appropriate** when occasioned by **certain** acts of **self-defense.** An individual or society might have to use violent force in physical self-protection, or to protect **vital interests** (those material objects upon which survival depends), or to protect **other** individuals or societies (that are **incapable** of protecting themselves) from the violent aggression of another. Such violent self-defense is moral if it is **unavoidable,** if it is in response to an act of **unprovoked** violence, and if it is **neither excessive** nor **punitive** in measure.

A society that permits its citizens to practice violent problem solving approaches will **necessarily** experience a **diminishing quality of life.** In particular, its intersocietal personal and institutional relationships will be impeded by **distrust**, a fear stricken social mentality will **prevail**, and the material wealth of its citizens and institutions will constantly be at **risk**; consequently, societies should **discourage** and **restrict** violence, not only to protect potential victims, but in **avoidance** of its broader detrimental effects.

To this end, societies devise methods of controlling their violent citizens (criminals). The primary object of such control should be to protect society from the immediate and future violent acts of such criminals. Methods of such control include **imprisonment** and **behavioral reconditioning.**

a. Imprisonment.

Imprisonment, through physical separation, does protect a society from the violent actions of its criminals; however, such imprisonment (particularly if **humane**) also subjects society to **substantial** material costs.

b. Behavioral reconditioning.

If violent individuals are permitted to re-enter society, it is in society's best interest to have behaviorally reconditioned them. Otherwise, such individuals will probably **continue** to commit violent acts.

Disregarding the criminally insane, most individuals employ violence because of faulty thought logic and inaccurate decision making premises. In order to **recondition** such individuals, it is necessary for society to:

> 1. **Isolate** and **expose** the **erroneous** logic/premises that underlie such individuals' violent/criminal problem solving approaches, and to **convincingly** inform them of the ineffectiveness of such approaches.

> 2. Inform such individuals of **accurate** and **functional** premises and decision making theory, for use in their future problem solving approaches.

> 3. Subject such individuals to **repetitive** *role-play* reconditioning, designed to **develop** and **reinforce** effective (non-violent) problem solving routines. To this end, such individuals should participate in hypothetical scenarios that allow them to **personally act out** moral problem solving approaches.

Punishment, as a reconditioning tool, is relatively **ineffective**. It **fails** to modify the thought processes that **underlie** a violent individual's actions. At best, punishment dissuades violence through the **threat** of retaliatory violence or associated discomfort, a methodology better suited for lower animals.

If an individual or a society **chooses** to employ punishment as a reconditioning tool, one should remain **consciously** aware of one's objective, that being the inducement or discouragement of certain actions, and **not** the **physical injury** of the subject individual.

A society's use of **Capital Punishment** establishes **dangerous** moral precedence in that it **signals** its citizens that violence (through **execution**) is an acceptable problem solving approach.

When violent individuals are **incapable** of behavioral reconditioning, they should be **permanently** separated from society through **imprisonment** or **banishment**. If such individuals are to be imprisoned, they should be encouraged to **perform labor** in support of their existence, thereby giving them a reason to live, and **reducing** society's material support burden.

The morality of violence is typically considered only as it applies to inter-human relationships; however, Man's violent acts against lower animals, plants, or inanimate objects also have **substantial moral consequences**. In fulfillment of his material needs, Man often employs violent problem solving approaches that impact other ecosystems and the general environment. Examples of such approaches include:

1. The **intentional killing** of plants or animals for use as human food, clothing, or industrial raw materials.

Specific techniques might include hunting, fishing, whaling, domestic livestock processing, commercial farming, logging, fur trapping, et cetera.

2. The **incidental killing** of plants or animals (such as insects, fish, dolphins, trees, et cetera) in the process of fulfilling Man's material needs.

Specific techniques might include the usage of pesticides, gill nets, the burning/razing of forested areas, the draining and filling of wetlands, hazardous waste contamination, et cetera.

3. The **intentional** or **incidental reconfiguration** of inanimate natural resources for commercial or territorial control purposes.

Specific techniques include strip mining, hydraulic pressure mining, commercial building site preparation, war damage, hazardous waste contamination, et cetera.

The morality of such actions should be considered from **two** points of view:

> 1. Mankind has evolved and flourished in **harmony** with and **dependent** upon a relatively **stable** ecosystem. If Man **substantially** disrupts (or alters) his surrounding ecosystems, the consequences might **negatively impact** Man's continued evolution or very existence.

> 2. The **predominant** use of violence against Man's environment encourages a **violence-oriented** problem solving **mentality**, therein inviting the opportunity for mankind itself to become the **victim** of such methodology.

Understandably, and naturally, Man must exploit his surrounding environment to survive. The **issue**, relative to such exploitation, is the morality of its **methods**; that is, do they serve **both** the **immediate and long-term** best interest of Man?

SUBJECT C. Racial Prejudice/Discrimination

Racial prejudice, as commonly practiced, occurs when one individual (or group) limits the rights of another individual (or group), based upon their comparative **racial characteristics**. At one time, racial prejudice may have served as a behavioral **survival mechanism**; in modern societies, it is an **impractical** and distasteful **anachronism**.

Primitive Man evolved in splintered groupings, distributed throughout environmentally **unique** geographic pockets. Such primate groupings, through selective breeding, **evolved** physical characteristics that were conducive to **survival** in their unique geographic environments. As such specialized body features (skeletal structure, skin pigmentation, hair texture, et cetera) became physically **pronounced** (through evolution), they were used to descriptively **categorize** individuals into primary and sub-**racial** groupings.

This book speculates that each such race, having evolved and maintained its unique **gene pool** of survival-conducive bodily characteristics, **instinctively** avoided interracial **cross-breeding**. Individuals did so for fear of diluting or altering their desirable genetic characteristics; consequently, **racial prejudice** developed and functioned (on an **instinctual** level) to **protect** racial genetics from the introduction of **foreign** and potentially **detrimental** genetic characteristics. In practicality, such prejudices probably extended beyond cross-breeding taboos to include social **privilege** limitations.

Cultural advancements in **tool usage, agricultural techniques,** and the **domestication of livestock** eventually afforded Man greater environmental adaptation **flexibility.** Man's newfound ability to alter, control, and adapt to his environment through technology necessarily **diminished** his dependence upon selective breeding and specialized (genetic) physical adaptations. Consequently, Man's instinctual racial prejudice tendencies have become **dysfunctional;** unfortunately, instinctual **habits** are difficult to retard.

Modern transportation and democracy have encouraged the global **dissemination** and **integration** of various racial groups. **Civilized people,** using education and law, wisely **discourage** Man's instinctual racial prejudices. Such enlightened nations, through social integration, typically enjoy commercial prosperity and cultural enhancement.

SUBJECT D. Etiquette/Courtesy

Etiquette refers to the **refined** mores of **dining, dress,** and **social interaction.** Although occasionally obscure in purpose, most acts of etiquette are based in civility and practicality.

The following etiquette suggestions are commonly practiced in Western civilizations:

1. Dining etiquette.

- Individuals should wash their hands before and after eating.

- When seated for dining, individuals should place a napkin across their lap and use it to wipe any food remnants from their fingers and lips.

- Gentlemen should remain standing until ladies, children, and elders have been seated.

- An individual should not begin eating until all others at the table have been served their meals.

- Individuals should use their eating utensils to cut their food into an edible size, cutting one bite at a time, approximately one square inch or smaller.

- Individuals should maintain an upright posture while eating.

- Individuals should refrain from placing their elbows on the dining table.

- Individuals should chew their food silently and with their mouth closed.

- Individuals should refrain from speaking while chewing their food.

- Individuals should eat in a relaxed manner, refraining from fast chewing or rapid food handling.

- When eating a bread roll, an individual should break off edible sized morsels and keep the larger uneaten piece on his bread plate.

- Individuals should refrain from slurping when drinking or spooning liquid food.

- Individuals should refrain from belching in public; if one must do so, he should cover his mouth and pardon himself.

- Individuals should announce their departure from the dining table by stating "excuse me."

- Individuals should refrain from smoking tobacco in the same room with non-smokers, particularly when others are dining.

- When invited to a dinner party, individuals should send flowers (early in the day of the occasion), or bring a small gift for the host or hostess, in appreciation of the invitation.

- Individuals should reciprocate dinner invitations.

When dining in a **restaurant**:

- Women, elders, and children should order first.

- Gentlemen might assist the seating of elders, women, and children by helping to slide in/out their dining chairs.

- Individuals should refrain from acting or speaking in a manner that distracts or disturbs other patrons.

- Any inter-patron problems should be resolved by the restaurant staff, not through inter-patron contact.

- Individuals should address the restaurant staff with courtesy.

- Individuals should respect a restaurant's dress code.

- Parents should refrain from bringing children (less than eight years of age) into *fine dining* settings.

2. **Interactive social etiquette.**

- Individuals should be courteous.

- Individuals should demonstrate respect for elders, understanding for children, and consideration for all.

- Gentlemen should open doors for women, children, and elders.

- Women, children, and elders should be favored when entering or departing elevators, and in limited seating or disaster evacuation situations.

- Individuals should refrain from critical comments about others, unless done in a constructive manner.

- Individuals should avoid acting or speaking in a manner that draws the unnecessary or underserved attention of others.

- Individuals should maintain balanced conversational interaction (see *Social Communication*).

- When conversing with a stranger, an individual should moderate his voice amplitude, not stand closer than one arm's length, and refrain from uninvited physical contact.

3. General grooming and dress etiquette.

- One's body and skin should be clean, and free of offensive odor.

- Individuals should maintain clean teeth and inoffensive breath.

- One's hair should be clean and groomed.

- Perfume or body cologne should not be detectable beyond an arm's length.

- One's clothing and footwear should be clean.

- One's manner of dress and grooming affects their sexual image. With this reality in mind, individuals should endeavor to project a sexual image that is appropriate for their age, marital status, and the specific social setting.

- Darker colors and heavier fabrics are typically worn in the fall and winter seasons, with lighter colors and lighter fabrics worn in the spring and summer.

- Individuals should favor clothing colors that compliment their personal skin, hair and eye pigmentation.

- Individuals should not usurp public attention through the shock effect of distasteful clothing or grooming.

4. Neighborhood courtesy.

Most individuals live in proximity to others; consequently, neighborhood courtesy is both appropriate and functional:

- Individuals, their children, and their pets should refrain from making any noises that can be heard beyond their home, particularly before 9:00 in the morning, or after 10:00 in the evening.

- Individuals should refrain from telephoning a private residence before 9:00 AM or after 9:00 PM.

- One's residence should be clean and attractive in appearance.

- Borrowing things from one's neighbor should be discouraged.

- Individuals should not permit their children or pets to soil or damage the properties of others.

- Individuals should treat their neighbor's children with patience and understanding.

- Individuals should offer help to a neighbor in need.

- When new neighbors move into a community, they should be welcomed with a gift or party.

- When a neighbor moves away, the community should say goodbye with a gift or party.

SUBJECT E. Indigence

Individuals become indigent for a variety of reasons, including: wars, economic collapse, natural disasters, illness, ineffective financial planning, et cetera. Regardless of the cause, indigent individuals must endeavor to survive. To this end, they might seek the assistance of **family, friends, charity,** or **their government**. If in absolute desperation, and in the absence of family, friends, or charitable institutions, such individuals might approach a **police officer** as a **starting point** in their search for survival assistance.

As soon as an **able-bodied adult** has secured temporary sustenance and shelter, he should **immediately** endeavor to establish self-sufficiency by seeking **any moral** form of work. To this end, it may be necessary to perform unpleasant work tasks, to work both a day and evening job, to use public transportation, to walk to one's place of employment, et cetera.

Any indigent individual that materially draws upon his family, friends, charity, or government has necessarily incurred a **personal obligation** to fully repay such debts, and to stand ready to provide **reciprocal** assistance. An individual should endeavor to repay such debts, as soon as he has attained **basic** financial stability, and **before** enjoying any luxury acquisitions.

Some indigent individuals, such as **children, mothers with infants**, and the **disabled**, are incapable of immediate self-sufficiency. In the absence of family support, a compassionate society should assume the obligation of materially assisting such individuals through government programs and charitable organizations.

A society's moral necessity to assist its indigent individuals is not altruistic; such assistance cleanses a society of elements that might lead to **broader** social illnesses. The ambition of social assistance programs must be tempered by the reality that they necessarily demand taking money from **those that have earned it**, and giving it to **those that have not**.

All individuals are **unique** in their desires and abilities; consequently, it is **natural** for the citizens of any society to **vary** in their personal material well-being. All citizens should enjoy an **equal opportunity** to realize their individual potential; however, it is **unrealistic** to expect (or to force) all citizens to be **equal** in material well-being. On the other hand, a society is at risk if it produces a **disproportionate** number of indigent individuals. **Imbalanced societies**, economic opportunity wise, inherently suffer social illnesses (poverty, crime, urban decay, pollution, disease, et cetera); consequently, the wealth of the **affluent few** is ultimately diluted and threatened by such negative effects.

SUBJECT F. Time Allocations

Successful living is largely dependent upon an individual's ability to intelligently **prioritize** his various life needs; and to make **appropriate** time allocations for the fulfillment of those needs. If one **misallocates** his time, he exposes himself to potential problems:

- If individuals expend **inadequate** time fulfilling their **health needs** (cleaning themselves, resting, eating, and exercising), they might suffer health problems, such as skin rashes, ulcers, hypertension, heart disease, neurosis, et cetera. Such problems tend to **interfere** with the fulfillment of one's other needs; for example, it is difficult to be a good spouse, parent, or provider, if one is ill. Worse yet, such problems might shorten one's life.

- **Family needs** are identified and fulfilled through personal interaction and communications. It takes time to properly relate to one's spouse and to raise one's children, and there are no **shortcuts** to this process.

Some individuals neglect their family needs by allocating **excessive** time to income production. From a financial point of view, the cost of a failed marriage or imbalanced children might far **outweigh** the material gains realized through excessive work. A failed marriage not only deprives one of his spouse's love, a divorce settlement might be materially **devastating**. Likewise, when parents dedicate excessive time to income production, they often fail to spend adequate time developing their children's abilities. As a result, such children tend to create **abnormal** material demands, and often continue to be **dependent** upon their parents into adulthood.

- **Conversely**, if individuals spend **inadequate** time fulfilling their **money needs** (working), they consequently **impact** the material fulfillment of their health, family, and play needs.

- When individuals spend **inadequate** time fulfilling their **play needs**, they tend to diminish their **overall** quality of life. Play permits one to develop and maintain healthy social interaction and basic survival skills. Additionally, play provides opportunity for ego gratification, relaxation, and diversion from discomfort or the mundane.

Assuming that one chooses to accept the priority sequence heretofore suggested (that being the fulfillment of *health* needs first, then *family* needs, then *money* needs, and finally *play* needs), one might consider applying the following respective **time allocations**:

1. Health time.

- Individuals need **eight hours of sleep** nightly (see *Health Considerations - Rest*), assuming that one expends about one hour preparing for bed, falling to sleep, and periodically re-awakening, fifteen waking hours then remain for the fulfillment of one's other daily needs (24 hours available, less 9 hours for rest = 15 hours remaining).

- Individuals should expend about **one hour** a day, **cleaning** themselves and performing bodily functions (see *Cleanliness*), leaving fourteen waking hours for the fulfillment of other daily needs (15 hours available, less 1 hour for cleaning/excreting = 14 hours remaining).

- Individuals should expend about **one-half hour for breakfast, one hour for lunch**, and **one hour for dinner** (see *Diet*), leaving eleven and one-half daily hours for other daily needs (14 hours available, less 2.5 for meals = 11.5 hours remaining).

- Individuals should expend a minimum of **one-half hour** a day for personal **exercise** (see *Health Considerations - Exercise*), leaving eleven hours for the fulfillment of other daily needs (11.5 hours available, less 0.5 hours for exercise = 11 hours remaining).

2. Family time.

- **In addition** to having breakfast and dinner with one's family, an individual should spend at least **one and one-half daily hours more** with his **spouse and family** (see *Communication in Marriage* and *Raising Children*), leaving nine and one-half hours for the fulfillment of other daily needs (11 hours available, less 1.5 hours for additional family time = 9.5 hours remaining).

3. Money time.

- An individual should be able to earn **enough money** (see *How much money is enough?*) by working **eight and one-half hours** a day (including commute), **five days each week**; this assumes that the individual is living in a modern Western society, with a healthy free market and capitalistic economic system, and has adequately prepared for his vocational endeavors. **One additional working day** might also be expended to accomplish **personal** work tasks, such as automobile or home maintenance, self-improvement study, et cetera. Such a work schedule leaves one hour per day for the accomplishment of other needs (9.5 hours available, less 8.5 working hours = 1.0 hour remaining).

4. Play time.

- An individual should expend at least **one hour a day** at **play** (see *Other Considerations - Play*).

The above suggested time allocations consume 159.5 hours per week, leaving eight and one half hours to be **flexibly** distributed over one's health, family, work, and play needs. On occasion, circumstances create need fulfillment **conflicts**, necessitating the **temporary** re-prioritizing of one's actions. For example, an individual might have a unique opportunity or obligation, prompting a conflict between his immediate work schedule and the fulfillment of his other basic needs. Likewise, a special health, family, or play need might interfere with one's normal time allocations. Consistent with this reality, it is **not** the intention of this section, to suggest **rigid** time allocations, but rather to provide the reader with **practical guidelines**.

SUBJECT G. Accomplishing Beyond the Norm

In order to accomplish beyond the norm of one's social group, **one must act *differently* than his peers.**

Most individuals are born into specific cultural and economic groupings. The members of such groupings tend to learn and share **common** behavior patterns. Notwithstanding genetic influences, a social group's behavior patterns determine its characteristic intellectual, athletic, artistic, musical, and other accomplishment levels, as well as its statistical incident of divorce, illness, and other problematic occurrences.

If individuals wish to achieve at any level **beyond** their group's norm, logically then, they must act **differently** than their peers. As examples:

- **Health.** An individual's family, friends, and associates might all consume a high fat/cholesterol diet and lead sedentary lifestyles, resulting in obesity and cardiovascular disease. If individuals wish to achieve a **better** health condition, they might simply consume a **different** diet (consisting of minimal fats/cholesterol), and engage in **different** exercise habits.

- **Family.** An individual's peers might commonly suffer unhappy marriages, due to infidelity or poor communications. If individuals wish to achieve a level of marital success **beyond** that of their peers, they might do so by acting **differently**, perhaps by **avoiding** situations that invite infidelity, and by **learning** effective marital communication techniques.

- **Money.** An individual's peer or ethnic group might be typified by inadequate vocational preparation habits. Consequently, he might suffer below average annual income, as compared to general society. If individuals wish to achieve material accomplishments **beyond** their group's norm, they **must** act **differently**, perhaps by making a **special effort** to acquire preparatory vocational training.

- **Play.** Each member of one's play group (perhaps an athletic team) might perform at relatively similar ability levels because they all employ the same practice schedules and play techniques. If individuals desire to accomplish **beyond** the norm of their group, they might act **differently**, perhaps by **increasing** the frequency of their practice, and by learning **enhanced** play techniques.

Granted, this simple concept of **doing something different** is **obvious**; unfortunately though, it is **incomprehensible** to most. Often, individuals will sit amongst their peers, complaining about their finances, their marriages, their health, et cetera, and then immediately **continue** the habit patterns that created their problematic circumstances.

Once individuals accept and begin to practice (typically in childhood) the habit patterns of their social group, regardless of the merit of such habits, it becomes very difficult for them to change their actions. To do so, one must employ **vision** and **self-discipline**. Vision is the self-induced ability to sense the potential benefits of doing something **different**; and self-discipline is necessary to overcome the psychological discomfort of breaking old habits and creating new ones.

It cannot be said loud enough or often enough: "**if individuals wish to accomplish beyond the norm of their peers, they must *act differently* than their peers.**"

SUBJECT H. Greed

Greed is a wealth acquisition **attitude** that results in the beholder's **self-damage**. In particular, greed occurs when individuals try to acquire wealth:

- Without putting forth **appropriate** labor.

- By **neglecting** their health, family, or play needs.

- By **infringing** upon the moral rights of others.

- By **spoiling** or wasting natural resources.

If individuals attempt to attain wealth through such means, they are typically **damaged** in the process, and the nature of such damage tends to **outweigh** the potential benefits of any wealth realized from such means.

The following are examples of various forms of greed:

1. Working long hours to produce excessive income.

Some individuals work an **inordinate** amount of hours to produce **more** income than is reasonably necessary to provide for their financial needs. In doing so, such individuals often deprive themselves of adequate time for rest, exercise, family interaction, friendships, or play, thereby **negatively** impacting their health or family relationships, and their overall quality of life.

2. Prostitution.

Prostitution is a form of income production in which the prostitute performs sexual acts in exchange for money or barter. In addition to the other moral consequences, such labor is necessarily **detrimental** to the prostitute's mental and physical health, and consequently greed motivated.

3. Gambling.

Gambling involves at least two parties: the party that runs the **game** (commonly referred to as the **house**), and the **gambler**. Because this form of income production typically depends upon the gambler's **ignorance** or **misunderstanding** of the game's financial **risk factors**, one might conclude that gambling is a greed-motivated form of income production.

In gambling, the house devises a game that requires the gambler to **wager** money, based upon the gambler's expectation that a certain **event** will occur. Should the designated **event** occur, the house pays the gambler a **pre-agreed to** amount of money (referred to as **winnings**). If the **event** fails to occur, the house keeps the gambler's wager.

In such gambling games, the statistical probability of the winning event actually occurring is **typically less than fifty percent**. In other words, the mathematical odds are **typically in the house's favor**. In effect, gambling relies upon gamblers to make an **irrational** investment of their money; that is, the gambler must wager on the occurrence of an event that is mathematically **improbable**.

Like the house, the gambler is **also** motivated by greed; that is, the gambler is typically attempting to acquire wealth **without putting forth appropriate labor**.

Some governments use gambling (lotteries) to create revenues. In doing so, they often employ commercial advertisements that extoll the virtues of gambling, such as "get rich by winning the lottery." One might question the moraliy of such fiscal methods, in that they propagate a greed mentality. **Enlightened** societies should encourage their citizens to attain wealth through **vocational preparation, creativity, and productive effort**; and they should inform their citizens that wealth, resulting from greed, **induces** individual and societal illnesses.

4. Greed Lawsuits.

Some individuals **misuse** civil legal processes to virtually **extort** money from their fellow citizens (see *Understanding Civil Law*). This method of income production typically follows one of two patterns:

> **A.** The perpetrating individual (**plaintiff**) files a lawsuit, based upon an **arbitrary, weak,** or **non-existent** claim, with the intention of forcing an **out-of-court cash settlement**.
>
> Such lawsuits name as many defendants as possible, with no particular regard for the defendants' actual guilt or innocence. The favorite defendant/victim of such lawsuits are **insurance companies**, because of their **deep pockets** (cash holdings).
>
> When sued, such defendants immediately incur substantial expenses for defense representation. Knowing this, the plaintiffs then use **court procedures** (such as **continuances**) to **manipulate** the trial process, with the specific intent of **driving-up** the defendants' representation expenses, hoping that the defendant will eventually **acquiesce** to an **out-of-court cash settlement** in lieu of incurring further defense expenses (attorney fees).
>
> **B.** The perpetrating individual files a civil lawsuit, based upon the occurrence of an **opportune** accident; for example, his child might have been injured on a public park *merry-go-round*. Such lawsuits name as many defendants as possible, including for example, the park maintenance staff, the City, the County, the State, the manufacturer of the merry-go-round, the doctor that treated the child, **and all of their respective insurance companies.**
>
> Although the subject accident may not have actually resulted **because of anyone's negligence** (with the possible exception of the parents), the lawsuit will demand that the defendants (jointly and separately) pay for the child's medical bills, and **several million dollars** more for emotional and punitive damages suffered by the child and parents.

The plaintiff will then endeavor to **hand-select** a jury that possesses a **"redistribute society's wealth"** mentality, hoping that such a jury will eventually grant him a several million dollar award (to be paid by the insurance companies).

Greed lawsuits **debase** a society's legal system, create **distrust**, and force **higher** insurance premiums (or non-coverage) upon all citizens. Individuals, attorneys, jurors, and judges should endeavor to discourage such actions.

5. Thievery.

Thievery is a greed-motivated form of income production, in which the perpetrating party (the thief) takes the material possessions of another individual (the victim), by means of force (robbery) or deception (fraud).

In addition to damaging innocent individuals, thievery subjects the thief to the risk of injury, imprisonment, or death, and it precipitates a distrusting and hostile society. Consequently, though it might meet a thief's **short-term** material needs, thievery typically **frustrates** the consistent fulfillment of a thief's **long-term** needs.

6. Labor abuse.

Some individuals realize business **profits** through the **unfair** labor exploitation of others. Such exploitation might be **psychological**, **physical**, or **economic** in nature.

Prostitution and pornography businesses are representative of both psychological and physical exploitation. Additionally, when individuals patronize such businesses (by engaging in sex with a prostitute, or buying pornographic materials, or attending sex shows), they are **contributing** to the continued exploitation of such employees.

Some employers subject their employees to excessive noise, heat, cold, hazardous materials, excessive working hours, or excessive mental or physical strain, in order to produce profits. Such actions are representative of physical exploitation.

When an employer profits by paying wages that are not **commensurate** with the value of an employee's labor contribution, or **insufficient** to meet the employee's reasonable living needs, the employer is exercising economic exploitation.

When a society **permits** the labor abuse of its citizens, it will eventually experience social illnesses that are **reflective** of such abuses; consequently, the wealth that is realized from such exploitation will necessarily be **diminished** by the **negative** effects of the **coincident** social illnesses.

7. Natural resource abuse.

Environmental pollutants are often created as a by-product of commercial industry. To increase profits, such pollutants are often disposed of in a manner that is **damaging** to the environment. Likewise, due to inconsiderate or **ineffective** planning, the commercial use of natural resources often **disrupts** important ecosystems, permanently **destroying** plant life, or driving animal life into **extinction**.

The profits resulting from such practices are greed-motivated in that polluted/damaged environments necessarily induce societal **illnesses**, and such illnesses necessarily **increase** societal maintenance expenses, consequently **diluting** the value of the profits enjoyed from such greedy practices. Furthermore, because such greedy practices tend to **rapidly** deplete or spoil natural resources, **all** commercial profits (both greed-based and legitimate) are put **at risk**.

Individuals, as **consumers**, should endeavor to **discourage** such greed profits; that is, one should **refrain** from **knowingly** purchasing any commercial item that has been produced in a manner that is environmentally harmful. Granted, such discretion might require self-discipline in that many environmentally damaging products are **less expensive** than alternative environmentally safe products. In such considerations, a responsible individual must look towards the **long-term benefits** of his actions.

SUBJECT I. Make it happen!

Individuals can either permit their lives to be loosely directed by **happenstance**, or they can take control, and *make it happen*. The latter approach tends to yield a **better** *quality of life*.

In fulfilling one's needs, individuals must often employ **procedural processes**, through which they become **dependent upon** the **performance** of others, or through which they are **subject to** the **judgement** of others. The manner in which one approaches such processes might **expedite** or **impede** the realization of his objectives. The following suggestions are intended to assist the reader in optimizing procedural processes:

- Individuals should not be **intimidated** by the **process**, itself; that is, they should not permit fear of the **process** to **deter** them from their end objective. For example, if an individual wishes to become a real estate agent, he should not be dissuaded by fear of the education and professional licensing requirements. When considered in its **entirety**, the process of such vocational preparation might seem intimidating; however, when performed **one step at a time**, such procedural processes are **comfortably** accomplished. This approach is equally applicable to **any** vocation (law, medicine, engineering, et cetera), or general goal. It should be remembered that all such processes are designed to accommodate the abilities of relatively **average** individuals.

- Individuals should act **carefully** when **relying** upon the performance of **others**. The accomplishment of certain personal objectives involves processes that depend upon the performance of others; for example, the employment of a **contractor** to complete some labor task, or the employment of an **attorney** to perform a legal task, or the instructing of one's employees to perform some productive task, et cetera. In such instances, an individual should **regularly** monitor the progress of such performing parties, thereby insuring that his objective is being accomplished in a **proper** manner. Such processes, if not **overseen** by the principal **beneficiary**, typically yield **mediocre** results.

- In completing some procedural processes, individuals must depend upon the **judgmental** or **approval** decisions of others. Representative of such processes are **civil or criminal court** trials, **loan, employment, rental,** or **membership application processing, licensing tests, building code inspections,** et cetera.

In such situations, one should endeavor to positively influence the outcome of the process, by:

> 1. **Properly** preparing the object to be judged (trial case, loan, employment, or rental application, et cetera).

> 2. **Subtly** influencing the thought process of the relative decision makers (judge, loan officer, landlord, et cetera). For example, if an individual is subject to an income tax audit, a structural building inspection, or the like, it might behoove him to develop a personal **rapport** with the auditor or inspector by discussing the weather, sports, family, et cetera. Such rapport building should be attempted, **prior** to commencing the decision making process; at the very least, one should exercise **politeness.** In this manner, the subjective element of any such decision might be subtly **directed** in one's **favor.**

Similar to the successful consummation of procedural processes, luck and opportunity do not **just happen.** Intent individuals **create** luck or **find** opportunities, through their efforts and attitudes; and then they **act** upon such situations to realize **beneficial** consequences! This phenomenon is true in **all** walks of life, from finding a good spouse, to creating a good business deal, to catching a big fish!

To realize the most from life, one should give it momentum by *making it happen*!

SUBJECT J. Taking Risks

The **mis-assessment** of risk can **diminish** one's quality of life, or worse yet, **shorten** one's life.

Risk is the probability factor of personal injury, material loss, or damage that is associated with an action. Be it **walking to the corner market, starting a new business,** or simply **swallowing,** every action has some associated degree of risk; consequently, risk is an integral part of life and every problem solving approach.

To be successful in life, individuals should **realistically** assess the risk associated with their planned problem solving approaches. Sometimes the associated risk is **disproportionate** to the potential gain. In such instances, an individual is wise to seek an **alternative lower risk** solution. As an example, an individual might consider purchasing either a motorcycle or an automobile for transportation. After comparing their respective accident injury statistics, one might decide that the motorcycle's relative cost savings do not outweigh its associated risk factor.

Certainly, the mis-assessment of an action's potential risk might expose an individual to **unnecessary** losses; likewise, a risk mis-assessment might unnecessarily **deprive** an individual of opportunity. For example, an individual might prefer to drive cross-country rather than use air travel, for fear of being injured in a airplane accident. In such an instance, the individual has unrealistically assessed the risk that is associated with air travel (in that it is actually less than driving an automobile), and has consequently deprived himself of the **time savings** opportunity afforded by air travel.

In summary, risk is an integral part of life; frivolous and unnecessary risks should be avoided, while appropriate opportunity related risks should be accepted.

SUBJECT K. Judging Human Nature

An individual's **nature** is the essence of his philosophical values, as reflected through his physical appearance, mannerisms, material possessions, relationships, and general actions.

Being social creatures, people are necessarily affected by the actions of others. By judging the *nature* of another person, an individual is **better** able to anticipate how that person will act in a mutual relationship, particularly with regard to risk assessment.

In many instances, such as business, individuals enter into relationships with others about whom they possess very little previous knowledge; consequently, it is beneficial to be able to **quickly** and **accurately** judge the nature of others. Granted, individuals are not always as they initially appear to be, and it could take days or years to thoroughly understand someone's true nature. Notwithstanding this reality, the following general guidelines are offered for use in those situations where a quick judgement must be made:

1. Physical Appearances.

An individual's physical appearance consists of his health condition, attire, and grooming. Certain appearances are generally associated with certain values:

- Health condition.

An individual's eyes, skin, and physique are generally indicative of his health condition, with alert eyes, firm unblemished skin, and a trim physique indicating **good health**. Conversely, bloodshot eyes with dark circles or bags, loose or blemished skin, or obese or emaciated physiques tend to indicate **poor health**.

Aside from indicating an individual's physical reliability, good health also tends to indicate the existence of personal **self-discipline**, a quality that generally underlies good health habits (cleanliness, diet, rest, and exercise). Conversely, poor physical health generally indicates poor self-discipline habits and unreliability, and consequently one should **take warning**.

There are, of course, exceptions to poor health appearances, such as allergies, genetic conditions, or unavoidable diseases. Although potentially disabling, such conditions are not necessarily reflective of poor personal habits.

- Attire and grooming.

If an individual's clothing and grooming are neat, clean, and conservative in style and color, one might assume that the individual is aware of, or practices, traditional values. On the other hand, if an individual's appearance is sloppy, dirty, or radical in style or color, one might assume that the individual's values are outside of society's mainstream. In such case, one should **take warning**.

2. Mannerisms.

- Handshake.

A firm handshake tends to indicate resolve and honesty, while a limp, damp handshake is commonly associated with weakness or deceptiveness.

- Eye contact.

Direct eye contact is generally indicative of an individual's forth-rightness and listening ability. Darting or furtive eye contact is generally indicative of a self-confidence or communication problem or dishonesty.

- Cigarette smoking.

Considering the common knowledge that cigarette smoking is potentially unhealthy, one might question the rationality and self-discipline of those that practice such a habit.

3. Material possessions.

If an individual's possessions (such as his desk, automobile, brief-case, office, home, et cetera) are clean, organized, and well-maintained, one might assume that the individual will treat his relationships and obligations in a similar manner. On the other hand, if an individual's possessions are dirty, in disarray, or in disrepair, then one might assume that the condition of such possessions are generally reflective of that individual's thought process and habits, and one should consequently **take warning**.

4. Personal relationships.

An individual's personal relationships are directly reflective of his nature, and the **most** telling of such relationships is one's **marriage**. If an individual has a healthy relationship with his spouse and children, it is generally indicative of the individual's ability to relate well to others. On the other hand, if an individual has "problem children," one might question the individual's social problem solving skills. Likewise, if an individual appears to be disloyal or hostile to his spouse, one should most certainly **take warning**, in that one's spouse should be his best friend, and if an individual will lie to (or mistreat) his spouse, he will certainly do worse to others.

In summary, an individual's physical appearance, mannerisms, and relationships are like a *ship's flag*, they are the only means by which a stranger can quickly assess the general values and intentions of another.

SUBJECT L. Dishonesty

Dishonesty is the act of **deceiving** others, for **personal motives**. Such motives often include **material gain**, or **discomfort avoidance**.

Dishonesty might accommodate the fulfillment of an individual's **immediate** objectives, however, such methods **frustrate** the fulfillment of one's **overall** needs. In simple terms, it is in one's best interest to act honestly because dishonesty usually **compound**s one's problems. For example, if an individual does **something wrong** and **lies** to avoid being reprimanded, he then has **two** problems: the initial offense, and the *lie*.

As another example, consider the student that has not prepared for his academic exams, and consequently chooses to **cheat** on his *tests*. Granted, he might obtain a passing grade in the class, however, he has probably **failed** to acquire the **knowledge** that was intended to prepare him for **successful living**.

Likewise, when an individual **wins** a *game* by **cheating**, he might fulfill his **immediate** ego needs; however, he necessarily **deprives** himself of the **greater** benefits of developing and refining **consistent** winning skills.

Though dishonesty might result in the perpetrator's **censure, banishment, imprisonment**, or **punishment**, there is a costlier effect: when an individual is dishonest, his **example** might prompt others to act **similarly**. By fostering a dishonest society, individuals chance falling **victim** to the dishonest acts of others.

In summary, dishonesty is **inherently immoral** because it is generally **ineffective** as a problem solving method (see *What is Immorality?* and *Greed*).

SUBJECT M. Coping With Death

Each person, to varying degrees, must cope with the **fear of premature death**, the **fear of eventual death**, and the **death of loved ones**. The manner in which individuals deal with these concerns impacts their quality of life. The following comments are intended to **ease** the process of such coping.

1. Coping with the fear of *premature* death.

The eventuality of death is **absolute**; however, rational individuals try to **avoid** death's **premature** occurrence. To this end, a healthy level of fear serves to assist individuals in the avoidance of, or escape from, potentially harmful situations.

Certain physical **actions** or **environmental conditions** expose an individual to the **possibility** of premature death. Examples of such circumstances might include:

- breathing polluted air	- water skiing
- driving on the freeway	- sky diving
- flying in an airplane	- playing *Russian Roulette*
- smoking cigarettes	- crossing the street

Each such event has an associated mathematical **probability**, relative to the **incidental** occurrence of one's death. For example, there might be a **one in six** (1:6) probability of premature death occurrence from playing *Russian Roulette*, or a **one in two hundred and fifty thousand** (1:250,000) probability of premature death occurrence from driving on the freeway.

The **degree** of incidental death probability associated with a particular circumstance becomes the **basis** for most individuals' rational fear of such circumstances; that is, an individual might **reasonably** associate a **greater** level of fear with a circumstance that occasions a 1:6 incidental death probability, as **compared** to a circumstance that occasions a 1:250,000 incidental death probability.

The **rational** fear of premature death can **prolong** one's life. On the other hand, an irrational fear of premature death might **degrade** one's **quality of life**. The rationality of one's premature death fears is reflective of his ability to discern and associate **accurate** incidental death probabilities relative to specific circumstances.

If individuals irrationally fear involvement in a particular circumstance because they have **misjudged** its realistic incidental death probability, those individuals might unnecessarily **deprive** themselves of the benefits that are commonly associated with the subject circumstance; consequently, diminishing the quality of their lives. As an example, one might have a disproportionate fear of flying in an airplane. As a result, he might deprive himself of the safety and time-saving benefits afforded by air travel, thereby potentially exposing himself to **higher** travel risks and **diminishing** the effectiveness of his time usage.

Such irrational fears might result from **misinformation** or **ignorance**. As an example, an individual might decline a life-saving operation because he is unaware of the benefits and relative safety of modern medicine.

Still other individuals might suffer an irrational fear of premature death as the result of **anxiety neurosis**, a psychological condition in which individuals mis-associate fear **sources** and **responses**.

Anxiety neurosis tends to occur when an individual is subject to a **continuing**, fear-inducing problem situation, for example, being held hostage. Anxiety neurosis might also result from the **internalization** of unresolved childhood experiences in which the individual suffered **extreme** fear. Regardless of its cause, the sufferer often experiences an emotional state of **free-floating anxiety**.

Individuals **normally** experience fear as **part** of their problem solving response to a particular situation. Such fear naturally helps to motivate or prepare individuals for **responsive** action; their pulse rates might rise, their breathing rates might increase, preparing their bodies for *fight* or *flight*.

Each new experience in life induces **some** associated anxiety. Examples of such experiences might include **public speaking**, **air travel**, **riding in an elevator**, et cetera. A rational individual experiences a fear response that is **proportionate** to the risk commonly associated with the subject activity. Comparatively, a sufferer of anxiety neurosis might experience a disproportionate fear response. In particular, such an individual might react as follows: The normal anxiety of a **new experience** stimulates and mixes with his free-floating anxiety; his mind, then, **mistakenly** associates the new experience with the discomfort of his **total** anxiety, therein causing the individual to disproportionately (irrationally) fear the new experience.

Individuals might **better** cope with such irrational fears by:

- Seeking professional counseling to determine if they are suffering from anxiety neurosis.

- Identifying the fear inducing source of their anxiety and resolving it.

- Exercising mental discipline to discern their pre-existing anxiety from reasonably experienced fear.

2. Coping with the fear of *eventual* death.

Eventual death, **unlike** premature death, is **unavoidable**; consequently, there is no justification for, or benefit to, fearing it. Granted, it is not in Man's nature, or best interest, to welcome eventual death. Naturally though, the concept becomes less difficult as one ages.

Individuals fulfill their needs through their mental and physical abilities, and enjoy the resulting pleasures through their senses. Experiences such as tasting food, catching a fish, reading a book, or having an orgasm, all result in pleasures that make life enjoyable.

As the aging process **deteriorates** one's body, it becomes more difficult to fulfill one's needs; consequently, **fewer** pleasures are realized. Aging also **dulls** certain senses, **diminishing** one's **appreciation** of some pleasurable experiences. Eventually, the natural fatigue and failing of bodily functions results in **pain**. When an aged individual consistently senses more pain than pleasure, with no realistic hope of improvement, the **nothingness of death becomes less repugnant**.

In the *end*, death is **instantaneous**; there is no further thought, or pain, or grief, or regrets, **or existence**.

3. Coping with the death of another.

Because of its inevitability, it is wise to **prepare** for coping with the death of another, particularly the death of a loved one. An individual's inability to deal with this eventuality can **unnecessarily** diminish his quality of life.

a. Understanding the discomfort.

When a familiar individual dies, it might disturb the survivor's **sense of reality**, his **routine**, or his very **survival**.

- Sense of reality.

An individual's sense of reality is formed from the intellectual and emotional integration of his **total** life experiences. One's interaction with his parents, siblings, spouse, children, friends, co-workers, and others, represents a **substantial** portion of his life experiences; consequently, one's sense of reality is strongly influenced by such relationships. When such a related individual dies, particularly if it is unanticipated, his passing necessarily affects the survivor's sense of reality. The effect might be subtle, for example, it might simply alter one's perception of death itself, making the survivor more sensitive to his own mortality. In general, the range of psychological impact varies from mild discomfort (grief) to extreme disorientation.

- Routine.

An individual's daily routine typically involves interaction with others. The death of a person with whom one **frequently** interacts will necessarily disturb the survivor's routine. When the death of another unexpectedly disrupts one's routine, a sense of discomfort or confusion might temporarily result, until a **new** routine is established.

- Survival.

Some relationships involve emotional or material **dependence** upon another, such as spousal or parental relationships. When one such party dies, the survivor(s) might suffer a temporary loss of emotional or material need fulfillment.

b. Adjusting to the *reality*.

The first step in coping with the death of another is to **acknowledge** the fact that **the individual has actually died**. This involves understanding the circumstances of his death and grasping the reality that he **no longer exists**. In particular, one should **dispel** any notions that the deceased has physically or spiritually relocated to some celestial place, and is consciously observing the survivor's earthly actions. Such fallacious thinking simply **interferes** with the healthy restructuring of the survivor's life.

Next, individuals must permit themselves to experience **grief**, thereby emotionally acknowledging that their lives have been involuntarily altered by the death of another. Experiencing grief, although certainly more tragic, is analogous to having the flu: when one has the flu, he might feel like he is going to die, but after the illness has run its course, one returns to normality and begins to enjoy life again. Similarly, when one is in grief, he might feel like he is going to, or wish to die, but after the shock of the loss has passed, and after he has re-established routines to compensate for the absence of the deceased, the grief will eventually pass and his life will again become enjoyable.

Finally, individuals must begin the **restructuring** of their lives; that being the adjustment of their reality, and the establishment of **new** routines. Routines which previously involved the deceased will naturally feel uncomfortable, **until** new patterns are established. Meal times, for example, might have been shared with a deceased spouse or child; consequently, a survivor's meal times might feel awkward until he gets used to eating alone, or until he establishes a replacement relationship. Likewise, the deceased might have been the survivor's business partner; consequently, conducting business might feel awkward until the survivor gets used to being in the office alone, or until he finds a new partner.

Re-establishing a sense of self-sufficiency after the death of one's spouse often poses a psychological challenge. In coping with this adjustment, one might consider Man's basic nature: upon birth, individuals become physically **unique** entities. Regardless of relationships with others, self-sufficiency is an **inherent** quality - it need only be **re-awakened**!

INDEX